INSIDERS'GUIDE®

OFF THE BEATEN PATH® SERIES

W9-BYH-263

Off the
Beaten Path®

NINTH EDITION

pennsylvania

A GUIDE TO UNIQUE PLACES

CHRISTINE O'TOOLE

INSIDERS'GUIDE®

GUILFORD, CONNECTICUT
AN IMPRINT OF THE GLOBE PEQUOT PRESS

The prices, rates, and hours listed in this guidebook were confirmed at press time. We recommend, however, that you call establishments to obtain current information before traveling.

To buy books in quantity for corporate use or incentives, call **(800) 962–0973,** or e-mail **premiums@GlobePequot.com.**

INSIDERS' GUIDE®

Streets paved in red brick listing on p. 11 reprinted from *Philadelphia Almanac and Citizens' Manual,* courtesy of the Library Company of Philadelphia.

Text design by Linda Loiewski
Maps created by Equator Graphics © Morris Book Publishing, LLC
Text illustrations by Carole Drong
Spot photography throughout © Masterfile

ISSN: 1536-6197
ISBN-13: 978-0-7627-4209-7
ISBN-10: 0-7627-4209-7

Manufactured in the United States of America
Ninth Edition/First Printing

To Jim, James, and Bill:
great Pennsylvanians.

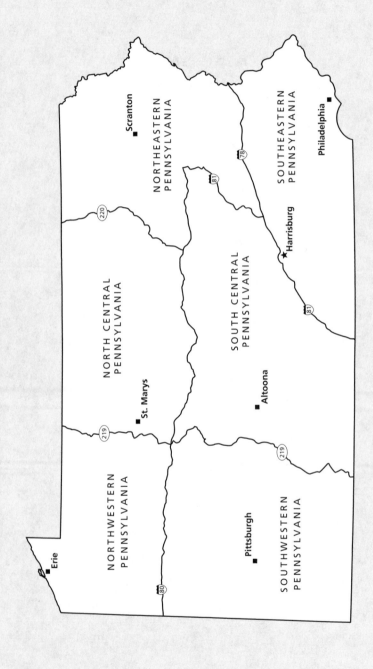

Contents

Acknowledgments

This book has helped me relive some favorite moments in Pennsylvania history—my own.

As a native who started east, moved west, and eventually became a travel writer, my personal and professional footprints run all through the state. For their help in mapping every opportunity along the way, I thank fellow writers like my twin, Carol Denny, and Jim O'Toole of the *Pittsburgh Post-Gazette,* my husband, intrepid companion, and best editor. Bruno Lavoissier provided valuable fact-checking.

To my father, Ned Hoffner, who bundled up seven kids and took them skiing in the Poconos, camping at French Creek, skating on frozen Delaware County ponds, and leaf-hiking at Ridley Creek, I owe a debt of gratitude for his boundless energy, example, and encouragement. He started me on this path.

Introduction

When I think of Pennsylvania, I think green.

Driving home to Philadelphia after a weekend at the beach, I used to roll down the window as I crossed the Delaware River and sniff the humid fragrance of an August night, so different from south Jersey's parched sand. On a spring drive down Route 6, I'll see a golden mountainside and know it's a week away from leafing out (unless it snows, of course—a distinct possibility in the Pennsylvania mountains). Whether observed from a bike seat in York County or a trail along the Chestnut Ridge, this state has simply terrific photosynthesis.

The natural end of all that transpiration is, of course, fall, and it's fabulous here. In October you bask in what I think is its most memorable weather: warm days, deep blue skies, and a palette of colors that Crayola (a Pennsylvania company) would kill for. Throw a few elk, bear, bikers, or golfers into that picture, and you've got the state at its finest.

Pennsylvania is an old state. Its central ridges and valleys are mind-bendingly ancient—about 250 million years old, geologically speaking. Evidence of human life in rock shelters in Washington County goes back at least 16,000 years. Ten thousand years ago Indians hunted mammoths and mastodons. Europeans first settled here in 1643. All those layers of history mean that however you slice it, there's always something new to enjoy and digest.

Spend lots of time in Philadelphia—it's as youthful as it is historic and has a collection of fabulous museums that would take weeks to visit. Walk around Old City, an authentic eighteenth-century neighborhood where young locals push strollers and bikes. In-line skate down Kelly Drive (but remove the skates when you get to the "Rocky" steps at the Museum of Art). Boo the sports teams—it's a tradition here—and ride the Market Street El, the Broad Street subway, or the trains to Suburban Station, because the Schuylkill Expressway can be a nightmare.

But Pennsylvania is a broad state. So, in planning your jaunt here, be broad-minded.

If you think state capitols are a snore, you'll be pleasantly surprised by Pennsylvania's neoclassical masterpiece on the banks of the Susquehanna. If you've ever seen the Grand Canyon, you owe it to yourself to compare it to Pennsylvania's version, a gorgeous gorge in Tioga County. And if you think Pennsylvania military history is all Gettysburg and Valley Forge, find out why the French and Indians battled for this land before the nation even existed—and why the British hacked their way through hundreds of miles of deep, mountainous forest (more greenery) to claim their fort at Pittsburgh.

Pennsylvania is green because it's well watered. Between the peaceful upper Delaware and Lake Erie, ribbons of white water and terrific trout streams cut through the woods. In the valleys of Susquehanna and Lancaster Counties, lush farms snuggle against every rolling hillside, enjoying magnificent thunderstorms. And streamside county seats like Franklin abide like Brigadoon, charmingly unchanged.

Although Pennsylvania's tourist attractions often focus on industry, agriculture is still its biggest business. So, since you're being broad-minded, try a U-pick orchard or produce from a roadside stand. Visit the annual Farm Show in Harrisburg, which celebrates everything that grows in the state, from apples to zucchini. (Sweet-faced kids leading sweet-faced cows, butter sculptures, and rodeos, too—all for free every January.)

Give Pennsylvania—specifically, recent governors Casey, Ridge, Schweiker, and Rendell—credit for the steady improvements in the state's 116 parks. Over the past few decades, the Department of Conservation of Natural Resources (DCNR) has worked to groom them and to create interpretive signs and exhibits. Nice job, DCNR (and thank you, Commonwealth taxpayers).

Old industries have new purposes here. Many abandoned short lines built to haul coal are now being converted to trails. A bonus: Most of them run alongside streams. Hundreds of peaceful miles that used to be rusting steel are now long, restful water-level pathways. (The state's prettiest country roads have also been linked to biking networks.) And in Elk County former strip mines have been converted to verdant meadows, creating a resurgence of elk. The herd is now one of the largest in the eastern United States—a rustbelt story with a wild ending.

Quick: What's the state's Web site address? If you're tailing a car with a Pennsylvania license plate, the answer's right in front of you: www.state.pa.us. Use that ubiquitous URL to find all things Pennsylvanian. Select the tourism page, "Visit PA" (www.visitpa.com), and type a keyword—say, apple—and you'll find the National Apple Museum in Biglerville, farm markets galore, even restaurants with apple desserts to die for. It really works.

Twenty years ago the state had a slogan that promised "You've Got a Friend in Pennsylvania." (Today you'll see front license plates in the same blue-and-gold style that say "You've Got a Friend in Jesus," a play on that old catch-phrase. When you see one now, you'll catch the reference. That's true native lore.) The old ad campaign caught on because it's common sense and the real thing. With twelve million residents, you really are bound to know *someone* here. And I can vouch for the part about friends, most recently while writing this book.

In Donegal a fellow in a pickup truck tugged my car out of a snowdrift and simply drove off with a friendly wave. Dennis Tice of the Bedford Visitors Bureau insisted that my family drive to Gravity Hill, the most memorable of all my off-the-beaten-path destinations. Two shy Smethport teenagers, the only employees, kept me, the only dinner guest, company at the Courtyard Restaurant while I ate. And Ken Fosco made the early United States Navy come alive for me on the US Brig *Niagara* while he guided me around. Ken's an enthusiast who'll never set sail (he gets seasick).

More help came from other authors. *Diners of Pennsylvania,* by Brian Butko and Kevin Patrick, is a great side dish for *Off the Beaten Path.* So is *Weird Pennsylvania,* Matt Lake's compendium of ghost stories, local legends, and other oddities from across the Commonwealth.

You might say that hospitality is a cornerstone of the state, but in Pennsylvania we prefer that you say "Keystone."

During colonial times Pennsylvania was the middle colony of the original thirteen colonies. It held the colonies together as the keystone supports the arch above a window or door, so it's the Keystone State and has been at least since 1800. Actually, technically, it's not a state at all. Officially Pennsylvania is a commonwealth, as are only three other states—Kentucky, Massachusetts, and Virginia. The word comes from Old English and means the "common weal," or well-being of the public. In Pennsylvania all legal processes are carried out in the name of the Commonwealth, although the word does not appear on the state seal.

How to Use This Book

Pennsylvania's hills come in three flavors. From west to east, the state's topography slides from the Allegheny Plateau (an Ice Age leftover) through the central Ridge and Valley region, and southeast through the Piedmont, until it flattens at the coastal plain along the Delaware River.

From above, the Ridge and Valley region looks like folds in a blanket. The long, wooded ridges run southwest to northeast, with beautiful farm valleys in between. Roads generally run along those ridge tops or through the valleys. That's why the six slices of the state—three northern segments and three southern—don't follow a grid. In most cases they are bounded by the major roads (more about them later), which, in turn, find a way around the state's rivers and valleys that can seem a bit slanted. If you want straight lines, go west; if you want surprises, stick around.

Pennsylvania Facts

BRIEF HISTORY OF EARLY PENNSYLVANIA

King Charles II of England gave William Penn, a Quaker, a large tract of land in the New World as repayment of a debt the king owed to William's father. The tract of land that became known as Pennsylvania, or "Penn's Woods," was settled in 1643. William Penn encouraged the Quakers and other persecuted groups to settle in Pennsylvania, saying "No person shall be molested or prejudiced for his or her conscientious persuasion or practice." In Pennsylvania, he promised, they could practice their religious beliefs in a democratic way. Over time, Pennsylvania's freedom appealed not only to Quakers but also to Amish, Moravians, Slovaks, Poles, Jews, Catholics, Hungarians, Italians, Irish, Greeks, and many other religious and ethnic groups.

Penn established a legislature, making his mark as one of America's great visionaries. "He was the greatest law-giver the world has produced," said Thomas Jefferson. Penn originally intended the capital of Pennsylvania to be located in Upland, now known as Chester. In 1682 the capital moved upriver to Philadelphia. But as settlers in Pennsylvania began pushing westward, legislators decided that the capital should be in a more central location, so they moved it to Lancaster in 1799 and finally to Harrisburg in 1810.

YOU TAKE THE HIGH ROAD, AND I'LL TAKE ROUTE 30

Pennsylvania has the nation's fourth-largest highway system—more than 44,000 miles of highways under state control. And the Keystone State has the eighth-highest count of highway miles—nearly 119,000 miles. Bottom line: It's *real* easy to get around. From four-lane highways with limited access to country roads that pass more cows than people, Pennsylvania has its share of concrete, macadam, and tarmac.

Most of Pennsylvania's busiest highways started out as Indian paths, as Indians had a genius for picking the most direct and level paths everywhere they went. The paths they created were no more than a foot or two wide, but they were later followed by European foot soldiers, then settlers with wagons, then modern road builders. Next stop: the interstates. When you drive any of the roads described below, you'll notice they often follow a ridgeline, a stream, a valley, or a mountain pass. You'll now know why.

Among all these roadways, five highways deserve special attention:

- **The National Road (Route 40)** was the first federally funded highway (1818 to 1835). It connected Washington, D.C., with points west, traversing Maryland, cutting across the southwest corner of Pennsylvania, running through Ohio and Indiana, and ending in Illinois. The National Road opened up land west of the Alleghenies and allowed a budding nation to expand westward. In the state's southwestern corner, what is now Route 40 had long been used by Indians before the European settlers paved it. In those early days the ridgeline route was called Nemacolin's Path for the chief who controlled these parts. (He was, in turn, controlled by the mighty Iroquois nation to the north.) You can see toll-houses in Petersburg and Searights and nearly fifty more structures that served as taverns and inns during the road's early years. The Stone House in Farmington and the Century Inn in Scenery Hill still welcome travelers after 200 years.

- **The Lincoln Highway (Route 30)** was the first coast-to-coast highway. When it was established in 1913, it was merely a line on a map, stretching from New York City to San Francisco by connecting existing roads. In 1925 the government began numbering highways. In 1928 the Lincoln Highway Association fabricated and installed (with the help of Boy Scouts) more than 3,000 concrete markers—one at almost every mile—across the entire country. Bands of red, white, and blue (with a big *L*) were painted on telephone poles to designate the highway. Alas, road widenings, snow plows, and natural disasters have destroyed all but about twenty markers. The Lincoln Highway Heritage Corridor (LHHC), a nonprofit organization, aims to encourage you to follow this ribbon of highway, where you'll discover nifty attractions that your grandparents might have seen. Within Pennsylvania, Route 30 covers 320 miles and thirteen counties. At its westernmost Pennsylvania point, it's 4 miles west of Hookstown; it runs east through the state and crosses the Benjamin Franklin Bridge, connecting Philadelphia to Camden, New Jersey. Reach LHHC at Box 582, Ligonier 15658. You can also call (724) 238–9030, fax (724) 238–9310, or visit www.lhhc.org.

- **Route 6** starts out mountainous in the east, then flattens out to a two-lane highway that strings together all the county seats of what's called the "northern tier." This is one of those in-between Indian paths: You'll notice the big mountains on either side as you drive through the Brokenstraw Valley, near the Allegheny National Forest. It may be a national road, but the speed limit is still 50 miles per hour most of the way.

- **Route 1** is a mostly stop-and-don't-go path through dreary suburban strip malls around Philadelphia—but be patient. Follow it south into Chester County and you'll find the heart of the Brandywine Valley—home to Wyeths, mushrooms, universities (Cheney and Lincoln), and farmland.

- **The Pennsylvania Turnpike.** Talk about the beaten path—this one's been beaten just about to death. Those who drive it may frequently admire the feats of engineering that took it through four mountains (and over a few more), two rivers, and the state's major cities. But they can't bring themselves to admire its congestion, seemingly constant summer construction, and frequently foggy conditions. (I won't even mention the tolls.) The Pennsylvania Turnpike developed the Sonic Nap Alert Pattern (SNAP), which is the placement of rumble strips along the edge of the right lane to alert drivers who are falling asleep. A better way to stay awake: Grab a map and plot a route that takes you off the turnpike as much as possible.

Delightful Driving Tours Recommended by the Pennsylvania Office of Travel and Tourism

Northern Zone

Route 6 from Smethport through Coudersport to Galeton

Route 44 from Coneville through Cherry Springs State Park to Oleona

Route 15 from Liberty through Mansfield to Tioga

Route 6 from Towanda to Factoryville

I–81 from Hallstead to East Benton

Central Zone

Route 26 from State College to Huntingdon

Route 62 from Tideoute (rhymes with "pretty suit") to Oil City

Route 322 from Clearfield to Potters Mills

Route 42 from Eagles Mere through Bloomsburg to Mount Carmel

Route 422 from Kittanning through Indiana to Ebensburg

Route 30 from Ligonier to Schellsburg

Southern Zone

Route 30 from Gettysburg to Bedford

Route 32 along the Delaware River from Easton to Yardley

Route 233 from Mont Alto through Pine Grove Furnace to Landisburg

Route 10 from Reading through Honey Brook to Cochanville

Route 445 from Fort Hunter through Pine Grove to Route 895 to Bowmanstown

The Mason-Dixon Line

The English astronomers Charles Mason and Jeremiah Dixon surveyed parts of the colonies in the 1760s and drew a straight line—the stripe that became the Mason-Dixon line. Pennsylvania touches the north side of the line; Delaware,

Maryland, and West Virginia touch the south. During the Civil War the North, the Union, comprised the "free states," and the South, the Confederacy, comprised the "slave states."

Welcome Centers

The Pennsylvania Department of Transportation (PennDOT) and the Pennsylvania Turnpike Commission operate welcome centers at highway entrances to the Keystone State. Knowledgeable and friendly hosts at the centers can offer directional assistance; provide detailed information about Pennsylvania's culture, history, scenic attractions, and activities; give you the weather forecast; report on road conditions; and arrange overnight accommodations. The centers have vending machines, picnic tables, restrooms, and pet areas. The welcome centers operate from 7:00 A.M. to 7:00 P.M. seven days a week, including most holidays. Following is a list of welcome center locations.

- Claysville, I–70 eastbound, 5 miles west of West Virginia border
- Easton, I–78 westbound, 1 mile west of New Jersey border
- Edinboro, I–79 southbound, 1 mile south of Edinboro exit
- Kirby, I–79 northbound, 5 miles north of West Virginia border
- Lenox, I–81 southbound, 4 miles south of exit 211 (old exit 64)
- Linwood, I–95 northbound, 0.5 mile north of Delaware border
- Matamoras, I–84 at exit 53 (old exit 11)
- Neshaminy, I–276 (Pennsylvania Turnpike), mile marker 51 westbound, 7 miles west of New Jersey border
- Shrewsbury, I–83 northbound, 0.5 mile north of Maryland border
- State Line, I–81 northbound, 1.5 miles north of Maryland border
- Tioga, Route 15 southbound, 7 miles south of New York border
- Warfordsburg, I–70 westbound, 0.5 mile east of Maryland border
- West Middlesex, I–80 eastbound, 0.5 mile east of Ohio border
- Zelienople, I–76 (Pennsylvania Turnpike), mile marker 21 eastbound, 21 miles east of Ohio border

Kids Welcome

Children and inner children will find plenty of playtime in Pennsylvania. Zoos abound (Philadelphia's is the oldest in the country, with 1,600 creatures; others in Pittsburgh, Hershey, and Erie are large and thriving). Philadelphia's purple Please Touch Museum, next to the Franklin Institute, is world-class; Pittsburgh's newly renovated Children's Museum includes a salute to a local hero, TV's Mister Rogers. Sesame Place, in Bucks County, has been voted one of *Parents* magazine's top picks for its rides and Muppets. The Crayola Museum in Easton is hands-on. And amusement parks? Pennsylvania boasts some that are twirled and true: Kennywood and Idlewild in the west, Hersheypark and Dorney Park in the east. Daredevils love Camp Woodward's skateboarding ramps and classes for extreme sports near State College, while toddlers prefer to feed the ducks at Dutch Wonderland in Lancaster County.

And while you're driving the kids from one to the other, tune in to *Kid's Corner,* a Sunday-through-Thursday radio show. More than 40,000 kids call in each month, making the Philadelphia-based show the most popular National Public Radio program for under-tens. Find it on WXPN-FM, 88.5, Philadelphia, and 104.9, Allentown; WXPH-FM, 88.1, Harrisburg; and WKHS-FM, 90.5, Worton, Maryland.

You've Got a Friend Who Eats in Pennsylvania: Eleven Keystone Food Firsts

1861   Julius Sturgis Pretzel Company, Lititz, becomes America's first commercial baker.

1894   Cracker Jacks are first manufactured in Philadelphia.

1900   Frank Fleer coats chewing gum in sugar. *Voilà:* Chiclets.

1902   Fast food is born at the Horn & Hardart Automat, 818 Chestnut Street, Philadelphia.

1904   The banana split makes its first appearance in Latrobe.

1918   Frank Fleer does it again: Dubble Bubble.

1920   Emil's, 1800 South Broad Street, Philadelphia, makes sandwiches for Hog Island workers and calls them hoagies.

1929   Sam Isaly of Pittsburgh creates the Klondike, the first ice-cream bar, selling it for a nickel.

1936   Frank Ludens of Reading concocts the Fifth Avenue candy bar.

1937   Good 'n' Plenty candy is manufactured in Philadelphia.

1968   Jim Delligatti, a McDonald's franchise owner, invents the Big Mac in Uniontown.

Fun Food Fact: Chocolate factories in Pennsylvania include Blommer, in East Greenville; Godiva, in Reading; Goldenberg, in Philadelphia; Hershey, in Hershey; Mars, in Elizabethtown; R. M. Palmer, in West Reading; and Wilbur, in Lititz. How sweet it is. According to the Chicago-based Retail Confectioners International, 45 of the group's 400 members are in Pennsylvania.

Pennsylvania's Official Designations

- **Animal:** White-tailed deer
- **Arboretum:** Morris Arboretum, Philadelphia
- **Beverage:** Milk

- **Bird:** Ruffed grouse
- **Dog:** Great Dane
- **Fish:** Brook trout
- **Flower:** Mountain laurel
- **Fossil:** *Phacops rana,* a small water animal
- **Insect:** Firefly
- **Motto:** Virtue, Liberty, and Independence
- **Ship:** US Brig *Niagara*
- **Tree:** Hemlock

Geography

- **Area:** 45,888 square miles
- **Campsites:** 7,000
- **Capital:** Harrisburg, in Dauphin County
- **Counties:** 67
- **Counties with no traffic lights:** Forest and Perry
- **Geographic center:** Centre County, 2.5 miles southwest of Bellefonte
- **Highest point:** Mt. Davis, 3,213 feet
- **Lakes:** 1 Great Lake (Lake Erie), 50 natural lakes (over 20 acres wide), and 2,500 artificial lakes
- **Largest county:** Lycoming, which is larger than Rhode Island
- **Lowest point:** Delaware River
- **Miles of Appalachian Trail:** 230 (The midpoint of the 2,144-mile Appalachian Trail, where it's traditional for hikers to eat a half-gallon of ice cream, is in Pine Grove Furnace State Park, Cumberland County.)
- **Rivers and streams:** 54,000 miles, more flowing water than any other continental state
- **Rivers with the hardest-to-pronounce names:** Schuylkill (say SCHOOL-kill) and Youghiogheny (rhymes with sock-a-SAY-knee) Rivers
- **Size:** 44,820 square miles of land, plus 735 square miles of Lake Erie
- **Species of fish:** 159
- **Species of trees:** 127
- **State forest districts:** 20; 2,200,000 acres
- **State game lands:** 294; 1,379,002 acres
- **State parks:** 116; 282,500 acres; miles of trails: 5,000

Government

- **U.S. representatives:** 19
- **State representatives:** 203
- **State senators:** 50

- **Municipalities:** 2,566 (more than any other state)
- **Sales tax on clothing and shoes:** Zero

Pennsylvania Firsts

- **First all motion-picture theater**—Nickelodeon, Pittsburgh, 1905
- **First Jeep**—Bantam Car Company, Butler, 1940
- **First educational public television station**—WQED, Pittsburgh, 1954
- **First hospital**—Pennsylvania Hospital, Philadelphia, 1751
- **First national capital**—Philadelphia, 1790
- **First newspaper**—*Pennsylvania Packet,* Philadelphia, 1784
- **First brewery**—Yuengling Brewery, Pottsville, 1829
- **First American theater**—Walnut Street Theater, Philadelphia, 1809
- **First computer**—University of Pennsylvania, Philadelphia, 1946
- **First zoo**—Zoological Society of Philadelphia, 1874

Agriculture (the state's largest industry)

- **Farmland:** 7.7 million acres
- **Farms:** 59,000
- **Leading farm products:** dairy products, mushrooms, apples, tobacco, grapes, peaches, cut flowers, Christmas trees, eggs
- **Rural population:** 3,700,000

Mascots of Major Sports Teams

- **Philadelphia Eagles**—Eagle
- **Philadelphia Phantoms**—Phantom
- **Philadelphia Phillies**—Phanatic
- **Philadelphia 76ers**—Hot Shot
- **Pittsburgh Pirates**—Parrot

Famous Natives and Residents

Louisa May Alcott, *novelist*

Marian Anderson, *contralto*

Samuel Barber, *composer*

John Barrymore, *actor*

Donald Barthelme, *author*

Stephen Vincent Benét, *poet and story writer*

Daniel Boone, *frontiersman*

Ed Bradley, *TV anchorman*

James Buchanan, *U.S. president*

Alexander Calder, *sculptor*

Rachel Carson, *biologist and author*

Mary Cassatt, *painter*

Henry Steele Commager, *historian*

Bill Cosby, *actor*

Jimmy and Tommy Dorsey, *bandleaders*

W. C. Fields, *comedian*

Stephen Foster, *composer*

Robert Fulton, *inventor*

Martha Graham, *choreographer*

Alexander Haig, *former U.S. secretary of state*

Marilyn Horne, *mezzo-soprano*

Lee Iacocca, *auto executive*

Reggie Jackson, *baseball player*

Gene Kelly, *dancer and actor*

Grace Kelly, *Princess of Monaco*

S. S. Kresge, *merchant*

Mario Lanza, *actor and singer*

Man Ray, *painter*

Margaret Mead, *anthropologist*

Andrew Mellon, *financier*

Tom Mix, *actor*

Arnold Palmer, *golfer*

Robert E. Peary, *explorer*

Betsy Ross, *flag maker*

B. F. Skinner, *psychologist*

John Sloan, *painter*

Gertrude Stein, *author*

James Stewart, *actor*

John Updike, *novelist*

Fred Waring, *bandleader*

Ethel Waters, *singer and actress*

Anthony Wayne, *military officer*

August Wilson, *poet, writer, and playwright*

Wallis Warfield, *Duchess of Windsor*

Andrew Wyeth, *painter*

When Autumn Leaves Start to Fall

In autumn 127 varieties of trees change from summer green into 127 spectac-
ularly brilliant fall colors. Choose this time to hike a nature trail—breathing the
clean, crisp air, experiencing the beauty of the red maples, comparing falling

leaves. If two feet is not the way you want to experience autumn in Pennsylvania, how about two wheels? If you know where to look, Pennsylvania offers hundreds of miles of scenic biking paths. Kudos to former Governor Tom Ridge, an avid cyclist, for asking engineers to link the Commonwealth's most level country roads. The result is a network of six less-traveled routes that take you near major cities but keep you far from clogged highways. You share the road, but safely. Routes A, E, S, Y, G, L, and Z are well marked. Check out the map at www.bikepa.com. For off-road riding, get some trail tips from the DCNR site: www.dcnr.state.pa.us/rails/index.html. And check the regional chapters of this book for local ideas.

ANNUAL TEMPERATURE AVERAGES (FAHRENHEIT): MAXIMUM/MINIMUM

	Allentown	Erie	Harrisburg	Philadelphia
January	35/20	33/20	37/23	39/24
April	61/39	54/37	62/42	63/43
July	85/64	79/62	86/66	87/68
October	64/43	61/44	65/45	67/47
	Pittsburgh	Scranton	Wayne County*	Williamsport
January	35/20	33/19	34/19	29/15
April	61/40	58/38	61/39	54/35
July	83/62	82/62	84/62	79/60
October	63/43	62/42	63/41	58/40

*Closest city: Binghamton, New York

Southeastern Pennsylvania: Philadelphia and Its Countryside

Philadelphia

How do you introduce a major metropolis to strangers without driving them around in your car? Do you start with the history? The planned geography? The parks and zoo? Or your favorite restaurants in a city overflowing with A-1 eateries in all price ranges?

Philadelphia has the fifth-largest metropolitan area in the country. The region comprises five counties in Pennsylvania (Bucks, Chester, Delaware, Montgomery, and Philadelphia) plus two in New Jersey (Camden and Gloucester). In the 1960s Walter Annenberg, who then owned the *Philadelphia Inquirer* and *Daily News,* coined the phrase "Delaware Valley," essentially for marketing purposes. The term stuck for decades but has recently fallen out of favor. Now it's safe, once again, to refer to the Philadelphia region or to the Philadelphia metropolitan area.

Philadelphia was not always a bustling urban center of five million people. When William Penn received a gift of a lot of forestland in the New World—hence, Penn's Woods, or Pennsylvania—he became a seventeenth-century land speculator.

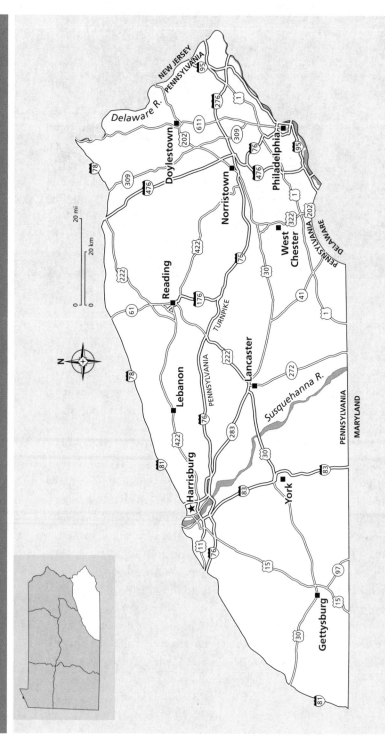

SOUTHEASTERN PENNSYLVANIA

Penn perceived his burgh to be a "greene countrie towne." In his 2-mile-wide-by-1-mile-north/south plan, he arranged for five squares to remain forever green. Four of those—Logan in the northwest, Rittenhouse in the southwest, Washington in the southeast, and Franklin in the northeast—remain gardenlike (and all but Franklin make delightful strolling areas, meeting places, or picnic sites). In the central square, cleverly called Center Square, the city built its *City Hall* in 1871. The building sits at the crossroads of the city and holds the mayor's office, city council, and courtrooms. The place is hardly off the beaten path, but few people think of it as a tourist destination, which it assuredly is. Treat yourself to a tour.

trivia

What better postmark than the signature of the nation's first postmaster? Get Benjamin Franklin's John Hancock on letters mailed from the U.S. Post Office at 316 Market Street, next to his home.

City Hall

City Hall is a bold example of what architectural historians call High Victorian picturesque eclecticism, designed in the then-popular French Second Empire style, similar to the Old Executive Office Building next door to the White House. The most dominant part of City Hall is the tower, soaring 548 feet above the ground. On top perches William Penn, sometimes called the tallest man in Philadelphia. Penn's 37-foot bronze likeness weighs more than twenty-six tons. He faces northeast, where the founder of Philadelphia and Pennsylvania made a legendary treaty with the Lenni-Lenape Indians in 1682.

AUTHOR'S TOP TEN FAVORITES IN SOUTHEASTERN PENNSYLVANIA

American Philosophical Society	The murals in Philadelphia
Chanticleer	Rosenbach Museum
Distelfinks	Statue of Ben Franklin on Penn's campus
Hawk Mountain	U.S.A. Weightlifting Hall of Fame
Mincemeat pie from Groff's Meats	
Mt. Gretna	

You can take one-and-a-half-hour tours weekdays at 12:30 P.M. Enter the east portal and go to the tour office on the first floor, where tours begin and where a gift shop offers souvenirs. For information on tours call (215) 686–2840, or visit www.philadelphiacityhall.org.

Beyond City Hall

Liberty Bell? Check. Independence Hall? Ditto. Most of Philadelphia's most popular attractions lie within Independence National Historical Park. Start your visit there with a stop at the ***Independence Visitor Center,*** a perfect orientation to the neighborhood. Check out the free movies, plot your itinerary on a giant map, buy your timed admission tickets to all the best attractions, and quiz the helpful staff for suggestions. It's open daily at 1 North Independence Mall West.

How to Order a Cheesesteak

Ordering a cheesesteak—that overstuffed hot sandwich of paper-thin sliced beef on a long, freshly baked Italian roll—can be intimidating, and not just because the counter man usually looks greasy and vaguely unhappy. This toothsome favorite, known elsewhere as a Philly steak, will hit your stomach like a hunk o' burnin' love. Most Philadelphians pledge allegiance to a preferred vendor—just ask the nearest local for the best shop within walking distance.

Cheesesteaks are messy. They're usually wrapped in paper for takeout (you should also grab lots of napkins and remove your tie). They are best eaten when you are absolutely famished, and washed down with a birch beer—a favorite local soda that tastes a bit like a Dr. Pepper.

Here's what you want to decide before that scary cook barks questions at you:

- Half or whole? A half sandwich is a six-inch slab; a whole is the equivalent of roughly two full meals.

- Cheese? Complicated. First decide if you want the cheese; if not, order a steak. If you want the classic provolone topping, order cheese. If you like soft processed cheese from an aerosol can, order with Whiz.

- Green stuff? A cheesesteak hoagie means topped with chopped lettuce and tomato. Specify your onions cooked or raw. Peppers can be either sweet or hot; mushrooms, always cooked.

- Sauce? In Philly parlance, sauce means spicy tomato sauce (feel free to specify lots or a little). You could ask for ketchup instead. Go for the burn.

After all that, don't be surprised if your order turns out wrong. Somehow, it's all good.

The Philadelphia Negro

In 1899 W. E. B. DuBois published *The Philadelphia Negro,* a meticulously researched, groundbreaking study of African-American life. The book, now a recognized classic in its field, was ignored by the people who sponsored it. The twenty-seven-year-old, spats-wearing, cane-carrying, Victorian-looking gentleman researched the 40,000 African Americans who lived amid more than a million whites in Philadelphia, then the second-largest city in the nation.

For more information phone (800) 537–7676 or (215) 925–7676, or visit www .independencevisitorcenter.com. Hours are 8:30 A.M.–7:00 P.M. July 1 through Labor Day; the rest of the year, 8:30 A.M.–5:00 P.M.

Just north of the Visitor Center, stop by the ***National Constitution Center*** (525 Arch Street, Independence Mall). The building by I. M. Pei, opened for the document's 220th birthday in 2003, is a marvel of high-tech, interactive displays interpreting all eight articles and twenty-seven amendments. Civic-minded kids can take the presidential oath in front of the Capitol on live TV or don Supreme Court judicial robes. In Signers' Hall mingle among clustered, lifelike statues of the document's forty-three signatories—authentic to their well-polished brass fingertips. Because it's so popular, best book your timed admission tickets ahead, either here or at the Visitor Center. Open daily. Admission is $9.00 for adults (extra for other special exhibits); $7.00 for children under twelve and seniors. For more information call (215) 923–0004, or visit www.constitutioncenter.org.

makeaphlash

Park your car and ride the *Phlash,* a small van that makes eighteen touristic stops in Center City. It operates every twelve minutes from 10:00 A.M. to 6:00 P.M. May 1 to November 30, and costs $1.00 per trip or $4.00 for an all-day pass. Call (215) 440–5500 or visit www .gophila.com/phlash for more details.

Most Old City tourists grab their souvenirs and snacks along Market Street. Dare to differ. Turn the corner onto Third Street and stroll north above Arch Street to find hipper alternatives.

This up-and-coming shopping strip offers Cafe Ole for Mexican food; Third Street Habit, Minima, and Three Sirens for funky women's clothes; and Indigo for cool Asian and African imports. At 160 North Third, stop at ***Petit 4 Pastry Studio.*** Fresh-baked fruit muffins, coffee, Sacher tortes, cheesecakes, cobblers, and desserts are made fresh daily. Four-star fabulous. Opens at 7:00 A.M., 8:00 A.M. weekends; closed Mondays. Call (215) 627–8440 for more information.

"Music is the most magical form of communication among people," said Wolfgang Sawallisch, former music director of the **Philadelphia Orchestra.** For over one hundred years the orchestra has been creating musical magic in Philadelphia and beyond. With Leopold Stokowski, Eugene Ormandy, and Riccardo Muti among its noted conductors, the orchestra has commissioned dozens of works of art, recorded scores of others, and entertained audiences from Ottawa to Osaka. By 1988 it was calculated that the orchestra had traveled enough to circle the earth a hundred times. A new concert hall, the Kimmel Center for the Performing Arts, opened in 2001 at Broad and Spruce Streets. It's a block away from the century-old Academy of Music, called the "Grand Old Lady of Broad Street." For more information and detailed schedules, visit the Fabulous Philadelphians at www.philorch.org.

trivia

The majestic plateau now topped by the Philadelphia Museum of Art was formerly a giant reservoir. Powered by the river, pumps raised water into reservoirs high atop the hill, which gave its name to the city park: Faire Mount.

The **Philadelphia Museum of Art** is a must-see. For an off-the-beaten-time opportunity, try Wednesday evenings, when, in addition to seeing the artwork, you can participate in a special event that includes a film, dance instruction, a gallery talk, and storytelling—all for the normal museum entrance fee of $10 per adult. Schedule varies. Light supper costs extra. Call (215) 763–8100 or visit www.philamuseum.org to find out what's on tap the Wednesday of your choice. Limited programming in July and August, but the cafe is open year-round.

In the art department, don't miss the **Clothespin** (as in "meet me at the Clothespin"), an oversize sculpture by Claes Oldenburg. It's at the corner of Fifteenth and Market Streets. Oldenburg's colossal **Button** is on the campus of the University of Pennsylvania, nearest the intersection of Thirty-fourth and Walnut Streets. And a few blocks west, at the pedestrian-only intersection of Locust Walk and Thirty-seventh Street, have a seat on the bronze bench next to the bronze statue of Benjamin Franklin, founder of the University. Ben's reading his *Pennsylvania Gazette,* leaning on his cane, and waiting for you to relax. He knows he's a photo op beyond compare.

For lunch you can't beat the **Reading Terminal Market.** Founded in 1892 at the terminus of the Reading Railroad, this is a traditional stall market with eighty-five merchants selling usual and unique kinds of fish, meat, produce, pastries, flowers, and more. That's far fewer than the 800 stalls that lined the place on opening day, but it's big enough to find precisely the spice or the sourdough roll you want. The market is particularly known for its Pennsylva-

On Location: Films Shot in Philadelphia

1940	*Kitty Foyle*	1989	*Dead Poets Society*
1940	*The Philadelphia Story*	1992	*The Age of Innocence*
1945	*Pride of the Marines*	1995	*12 Monkeys*
1958	*The Blob*	1996	*Up Close and Personal*
1959	*The Young Philadelphians*	1998	*Wide Awake*
1963	*David and Lisa*	1998	*Requiem for Murder*
1966	*The Trouble with Angels*	1998	*The Sixth Sense*
1970	*Rocky*	2000	*Unbreakable*
1976	*Nasty Habits*	2002	*Signs*
1980	*Atlantic City*	2005	*In Her Shoes*
1981	*Blow Out*		
1981	*Taps*		
1983	*Trading Places*		
1984	*Birdy*		
1984	*Lost in America*		
1985	*Witness*		
1987	*Echoes in the Darkness*		
1988	*Clean and Sober*		

Hop a minibus tour of the city's prime film locations. The Philadelphia Film Office offers celebrity dish, movie clips, and more in a three-hour glimpse behind the scenes. Cue the *Rocky* soundtrack. For more information call (215) 686–2668, or get a preview at www.film.org.

nia Dutch vendors, who bring cheese and carrots from the surrounding countryside each day. It's open daily except Sunday from 8:00 A.M. to 6:00 P.M. (see www.readingterminalmarket.org). Many stands sell delicious lunches at reasonable prices. Get your Philadelphia soft pretzel here.

Another in-your-face Philadelphia shopping tradition is the loud, messy, and lively **Italian Market.** It sprawls on both sides of South Ninth Street between Christian and Wharton Streets, with four cheese stores, four fish stores, seven butcher shops, forty different international food vendors, and a larger-than-life mural of beloved former mayor Frank Rizzo, here called The Big Bambino. For more than one hundred years, this district has been the city's favorite place to rub elbows and pinch tomatoes. Open every day but Sunday. Get the details at www.phillyitalianmarket.com.

Don't overlook the excitement of other ethnic neighborhoods. The city's Asians, Latinos, and African Americans welcome you, too.

Enter Chinatown at **Friendship Gate,** at Tenth and Arch Streets, and grab a meal and your bearings at **Joseph Poon Chef Kitchen** at 1010 Cherry Street. Poon, a larger-than-life celebrity chef, leads three-hour "Wok 'n' Walk" tours of his neighborhood by appointment. They include a four-course lunch and local

Philadelphia Stars

Mario Lanza, singer and actor

The Nicholas Brothers, Fayard and Harold, dancers

Jeanette McDonald, actress

Katharine Hepburn, actress who attended Bryn Mawr College

Candice Bergen, actress who attended the University of Pennsylvania

Bill Cosby, who needs no introduction

Will Smith, actor

W. C. Fields, comedian

Elaine May, comedienne, born here

Grace Kelly, actress, later Princess of Monaco

Sidney Lumet, movie director

Brian dePalma, movie director

Richard Brooks, directed films *In Cold Blood* and *Blackboard Jungle*

Garrett Brown, invented the Steadicam

Sylvester Stallone, actor and director, attended high school here

Kevin Bacon, versatile movie actor who's within six degrees of practically everyone

The Barrymores, brothers Lionel and John, great film actors of the 1930s and 1940s

Peter Boyle, who graduated from LaSalle University here, with film and TV roles from *Frankenstein* to *Everybody Loves Raymond*

M. Night Shyamalan, who directed three movies set here: *The Sixth Sense, Unbreakable,* and *Signs*

color: everything from a Tai Chi demonstration to a vegetable-carving lesson. Lunch and the tour is $45 per person. For more details call (215) 928–9333, or visit www.josephpoon.com.

Nearby at 700 Arch Street, explore the African-American community's heritage at the ***African-American Museum in Philadelphia,*** with four galleries. Open Tuesday through Saturday, 10:00 A.M. to 5:00 P.M., and Martin Luther King Day. Admission is $8.00 for adults, $6.00 for seniors and children. Call (215) 574–0380, or visit www.aampmuseum.org. The Philadelphia Dance Company, known locally as Philadanco, is one of the country's foremost African-American performing groups; it's headquartered at 9 North Preston Street in West Philadelphia.

The Philadelphia Latino community calls the Fifth Street and Lehigh Avenue corridor "El Centro de Oro," or its heart of gold. Here you'll find Taller Puertorriqueño, a Puerto Rican cultural education organization; Asociación de Musicos Latinos Americanos (AMLA), a center for Latin music; and great bodegas and cafes.

The Benjamin Franklin Parkway holds some of the jewels of Philadelphia—the majestic Museum of Art, the Franklin Institute, the Rodin Museum, the Museum of Natural Sciences, and the Free Library (founded by Ben himself). But don't overlook some smaller gems with world-class special collections (see a full listing under "Culture Files" at www.gophila.com).

One of the city's oddest museums is preserved, quite literally, off North Broad Street, three blocks from the Temple University campus. The *Wagner Free Institute of Science* (1700 West Montgomery Avenue) is an institution housing the private collections of the altruistic William Wagner. Since its founding in 1855, it has offered free public education courses. Fossils, taxidermy mounts, skeletons, insects, minerals, geodes, and shells—Wagner meticulously amassed a collection now displayed in a grand three-story Victorian library. It even claims the first American saber-toothed tiger. It's both spooky and spectacular, a perfect setting for a horror movie. Admission is still free, though the Institute suggests a donation. Hours are Tuesday through Friday 9:00 A.M. to 4:00 P.M. Visit www.wagnerfree institute.org.

scootifyoudare

Roll along the Benjamin Franklin Parkway aboard an invention he'd adore: a Segway scooter. Tour the museum district and the Kelly Drive waterfront on these self-balancing scooters. Reservations only. For more information call (877) 454–3381 or glide to www.iglidetours.com.

In the Rittenhouse Square area, a beautiful spot for strolling and shopping, stop by the *Rosenbach Museum* at 2008–10 Delancey Place. It's the palatial town home formerly owned by two brothers: Philip Rosenbach, who collected rare furnishings; and A. S. W. Rosenbach, who collected rare books and manuscripts. Today you can gape at rarities on display from the museum's vast holdings: the original manuscript of James Joyce's *Ulysses,* Shakespeare folios, rare

American Bandstand

American Bandstand, the TV show you watched after school in the late fifties if you were between the ages of ten and twenty, was a Philadelphia phenom. The rock 'n' roll dance party, which went national in 1957, starred sock-hoppers and Dick Clark, the host with the most. The 1947 building (now demolished) at Forty-sixth and Market Streets in West Philadelphia, where Chubby Checker chugged and played, was one of the first facilities designed and constructed exclusively for television productions.

Americana, and works by children's author/illustrator Maurice Sendak (for whom the museum's new addition was named). The museum is open Tuesday through Sunday 10:00 A.M. to 5:00 P.M. (Wednesday until 8:00 P.M.); closed Monday and national holidays. Admission is $8.00, $5.00 for students and seniors; guided tours are available on the hour. Call (215) 732–1600, or visit www.rosenbach.org.

Like the Rosenbach, the **Pennsylvania College of Physicians Mutter Museum** is housed in a Rittenhouse Square town house and has its own unique niche, but there all similarities end. In fact, "endings" might be a good theme for this bizarre collection of skulls, lesions, a giant distended colon, the secretly removed tumor of Grover Cleveland, and much more. Both medical and morbid, for certain members of certain families (parents of teenage boys, are you listening?) it would be engrossing, as well as gross. The museum at 19 South Twenty-second Street is open daily from 10:00 A.M. to 5:00 P.M. Adult admission is $9.00. Call (215) 563–3737, or visit www.collphyphil.org.

hometownboy

"What a backyard I had growing up. Boathouse Row, Independence Hall. Come play in my old backyard. You'll love it, and I know it'll love you."

—Kevin Bacon

The **Art Alliance,** located on Philadelphia's fashionable Rittenhouse Square, displays innovative visual art. Built as a private home in 1906, the building was given to the Art Alliance in 1925. People initially joined the organization so they could imbibe alcohol on Sundays—the building was a speakeasy during Prohibition. The facility at 251 South Eighteenth Street is open Tuesday through Sunday from 11:00 A.M. to 5:00 P.M. Admission is free, with a donation suggested. Opus 251, a cafe on the premises, serves lunch from 11:30 A.M. to 2:30 P.M. (from 11:00 A.M. Friday and Saturday), and dinner from 5:30 to 10:30 P.M. daily, except Monday. For more information call the Alliance at (215) 545–4302, or visit www.philartalliance.org.

For those intrigued by Lewis and Clark, a visit to Independence National Park is definitely in order—not to gawk at the Declaration, but to view artifacts of the famous 1803–04 expedition at the **American Philosophical Society** next door at 105 South Fifth Street. Among the society's founders were Benjamin Franklin and Thomas Jefferson. The society, which directed scientific preparations for the Corps of Discovery, owns Lewis's original journals and exhibits them each summer. Rembrandt Peale's famous portraits of the explorers are displayed with those of other early American heroes a block away. (Pick up a nifty walking guide detailing other neighborhood sites connected to the historic journey at the park's visitor center.) The society presents displays in the library lobby and the next-door Philosophical Hall. Visit Thursday through Sunday from noon to 5:00 P.M. (and Wednesday from March 1 to Labor Day); admission is free. For more information call (215) 440–3400, or visit www.amphilsoc.org.

Another undiscovered urban treasure is the **Atwater Kent Museum,** whose collection details the people, places, and products of Philadelphia's 300-year history. There's a gift shop, too. Open daily except Tuesday, 10:00 A.M. to 5:00 P.M.; closed major holidays. Admission is $5.00 for adults. The museum is located at 15 South Seventh Street, just around the corner from Independence Hall. For more information call (215) 685–4830, or visit www.philadelphiahistory.org. If you can't find it—check your map again. Don't bother to ask Philadelphians, even those walking by the front door. They've never heard of the Atwater Kent.

Go to jail. Go directly to jail. Do not pass *Go*, and do not miss a tour of the **Eastern State Penitentiary** at Twenty-second Street and Fairmount Avenue. You can stay for a short time, unlike Willie Sutton (who robbed banks because, he said, that's where the money was) and Al Capone. This was the world's first *penitentiary,* a place where criminals could be *penitent.* Constructed in the 1820s to rehabilitate criminals through solitary confinement, the castlelike penitentiary that was once the most expensive building and most

Follow Philadelphia's Red Brick Roads

For a trip back in time, visit these twenty streets still paved in red brick.

Abbotsford Avenue (100 block)	Lofty Street (200)
Bodine Street (South 900)	Maiden Street (100)
Burbridge Street (6300)	Montgomery Avenue (2900)
Carlisle Street (5100 to 5300)	Orianna Street (300)
Chang Street (North 900)	Pechin Street (4500)
Estaugh Street (West 100)	Perkiomen Street (800)
Fulton Street (South 600)	Rector Street (100)
Gates Street (100)	Smick Street (4800)
Hedge Street (5300)	Wyneva Street (West 100)
Jessup Street (South 200)	Zeralda Street (300)

famous prison in the world is now a crumbling, empty block of sky-lit cells and guard towers. Regular tours are held April through November. For a $9.00 admission fee ($7.00 for students and seniors, $4.00 for kids), you get an audio tour from 10:00 A.M. to 5:00 P.M. Wednesday through Sunday. At other times groups of twenty or more can book ahead. Call (215) 236–3300, or visit www.eastern state.org.

> ## trivia
>
> Near Wissahickon Creek in northwest Fairmount Park you'll see Hermit Street, Hermit Lane, and Hermit Terrace. The streets commemorate a brotherhood of seventeenth–century German mystics led by Johannes Kelpius, who lived in a cave nearby.

At Forty-third Street and Baltimore Avenue, in the pocket-sized Clark Park, is a *statue of Charles Dickens,* the only known sculpture in the world of the English author of classics such as *David Copperfield* and *Great Expectations.*

For over a hundred years, men (and, of late, women and children) have strutted along Philadelphia's major thoroughfares on the first day of the year, commemorating winter with costumes, comedy, and uncommon music. It's the internationally recognized *Mummers Parade.* The annual parade is an hours-long extravaganza of otherwise-normal people dressed in glitter, feathers, and organza. They march, they dance, they strut—and they compete for valuable prizes. (And the next day, legend says, they start preparing next year's pageant.) Thousands of enthusiastic revelers line city sidewalks at dawn each January 1 as the clubs, or "brigades," of Mummers dance to the music of banjos. Stilts, sequins, and serenades make it worth everyone's while to brave the cold. Kids drag their parents—or vice versa—and everyone, paraders and spectators alike, enjoys the occasion. Visit www.mummers.org or the *Mummers Museum,* 1100 South Second Street. The phone number is (215) 336–3050.

Fairmount Park

Philadelphia boasts *Fairmount Park,* the biggest planned urban park system in the world, with more than 8,700 acres of parkland, including natural and historical features, cultural attractions, recreation areas, and waterways. Every Philadelphian lives within a few minutes of a park, and it's a rare citizen who doesn't have a favorite tree, path, or picnic spot. Out-of-towners who come here to see the Liberty Bell and then trot off to New York or Washington are missing a jewel if they skip the park.

The park comes closest to downtown along Kelly Drive. Renamed for a famous Philadelphia rower (and brother of Princess Grace of Monaco), the road closes to traffic on Sundays so bikers, runners, and bladers can enjoy the river-front scene from its east bank. Alongside are crew teams practicing for the city's many regattas; they finish their races close to **Boathouse Row,** the oft-photographed stretch of Victorian riverfront buildings. Bathed in floodlights at night, they're best seen either from West River Drive (where you can't stop your car to enjoy them) or from the promenade outside the Fairmount Waterworks.

The **Fairmount Waterworks Interpretive Center,** located in the largest cream-colored building in the group below the Museum of Art, is a great free introduction to what was once a worldwide wonder. In 1821 the city created an ingenious system that used waterpower to pump water. Waterwheels, installed in the dam below the Engine House, used thirty gallons of water to lift one gallon out of the river. The dam was the largest in the world and cre-ated a lake in the Schuylkill that was six miles long—which is why it's been a favorite rowing venue ever since.

The center does a lighthearted job of showing kids how water is treated and transported (even the restrooms are educational, with displays on "The Journey of Your Flush"). Don't miss the wonderful short film that explains how the city turned the waterworks into a profit-making venture that beautified the entire riverbank, with parks, fountains, and promenades. The center is at 640 Waterworks Drive and is open Tuesday through Saturday from 10:00 A.M. to 5:00 P.M., Sunday from 1:00 to 5:00 P.M. (except for city holidays). Call (215) 685–0723 or visit www.fairmountwaterworks.org. The Waterworks Restaurant, www.the waterworksrestaurant.com, alongside promises fine dining and great views.

The perfect trip to Philadelphia includes a visit to **Valley Green**—if you can find it. It's the best—absolutely the best—part of the superb park system. It's in the Wissahickon Valley, Wissahickon being an anglicized blend of two words used by the Lenni-Lenape Indians: One meant yellow stream, the other meant catfish creek. (Anglers still occasionally lure catfish.) At Valley Green so many toddlers feed the ducks so many days of the year that the mallards can safely rely on human handouts for sustenance. A 5-mile-long, dirt-and-gravel path called **Forbidden Drive** passes through Valley Green. It's called For-bidden Drive because it has always been forbidden to automobiles and limited to walkers, runners, and horses, and now bikers and bladers. Valley Green, a totally un-urban Eden in the upper northwest section of the city, is always open. Study your map. Take Germantown Avenue northwest to #7900, turn left on Springfield Avenue, and follow signs (and the topography down-hill) to the valley. Or take Henry Avenue northwest to #7900, then turn right on Wise's Mill Road, following signs to the valley. If you're on foot, access Forbidden Drive anywhere and stop for coffee or crepes at the **Valley Green Inn.** Call (215) 247–1730, or visit www.valleygreeninn.com for reservations.

The Mural Tour

Early in 1999 Philadelphia surpassed Los Angeles as having the most urban murals of any city in the country. On exhibit twenty-four hours a day, with no admission fee and no waiting lines, 2,300 murals tell the story of the city's vitality, history, and dreams. The brainchild of Jane Golden, the Mural Arts Program (215–685–0750; www.muralarts.org) has created 1,900 of those murals, inspiring hundreds of disadvantaged youths to work with professional artists. To everyone's pleasure, as the murals go up, graffiti decreases. Here, with permission from the Mural Arts Program, is a self-guided tour of eleven popular murals. By car this tour takes about an hour. Or take the tour by trolley from April to October. Tickets are $20 for adults, $17 for students, and $10 for children five through ten.

Start at the Tourist Center at Sixteenth Street and J. F. Kennedy Boulevard.

Go west on Kennedy Boulevard toward Twentieth Street, moving into the left lane as you drive.

Turn left on Twentieth Street.

In 1 block turn right on Market Street.

Continue 0.9 mile, across the Schuylkill River. Turn right on Thirty-third Street.

In 0.4 mile turn right on Hamilton Street.

In 2 blocks turn left on Thirty-first Street.

In 1 block turn left at Spring Garden Street. Look for **Tuscan Landscape** on your left.

Get in left lane and turn left at light on Thirty-second Street (sign may be missing).

In 4 blocks turn right at Powelton Avenue. In 0.7 mile, look across Fortieth Street for **Boy with Raised Arm.**

Continue west on Powelton Avenue to third light, where it intersects with Market Street and Forty-fourth Street. Look across the intersection for **A Celebration of Community.**

Turn left onto Market Street. Go 1.7 miles, crossing the Schuylkill River, and turn right on Twenty-third Street.

In 0.6 mile cross South Street. Continue south, as Twenty-third Street bears right and becomes Grays Ferry Avenue.

Go 0.7 mile and turn left on Twenty-ninth Street.

Go to second stop sign (Wharton Street) and look across intersection for **Peace Wall.**

Continue on Twenty-ninth Street to second stop sign; turn left on Dickinson Street. Go 1.3 miles and turn left on Broad Street (which would be Fourteenth Street).

Follow Germantown Avenue farther north and you'll climb to **Chestnut Hill,** a well-heeled historic district. Cobblestoned, tree-lined Germantown Avenue is loaded with blocks of pleasant shops and cafes; nearby lie the leafy campuses of private schools such as Germantown Academy and Chestnut Hill College. Among the dozens of cafes, Campbell's Place, 8337 Germantown Avenue (215–242–2066), is a good choice for casual fare; find details on dozens of others at www.chestnuthillfood.com.

Chestnut Hill is also the home of the **Morris Arboretum** of the University of Pennsylvania, a romantic ninety-two-acre garden that emphasizes sculpture,

At first light (Reed Street), look across intersection to see **Mario Lanza.**

Continue on Broad Street about 0.8 mile; turn right on South Street.

At Sixth Street turn right and face **Brazilian Rainforest.**

Continue on Sixth Street and turn right on Christian Street.

Cross Seventh Street and look right for **Moonlit Landscape.**

Continue on Christian Street and turn right on Ninth Street.

Go 6 blocks and turn right on Pine Street.

Turn left on Seventh Street, and stay on it for 1.9 miles. You will run into Washington Square. Follow Seventh Street clockwise around the square, staying in the right lane. At Race Street, bear left around Franklin Square. Stay on Seventh, in the middle lane. Go straight, driving under the multilane I–476 overpass.

At Brown Street, look across intersection on left to see **Immigration and the Dignity of Labor.**

Continue north on Seventh. Turn left at Poplar Street.

Turn left on Eighth Street.

In 2 blocks turn right on Fairmount Avenue.

Turn left on Twelfth Street.

In 2 blocks turn right on Mt. Vernon Street.

In 1 block turn sharp left on Ridge Avenue.

In 1 block at Green Street, look left to see **Dr. J.**

Turn left on Green Street.

Turn left on Eleventh Street.

In 1 block turn left on Mt. Vernon Street.

When Mt. Vernon ends at Broad Street, turn left.

Go 3 blocks to intersection of Spring Garden Street. Look across intersection on left for **Common Threads.**

Continue on Broad Street for 8 blocks to intersection with Vine Street. Look across intersection for **A Tribute to the Family.**

When Broad Street ends at City Hall, turn right onto J. F. Kennedy Boulevard. Go straight, crossing Fifteenth Street, to return to Tourist Center on your right.

The mural project also creates three-dimensional art. See artist Bob Phillips's **Metamorphosis,** a series of forged steel butterflies, chrysalis lamps, ornamental railings and mosaics on the bridge that crosses the CSX tracks between Thirty-first Street and Fairmount Park.

trees, and research. It's a quarter mile off Germantown Avenue at 100 North-western Avenue. You can enjoy lunch alfresco, or at least under a tent, during warm weather at the cafe next to the Widener Visitor Center. The Arboretum is open weekdays from 10:00 A.M. to 4:00 P.M. Admission is $10.00 for adults, $8.00 for seniors, $5.00 for students; kids under three are admitted free. Call (215) 247–5777, or visit www.upenn.edu/arboretum.

In nearby Elkins Park (take Route 611 north from the city) is Frank Lloyd Wright's ***Beth Sholom Congregation.*** Dedicated in 1959, months after Wright's death, the building is a hexagonal pyramid of glass. The design is based, in part, on ideas put forth by the synagogue's distinguished and forward-looking first rabbi, Mortimer Cohen. The building was intended to be self-contained and to stand apart from its suburban surroundings. It succeeds. Wright designed the fittings, too: the lighting, the seating, and the placement of the religious symbols. When the Museum of the Diaspora in Tel Aviv created a permanent exhibit of synagogues to represent eighteen centuries of Judaism, it chose Beth Sholom for the twentieth century. Tours of the sanctuary, at Old York and Foxcroft Roads, are given Sunday through Thursday by appointment only. Call (215) 659–3009. To attend religious services, call (215) 887–1342.

Pennypack Environmental Center manages a one-hundred-plus-acre nature center that was dedicated as a bird sanctuary in 1958. Near the building are a bird blind, an herb garden, a composting area, and a campfire area. Organized programs include bird walks, botany hikes, and craft sessions. The Environmental Center is located in the far northeast section of Philadelphia on Verree Road, 1 mile north of Rhawn Street and 1.5 miles south of Red Lion Road.

Got a few hours' layover between planes? Go fishing. It's actually possible, from Philadelphia International Airport, to hop in a cab and be transported across the highway into a national wildlife refuge. This one, the *John Heinz National Wildlife Refuge at Tinicum,* was created to save the largest remaining freshwater tidal marsh in the country. As planes soar overhead, 300 species of birds fly below. The interpretive center at 8601 Lindbergh Boulevard is open daily. Additional information can be found at http://heinz.fws.gov.

Another patch of green—one of the city's most venerable—lies a few miles down Lindbergh Boulevard. From its surroundings—the Philadelphia Gas Works and other flat and charmless industrial sites—you'd never guess that the

ON THE BEATEN PATH ATTRACTIONS WORTH VISITING

Academy of Music,
Philadelphia

Independence Hall,
Philadelphia

Liberty Bell,
Philadelphia

Pennsylvania Academy of Fine Arts,
Philadelphia

Philadelphia Zoo

Rodin Museum,
Philadelphia

National Constitution Center,
Philadelphia

site is a landmark in the history of botany. ***Bartram's Garden,*** the eighteenth-century home of the naturalist Bartram family, is an idyllic Schuylkill River plantation that preserves native wildflowers, trees, and wetlands.

Father and son John and William Bartram are credited with sharing the plants of the New World with European scientists; John was named King George III's royal botanist in 1765. Both he and his son identified new species on field trips up and down the East Coast, cultivated over 200 of them, and saved at least one from extinction: the *Franklinia,* a tree named for their good friend and frequent visitor Benjamin Franklin. (Thomas Jefferson and George Washington stopped by, too). Today visitors can stroll the plantation and river trail, admiring the skyscrapers of downtown Philadelphia from a peaceful meadow. A map brochure identifies the locations of famous specimens, such as the country's oldest living ginkgo tree (circa 1785).

Boat trips along the Schuylkill from the Garden to the Fairmount Water-works depart from the Garden dock on weekends in warm-weather months. Reservations are required; tickets are $15 for Garden members, $20 for nonmembers. Check the schedule on the Garden Web site.

Bartram's Garden is open daily from 10:00 A.M. to 5:00 P.M., except for city holidays. Admission to the grounds is free. Forty-five minute guided tours leave the Museum Shop hourly and cost $5.00 for adults, $4.00 for seniors and students; children under twelve free. The Garden is located at 54th Street and Lindbergh Boulevard but is hard to find; call first for directions at (215) 729–5281, or visit www.bartramsgarden.org.

notjustforbreakfast

No matter what time you get up, cereal's the perfect breakfast. And that's why students at the University of Pennsylvania love **Cereality,** a restaurant that serves nothing but. Cereality will mix any combination of your favorites—say, Captain Crunch and Count Chocula with granola and raisins—all day long at 3631 Walnut Street, in the middle of Penn's campus. What's playing on the overhead TV? Cartoons, of course. Call (215) 222-1162.

Philadelphia gave birth to the nation's first horticultural society in 1827 and its first flower show in 1829. At the first show, twenty-five members of the Penn-sylvania Horticultural Society showed off their magnolia bushes, peonies from China, an India rubber tree, the Coffee Tree of Arabia, and sugarcane from the West Indies. Today the ***Philadelphia Flower Show*** is an international success: ten acres of soil, picket fences, orchids, and more—spectacular, enviable gardens created by nurseries and florists enlivening the Pennsylvania Convention Center. Crowds of more than 300,000 people cross-pollinate at the early-March flower show, the world's biggest indoor flower show. They bring pens and notepads, cameras, sketchbooks and charcoal. For more information call (215) 988–8800, or visit www.theflowershow.com.

Inner Suburbs

A scant block outside the city limits is the ***Barnes Foundation,*** one of the finest private collections anywhere of French modern and postimpressionist paintings. An extraordinary number of masterpieces by Renoir (180), Cézanne (69), and Matisse (60) provide the framework, with occasional gems by Picasso, Seurat, Modigliani, Degas, and others. The surrounding arboretum, rose garden, and lilacs make this place a special treat. The Barnes, well known but difficult to find, is located at 300 North Latchs Lane, Merion. The twelve-acre property was never designed as a public museum, and founder Albert C. Barnes himself stipulated that the collection should not be moved, nor could any individual paintings be rearranged. A 2004 court decision overrode his will. The Barnes will move to a new home downtown, on the Benjamin Franklin Parkway, but no one knows just when. Meanwhile, it's open Friday through Sunday from 9:30 A.M. to 5:00 P.M. Call (610) 667–0290 a month or more before your visit for driving directions and timed tickets. Sometimes it books up months in advance (reserve online at www.barnesfoundation.org). Adults pay $10 to enter—when they can get in.

Nearby ***Harriton House*** was the northernmost tobacco plantation operated on the slave economy. It's at 500 Harriton Road, Bryn Mawr. It's scheduled to be open 10:00 A.M. to 4:00 P.M. Wednesday through Saturday, but call ahead (610–525–0201), or visit www.harritonhouse.org.

Right in the middle of the beaten path is ***Valley Forge National Historical Park,*** where George Washington and his 11,000 soldiers slept fitfully during the winter of 1777–78. If you are a history buff, an enthusiastic kid studying the Revolution, or just a healthy visitor out for a country walk—if you are, in fact, anything but a British loyalist—you'll enjoy the natural and historical beauty of the park. The park grounds are open daily year-round from 6:00 A.M. to 10:00 P.M. The visitor center and Washington's Headquarters are open 9:00 A.M. to 5:00 P.M. daily except Christmas Day. Valley Forge National Historical Park, 1400 North Outer Line Drive, King of Prussia, (610) 783–1077.

Not far away is the ***Mill Grove Audubon Wildlife Sanctuary,*** on a bluff overlooking Perkiomen Creek. The museum features an array of wildlife art by John James Audubon, in a rural setting with 3 miles of trails. The first American home of Audubon, the museum charges $4.00 for adult admission, $3.00 for seniors, and $2.00 for children. It's open Tuesday through Saturday 10:00 A.M. to 4:00 P.M. and Sunday 1:00 to 4:00 P.M. The grounds are open daily except

Monday, from 7:00 A.M. to dusk. Find it at the intersection of Audubon and Pawlings Roads, Audubon. Call (610) 666–5593 for details about naturalist programs, some of which are perfect for children.

Consider, too, scheduling a visit to the **Wharton Esherick Studio.** This Philadelphia-born artist spent much of his life in this curious, rustic five-story structure, creating designs mostly in wood. Like Barcelona's famed Antonio Gaudí, Esherick eschewed straight lines and right angles. If you love the sensuality of delicately curved wooden forms, you'll flip. The two-story spiral staircase, carved from a single piece of wood, defies description but begs to be touched, as do many of the displayed pieces the artist designed for the 1940 World's Fair in New York. The studio, built over the course of forty years, features oddly shaped scraps of patchworked wood on the floor and a cantilevered deck. The hour-long guided tour is not recommended for young children. Tours of this National Historic Landmark for Architecture are available March through December, 10:00 A.M. to 5:00 P.M. Saturday, and 1:00 to 5:00 P.M. Sunday; groups midweek by appointment. Adult entry is $10.00 and includes a one-hour guided tour. The studio is on the Horseshoe Trail near Country Club Road. Write to Box 595, Paoli 19301, or call (610) 644–5822 for reservations and driving directions.

While nearby Longwood Gardens gets the tour buses and big crowds, **Chanticleer,** in Wayne, attracts the folks who garden for fun. Its British designer, Chris Woods, spent twenty years transforming an estate on the city's posh Main Line into a contemporary garden that arouses the senses.

Open to the public since 1993, Chanticleer's two manor houses are surrounded with bold shapes, modern contrasts, and a lighthearted approach. The result looks like a hip children's picture book. No placards with Latin plant names here—just oceans of color and shapes, punctuated by witty garden sculpture. Stroll an easy mile-long path, linking eight separate plantings, that winds down a gentle green slope. Beds close to the circa 1913 house (the former home of the Rosengarten family) are pleasingly structured. Those at a distance, like the Woods and the Water Garden, flourish seemingly undisturbed, with swaths of single colors, like red clover or blue camas, punctuating the lawns.

trivia

Philadelphia's newest superhighway relieves some of the load on the others, Interstate 95 and the Schuylkill Expressway. The Blue Route, another name for Route 476, cuts through the western suburbs from Chester, near the Philadelphia International Airport to Plymouth Meeting in northern Montgomery County. It's "blue" because two other routes—a red one and a yellow one—were also proposed.

A Day on the Main Line

Built to shuttle the wealthy in and out of Philadelphia in style, the *Main Line* train became synonymous with old money and grand estates. The stops along the way—like Haverford, Bryn Mawr, Rosemont, and Villanova—also correspond to gracious college campuses and chic shopping and are well worth a drive west along Route 30, known here as Lancaster Avenue. One chic collegian, Libby O'Toole, shared some of her favorite spots.

Start in Bryn Mawr, where the area's most beloved toy store fronts the street at number 839½. Pun's Toys has gotten "best of" honors from local magazines and lots of lucky kids. Skip the cartoon action figures—Pun's has marvelous tin soldiers from centuries of wars, velvety plush creatures, juggling equipment, puzzles, puppets, and more. It's open seven days a week (Monday through Friday 9:30 A.M. to 6:00 P.M., Saturday 9:30 A.M. to 5:30 P.M., Sunday 11:00 A.M. to 4:00 P.M.). Call (610) 525–9789.

For handpainted Italian ceramics, try Via Bellissima, at 853 West Lancaster Avenue; it's open Monday through Saturday 10:00 A.M. to 5:30 P.M.; call (610) 581–7414. One block down the street, grown-up girls love Skirt, a tiny boutique crammed with everything from this year's most sophisticated prom dresses to designer flip-flops. It's open Monday through Saturday 10:30 A.M. to 6:00 P.M.; call (610) 520–0222, or browse www.shopskirt.com.

Continue past the gray Gothic Villanova University campus to Wayne. The corner of Conestoga Road and Lancaster is home to The Flag Lady (398 West Lancaster Avenue; (610) 964–6280; www.flagladygifts.com), with Vera Bradley specialties, seasonal decorations, and holiday accessories that Main Line matrons love. The matron's teenage kids prefer South Moon Under, with men's and women's clothing and hip dorm-housewares like picture frames and candles (205 West Lancaster Avenue; 610–964–9064; www.southmoonunder.com).

Stash the shopping bags and relax for a meal at Georges'. This bistro by Georges Perrier, founder of Philly's four-star Le Bec-Fin, has a bar with a roaring fire and a casual dining room (503 West Lancaster Avenue; 610–964–2588; www.georges onthemainline.com). Or relax with tea on the Victorian veranda at the Wayne Hotel. This restored century-old landmark is a charmer, with four floors of elegant guest rooms and a main floor restaurant, Taquet (139 East Lancaster Avenue; 610–687–5000; www.waynehotel.com).

Chris Woods's whimsical sensibility takes a theatrical turn in the Ruin Garden, three open-air garden rooms that were built on the foundation of a prior residence on the property. A large fountain, inspired by ancient sarcophagi, dominates the Great Hall, mirroring the surrounding trees in its dark waters; huge sculpted stone books spill over the floor of a library; and in the Pool Room, marble faces gaze tranquilly from the watery depths of another fountain.

Chanticleer is located at 786 Church Road, Wayne; call (610) 687–4163, or visit www.chanticleergarden.org. It's open April through October, Wednesday through Saturday, 10:00 A.M. to 5:00 P.M. (until 8:00 P.M. Friday, June through August). Admission is $5.00. Docents lead two-hour tours twice daily Wednesday through Friday, but you'll enjoy a solitary stroll just as much.

Art aficionados adore the **Brandywine River Museum** (Route 1, just south of Route 100, Chadds Ford), one of the largest and most comprehensive collections of works by N. C. Wyeth, Andrew Wyeth, Jamie Wyeth, and Howard Pyle. The exhibition changes often, so you might see your favorites (like Jamie's *Pig*) next to works you've never seen. It's open every day except Christmas, 9:30 A.M. to 4:30 P.M., and admission is $8.00 for adults. Call (610) 388–2700, or visit www.brandywinemuseum.org.

At **Longwood Gardens** (Route 1, P.O. Box 501, Kennett Square 19348), the extravagant, elegant, exquisite horticultural displays are open every day of the year, from 9:00 A.M. to 5:00 P.M. January to March, and staying open until 6:00 P.M. April through October, with extended hours in summer and at Christmas. The conservatory opens at 10:00 A.M. Exotic flowers thrive in hothouses, and illuminated fountains highlight summer concerts. Longwood is a carnival of twenty indoor gardens, 400 performing-arts events each year, a gift shop, and a restaurant. Daily programs and classes enhance your gardening know-how. Admission is $14 for adults (with discounts on Tuesday and in midwinter and a $1.00 holiday surcharge). Call (610) 388–1000, or go to www.longwoodgardens .org for details.

In addition to being the cradle of liberty, Philadelphia is also the birthplace of the helicopter industry. That's why you'll find the **American Helicopter Museum,** a sure-fire kids' favorite, twenty minutes from Route 1 in West Chester. You'll learn about the history of the chopper and see vintage machines and the only V-22 Osprey on public display in the United States; you can even hop into a helicopter for a quick flight. Family rides are offered the third Saturday of the month for $35 per person; individuals over age twelve can fly any clear weekday between 1:00 and 1:30 P.M. *Philadelphia Magazine* voted the museum its "best scientific outing for kids" a few years back, for the number of things that they can get into—wind tunnels, instrument cockpits, and hands-on exhibits. The museum is off Route 202 at 1220 American Boulevard, adjacent to the Brandywine Airport. It's open Wednesday through Saturday 10:00 A.M. to 5:00 P.M., and Sunday from noon to 5:00 P.M. Admission is $6.00 for adults, $5.00 for seniors, and $4.00 for children. Call (610) 436-9600, or fly to www.helicoptermuseum.org.

Armchair shoppers love **QVC,** the cable television network that hawks everything from zirconium to cookware. When they leave home, they flock to its West Chester studios for a glimpse into its inner workings. Daily guided walking tours take them to an observation deck overlooking the broadcast area. The station is at 1200 Wilson Drive. Tours are available hourly from 10:00 A.M. to 4:00 P.M.; an impulse ticket purchase is $7.50 per adult, $5.00 for kids six to twelve. Call now, as they say: (484) 701–1000; or visit www.qvc.com. Bring identification.

Follow Route 1 south until you get to **Lincoln University,** just northeast of Oxford. Lincoln, founded in 1854, is the nation's oldest historically black college. Originally named Ashmun Institute, it was renamed in 1866 to honor President Abraham Lincoln.

If you'd rather bike, walk, or skate than drive, try the **Schuylkill River Trail** to get from here to there. It extends 22 miles from Center City Philadelphia along the Schuylkill River to Valley Forge. (When completed, the trail will be 100 miles long.) If you live in the area, consider walking the trail in spurts till you cover it all.

Nothing could be farther off the beaten path than the **Museum of Mourning Art** at Arlington Cemetery in Drexel Hill (2900 State Road). Would you believe emblems of the skull and skeletons, hearses, and mourning jewelry can be found in a museum? Open weekdays from 8:00 A.M. to 4:30 P.M. Call (610) 259–5800.

On the northern edge of the metropolis, Doylestown, the Bucks County seat, offers a concrete-and-tile monument to one man's life. It's **Fonthill,** the home of Henry Mercer. Mercer (1856–1930) was a polymath of astounding energy. After training as an attorney and following a career as a globe-trotting archaeologist, he turned artist, designing and producing thousands of tiles at the height of the American Arts and Crafts movement. (The floor of the state capitol is inlaid with hundreds of the results.) Mercer crammed the walls and ceilings of his castlelike abode with his own work and added extensive displays of pottery, lighting, and furniture. One writer called the result "Colonial Williamsburg on amphetamines." It's less crazy when you learn that Mercer always intended his home to be a museum. The next-door Moravian Pottery and Tileworks and the **Mercer Museum** a few blocks away comprise the town's "Mercer Mile."

Both Fonthill and the Mercer Museum are open daily (the museum is open Tuesday evenings, too) but are closed on certain holidays. Call Fonthill at (215) 348–9461 and the Mercer Museum at (215) 345–0210, or visit www.mercer museum.org. Admission is $12 for both.

Upscale flea market may be a contradiction in terms, but it aptly describes nearby **Rice's Market** (6326 Greenhill Road, New Hope; 215–297–5993; www.ricesmarket.com). There's been a weekly Tuesday market on this thirty-acre site since 1860. It's a Bucks County tradition, located midway between Doylestown and the Delaware River, with vendors hawking everything from antiques to zucchini. Get there early.

As you travel west, drop south to Chester County and **Historic Yellow Springs** (1685 Art School Road, P.O. Box 62, Yellow Springs 19425). This village "has a connection with every era of American life," says staffer Pat McGlone. During the Revolutionary War, Washington's troops traveled here from Valley Forge for the medicinal waters. During the Civil War, Union troops recuperated at its hospital. Sixty years later, lured by the bucolic surroundings, the Pennsylvania Academy of Fine Arts established its landscape school here. In 1958 Steve McQueen spent his honeymoon at the Springs while filming *The Blob* in the village (then briefly a movie-making center). Nowadays the beautifully restored Inn at Yellow Springs serves exquisite French dinners, and the remaining buildings host art programs. For directions and details call (610) 827–7414, or visit www.yellowsprings.org.

Pennsylvania Dutch Country: Plain and Fancy

About 300 years ago, groups of religious refugees from the Rhine region of Germany migrated to southeastern Pennsylvania. These settlers, mostly peasant farmers, came to take advantage of the religious freedom offered by William Penn. They included Amish and Mennonites—people of "plain" dress—and Lutherans and other Reformed groups of more worldly attire, sometimes called "fancy." Over time these people became known as "Pennsylvania Dutch," with the *Dutch* really a misinterpretation of the original *Deutsch*.

Wilkum to Lebanon and Lancaster Counties and the scenic Pennsylvania Dutch Country, where life moves at a slower pace and centers around time-honored traditions and values. Here you find beautiful scenery punctuated with one-room schoolhouses and wooden covered bridges, modern farm machinery pulled by mules, homemade clothing and quilts hanging to dry. You hear the clip-clop of horses' hooves on quiet country roads. The plain folks are less materialistic and less hurried than their urban counterparts, yet the highways through Lancaster County have grown touristy, as various people attempt to capitalize on the otherworldliness of these self-effacing settlers. Virtually any T-shirt shop, quilt boutique, or restaurant in the area can hand you a brochure with a self-guided driving tour. For a glimpse of a real Pennsylvania Dutch family, enjoy the movie *Witness* and leave these people alone.

Begin exploring off Route 72 in Lebanon County. It's the less-traveled part of the region, with equal numbers of "English" and Amish residents. While Lancaster

County, to the south, hawks its "real Pennsylvania Dutch" attractions with ferocity, Lebanon County treats its Amish neighbors with deference and respect. Farms seated on the richest soil in the country sport immaculate barns and flourishing gardens. Stern biblical quotes flank mailboxes. In the quiet, a syncopated trot heralds horse-drawn buggies before they come into view.

The region's German dissenter roots still flourish. In Schaefferstown, bright signs adorned with distelfinks, the folk-art icons of the region, adorn adjacent museums. The modest Gemberling-Rex House and Brendle Museum display 250 years of village history. They're not open often, so plan ahead (717–949–2244; www.hsimuseum.org). A historic tavern operates nearby: the Franklin House (Route 419 on the town square in Schaefferstown; 717–949–2122). It offers German platters and sandwiches for weekend lunches and serves dinner daily except Monday; call for hours.

Six miles north of Schaefferstown, there's a place to test an old adage. Give a man a fish, says the old saw, and you feed him for today; teach a man to fish, and you feed him for a lifetime. ***Arrowhead Springs*** varies the proverb: Visit a trout farm to fish, and you'll end up feeding the multitudes.

For the under-ten crowd, every activity is about immediate gratification. That's why the Gameboy gang flocks with their parents and grandparents to this manicured commercial hatchery in Newmanstown. Its sparkling spring-fed lake, stocked with over 5,000 pounds of rainbow and golden trout, provides a can't-miss intro to angling and a Grandma Moses setting. Around the circular one-acre pond, hand-tied flies and waders are scarce. More standard gear includes juice boxes, coolers, and cameras. You can bait your hook anyway you choose (marshmallows work well, if anglers

trivia

Baldwin's Book Barn in West Chester is just that: an 1822 barn crammed with 400,000 titles, both new and antique. Call it the anti-Amazon. Open daily; call (610) 696–0816, or visit www.bookbarn.com.

don't eat them all), and the Ludwigs, who own the place and keep it immaculate, will rent you rods, clean your catch, and send it home with you for dinner. The only real challenge here is getting the kids to bait the hooks, and there's no fishing license required. Picnic area and grills are available on the spacious green lawns, and everything's wheelchair accessible. Arrowhead has a separate trophy pond, which stocks ten-plus-pound behemoths; it's usually open from mid February through midsummer.

The hatchery is open Monday through Saturday 9:00 A.M. to 4:00 P.M. through mid-November; closed Sunday. Admission is just $1.00 per person (children under five free); trout is $3.50 per pound; rental rods are $4.00; tackle and bait are sold on-site. Arrowhead Springs is located at 118 West Bethany Road in Newmanstown (610–589–4830; www.arrowheadsprings.net).

Pennsylvania has more than one hundred private fishing lakes; for a full list, visit http://sites.state.pa.us/PA_Exec/Fish_Boat/lakesreg.htm.

Head north toward Cornwall, a village with charm, history, and a pretty nice bike trail. You may have noticed how many eastern Pennsylvania towns end in "Forge" or "Furnace." There's plenty of iron ore below this land, mined since the eighteenth century. The *Cornwall Iron Furnace* is the only surviving furnace of its kind in the Western Hemisphere and was put to work during the American Revolution. Now a well-done state museum, it offers thoughtful displays about the region's development. The surrounding homes—grand for the owners, modest for the ironworkers—still stand. The redbrick museum is at Rexmont and Boyd Streets (717–272–9711; www.cornwallironfurnace.org). It is open Tuesday through Saturday from 9:00 A.M. to 5:00 P.M. and Sunday from noon until 5:00 P.M., with the last tour beginning at 4:00 P.M. each day. Admission is $4.00 for adults, $3.50 for seniors, and $2.00 for youths.

Moving all that iron eventually required a short-line railroad that's now gone rails-to-trail. The Lebanon Valley Trail is now about 5 miles long between the Lancaster county line to Cornwall; an extension into Lebanon is planned. Check progress at www.lvrailtrail.com. The 1830-era *Cornwall Inn* (717–306–6178 or 888–313–3963; www.cornwallinnpa.com), a bed-and-breakfast at the Cornwall trailhead, was once the Cornwall mining company store. It has rooms and family-friendly suites from $125.

In the 1890s the Pennsylvania Chautauqua Society, attracted by the region's natural beauty, founded *Mt. Gretna.* The landscape is still just as inviting—gently wooded mountains, a stream, and a lake. Throughout the summer, the Chautauqua's genteel educational and cultural tradition lives on with music, theater, and arts events, and the Arts and Crafts–style cottages are treasured family heirlooms (a few can be rented, too). Follow Route 72 west from Cornwall to discover its charms.

The most well-known local attraction is the professional summer stock theater at the Gretna Theatre, where plays have been performed since 1927. Within strolling distance, on paths covered with pine needles, are the Greek Revivalist Hall of Philosophy (for lectures and chamber music), a gift boutique, and The Jigger Shop, an old-fashioned soda fountain that feels like the soul of the village. Among the highlights here are old-fashioned birch beer from a keg; fountain drinks you thought you'd forgotten, like lime rickeys; and chrome-bound counter stools that twirl until you're dizzy. The waiters and waitresses sport their colleges on their name tags (tip generously). Enjoy your lunch on the spacious deck.

Mt. Gretna's lake across the road is another throwback—a sand-bottomed freshwater lake with a beach, broad lawns, picnic pavilions, and a stationary diving platform with swing ropes in the middle.

They say you can't revisit the past. Mt. Gretna proves them wrong. Get all the details at www.mtgretna.com.

Heading south, you'll see another monument to religious expression at **Ephrata Cloister.** At the zenith of this community in the 1740s and 1750s, about 300 German members worked and worshiped here. Today the National Historic Landmark is open for tours at 632 West Main Street in Ephrata.

The charismatic founder of this community, Conrad Beisel, settled along the Cocalico Creek in 1732. He was followed by two groups of followers: celibate men and women, who lived in dormitories, and married couples with families. All expected that the Second Coming was imminent. The monastic Anabaptist community invented its own a cappella music, created Germanic calligraphy known as Frakturschriften, and operated a printing press. By 1813 its celibate members had died; children raised in the community were less enthusiastic about the celibacy tradition, and the community dwindled. Its buildings remain. Visit Monday through Saturday from 9:00 A.M. to 5:00 P.M. and on Sundays from noon to 5:00 P.M. Ephrata Cloister is closed on Mondays in January and February, and on Columbus Day, Veteran's Day, Thanksgiving and the day after Thanksgiving, Christmas, and New Year's Day. Admission is $7.00 for adults, $6.50 for senior citizens and $5.00 for youths six to seventeen; children under six are admitted free. For more information call (717) 733–6600, or visit www.ephratacloister.org.

world's largest chickendance?

It was a noble goal. At the 2003 Pennsylvania Farm Show, the organizers attempted to break the Guinness World Record for the number of people doing the chicken dance at the same time. Alas, the crowd wiggling their behinds and flapping their arms at Harrisburg's Farm Show Complex fell a few feathers short of the required 72,000. Better luck next time.

At the **Landis Valley Museum** north of Lancaster, you can see eighteen historic buildings filled with the arts and crafts, tools, and tales of German immigrants. It's open Monday through Saturday 9:00 A.M. to 5:00 P.M. and Sunday noon to 5:00 P.M.; closed major holidays. Adult admission is $9.00. From downtown Lancaster, take Route 272 north to 2451 Kissel Hill Road. For more details call (717) 569–0401, or visit www.landisvalleymuseum.org.

The city of Lancaster served as the capital of the United States for almost an entire day. It was September 27, 1777, and British invaders were threatening the capital in Philadelphia. The Continental Congress and the Executive Council of

Pennsylvania fled to Lancaster, where they held one session of congress. Believing that the British were in hot pursuit, congress moved across the Susquehanna River to York. Find out more at the *Discover Lancaster County History Museum* (2249 Route 30 East, Lancaster). The museum is open daily from 9:00 A.M. to 4:00 P.M. Entry costs $7.25 per adult. Call (717) 393–3679, or visit www.discoverlancaster.com.

trivia

Regionally, the acceptable pronunciation of the town name is LANG-custer, not LAN-cast-er.

In western and southern Lancaster County, the hills are more pronounced and the views more dramatic. Along the Susquehanna River you'll find many scenic overlooks that offer breathtaking views of the river far below.

A National Historic Monument, the *Fulton Opera House* in Lancaster was built in 1852. A gem of Victorian architecture, the theater's lush interior includes a magnificent main lobby with a sweeping staircase and crystal chandelier. Sarah Bernhardt, Al Jolson, W. C. Fields, Mark Twain, and others performed here. Read more history or order tickets at www.fultontheatre.org.

mindthegap

As a shortcut between Lancaster and the Delaware River, Route 30 leaves a lot to be desired. There's simply too much traffic, too many strip malls, and too few swaths of open land. That's why we prefer Route 41, which drops south from Route 30 through beautiful farmlands. Start at the tiny village of **Gap** (home of the Gap Diner), and continue past West Grove and over the state line to the Delaware Memorial Bridge. As highways go, it's a byway—restful and scenic.

Lancaster County features one of the largest concentrations of antiques in the country. In Adamstown, the "Sunday Antiques Capital of the United States," more than 7,000 antiques dealers gather to display and sell their merchandise. Every Sunday from 7:30 A.M. to 4:00 P.M., Adamstown (www.antiquescapital.com) becomes the essential antiquers' paradise. Dozens of shops line Route 272, with *Renninger's* (www.renningers.com) one of the best known and best loved. If you crave memories from any bygone era—even the 1990s—here's where to find what you're looking for. Take the Pennsylvania Turnpike to exit 286 (old exit 21), then go north on Route 272.

Since 1875 *Groff's Meats* has been selling wholesale and retail meat in Elizabethtown. The fourth generation of Groffs—two brothers and two sisters—now run the business. Groff relatives and employees buy and slaughter cattle and pigs, then lovingly and painstakingly convert them into hams, bacon, sweet bologna, and, in the fall, mincemeat: a super-secret family recipe of beef and suet, local apples, raisins, sherry, rum concentrate, and spices. No minces are killed to make this concoction. Groff's Meats makes five and a half tons—*tons*—of mincemeat a week during mincemeat season, which coincides roughly with autumn leaves. (If storage space fills up, they might skip a week.) Visit Groff's Meats at 33 North Market Street, Elizabethtown, or place a two-pound or thirty-five-pound order by calling (717) 367–1246.

You want corn chips? You want onion rings? **Herr Foods** is the third-largest snack-food company in the country, employing a thousand people and distributing its munchies in ten northeastern states. The factory tour includes a twenty-five-minute video (great for kids). Then you walk through windowed corridors, watching people and machines washing, peeling, slicing, cooking, and seasoning the food—then bagging, boxing, and preparing it for shipment. Drool no more. Reach onto the conveyor belt and pick up a free handful of fresh, warm chips. Yum. Herr's is at the intersection of Herr Drive and Route 272 in Nottingham, just south of Lancaster. The visitor center is open weekdays year-round except for major holidays, 8:00 A.M. to 5:00 P.M. Monday through Friday. The free hour-long tour runs on the hour from 9:00 A.M. to 3:00 P.M. Monday through Thursday and 9:00 A.M. to noon Friday. Call ahead (800–637–6225), or visit www.herrs.com for reservations.

Visit the demonstration garden and see the agricultural experiments taking place at the **Rodale Institute.** Rodale, which publishes *Prevention* and other magazines, welcomes visitors. Take a self-guided tour Tuesday through Saturday 10:00 A.M. to 4:00 P.M. From May through October the gardens are also open Monday 10:00 A.M. to 2:30 P.M. Rodale is closed Sunday. Call (610) 683–1400, or visit www.rodaleinstitute.org.

Reading

People in the East know Reading for its outlets, its Pennsylvania Dutch heritage, and its antiques marts. But few people recognize that in some ways, Reading *is* the East—the East as in Orient, China, and pagodas. At the top of Mt. Penn, the seven-story **Pagoda** dominates the town's skyline. In the early 1900s William Abbott Witman bought this land to quarry its stone. But the quarrying operation defaced the mountain, which he hid by building, of all things, a pagoda, hoping it would become a luxury hotel. When Witman's license to serve alcohol was denied, the building fell into the hands of a bank. In 1910 an investor bought the full catastrophe, then sold it to the City of Reading for a dollar. You can visit, free, daily from 11:00 A.M. to 5:00 P.M. A gift shop is open Monday, Friday, Saturday, and Sunday on the fourth level. To get there, start in Reading and drive uphill. For precise driving directions call (610) 375–6399 during operating hours.

trivia

The white streak through the center of the valley below Hawk Mountain is the River of Rocks, boulder-sized leftovers from the glacier that pushed past this region 11,000 years ago. Visitors can hike a 4-mile circuit around the formation, circling down into the valley and back. Other hikers are just passing through: This is one of the most difficult stretches of the Appalachian Trail.

If you prefer valley views to mountain views, the old Wanamaker, Kempton & Southern Railroad still operates steam engines near Hawk Mountain. The 6-mile ride boards just past the intersection of Routes 143 and 737 on 737, just north of Kempton, on weekends from May through October. Tickets are $7.00 for adults and $3.50 for children under eleven. For a schedule call (610) 756–6469, or board www.kemptontrain.com.

Each fall 18,000 raptors get a bird's-eye view of **Hawk Mountain Sanctuary.** On routes that can begin at Hudson's Bay and end in Argentina, they soar down the Kittatinny Ridge, the southernmost ridge in the Appalachians, before cutting across Texas into Mexico, where they mass into millions.

Hawk Mountain is one of the best places in the world for humans to catch the timeless spectacle. At this central Pennsylvania bird sanctuary, located off Route 61 near Pottsville, volunteers from all over the world annually track the flight paths of sixteen species, from tiny kestrels to bald eagles, for the longest record of raptor population in the world.

Migration is hard work. Hawks, falcons, and eagles make it look easy, gliding at eye level past the sanctuary in numbers that can reach 1,000 per day in mid-autumn. It's easy to copy their laid-back style and sample their view by kicking back on a fall afternoon on the sunbaked boulders atop Blue Mountain. From the sanctuary's 1,300-foot summit, the views can extend some 70 miles. The Indian blanket of orange, yellow, and red foliage draping the ridge-and-valley landscape is *echt* ("pure") Pennsylvania.

Are you guaranteed to spot a golden or bald eagle? No. But here's a tip: Visit when the winds blow. "When there's a cold front over the Appalachians, we usually get northwest winds, and birds conserve energy by riding that deflected air current," says khaki-clad Jeremy Scheivert, an education specialist at the center.

Trails are open dawn to dusk; adults pay $5.00 to enter, $7.00 on autumn weekends. From Interstate 78, take the Hamburg exit (exit 30; old exit 10). Drive north on Route 61, then veer right to go north on Route 895. Turn right at Drehersville. You can write to the Hawk Mountain Sanctuary, 1700 Hawk Mountain Road, Kempton 19529; call (610) 756–6961; or visit www.hawkmountain.org.

Daniel Boone, the legendary pioneer, was born and raised in Birdsboro. You can visit the **Daniel Boone Homestead** (mailing address: 400 Daniel

Daniel Boone Homestead

Boone Road, Birdsboro 19508) and learn about the lifestyles of different cultures in eighteenth-century rural Pennsylvania. From Reading, take Route 422 east to 400 Daniel Boone Road, Birdsboro. Hours are Tuesday through Saturday 9:00 A.M. to 5:00 P.M. and Sunday noon to 5:00 P.M. (reduced hours in January and February). The homestead is closed Monday except Memorial Day, Independence Day, and Labor Day. You may visit the grounds for free or pay $4.00 for a guided interior tour. Call (610) 582–4900 for more details.

Fleetwood, northeast of Reading (take Route 12 northeast, then go north on Route 662), is the home of the first Fleetwood Cadillac. A factory still produces upholstery here.

Capital District

My husband used to joke that my intellect was like the Susquehanna River: broad but shallow. It's a good description, both of my brain and of the river at Harrisburg. Here little forested islands dot the stream, and the only boats that can maneuver are of the pontoon variety. But Harrisburg's small downtown makes good use of its waterfront, and its state capitol complex, lavishly restored and expanded over the past few decades, is no snore—it's a stunner.

In 1906 President Theodore Roosevelt dedicated the gleaming granite capitol, declaring it "the handsomest building I ever saw." Lots of folks would argue that it outshines even the U.S. Capitol, which stylistically shares its distinctive flights of steps and domed rotunda.

Free tours start at the foot of the grand staircase, copied from St. Peter's Basilica in Rome and the Paris Opera House. Look up—272 feet—to admire the grand dome, flanked by gleaming mosaics of women depicting virtue, justice, and other good qualities of the commonwealth. Look down, too: Interspersed with the terracotta floor tiles throughout the building are 377 mosaics by Henry Mercer's Moravian Tileworks. These mosaics depict a visual timeline of Pennsylvania, from its native animals, like the elk and robin, to the factory and automobile.

Images of women abound in the capitol, which adopts different styles for its major chambers. In the state senate chamber, you'll find the mural *Unity* by muralist Violet Oakley in which goddesses holding up light fixtures preside in pre-Raphaelite style. In the Italianate house chamber, women representing "The Hours" are featured in the dome painting by Edwin Austin Abbey, and still others are found glowing with light in the stained-glass windows designed by Philadelphian William Brantley Van Ingen.

The capitol's newer east wing houses offices, a skylit cafeteria, and the welcome center's lighthearted interactive introduction to state government (the state dog is the Great Dane because William Penn owned one). Don't miss the wonderful Rube Goldberg contraption called "Making a Bill."

Guided tours are offered every half hour Monday through Friday 8:30 A.M. to 4:00 P.M. Weekends and most holidays (except major ones), tours are offered at 9:00 A.M., 11:00 A.M., 1:00 P.M., and 3:00 P.M. Call the tour guide office (800–868–7672), or visit www.legis.state.pa.us.

Security precautions prevent visitors from parking in the garage under the capitol, and on-street parking is fiendishly difficult. Leave your car instead on **City Island,** a short walk across the Walnut Street pedestrian bridge from downtown. City Island is the site of Riverside Stadium, the summer home of the Harrisburg Senators, an Eastern League AA pro team (check the schedule at www.senatorsbaseball.com). But it's got plenty of other fun. The *Pride of the Susquehanna* paddleboat departs for river tours from its marina (call 717–234–6500). A miniature steam train, minigolf, food stands, athletic fields, and paved trails are open most of the year. If you're feeling unathletic, just take a horse-drawn carriage ride from the Harrisburg Carriage Company (717–234–1686).

Farther from downtown, Harrisburg's attractions dwindle, but firebugs may enjoy the **Pennsylvania National**

trivia

Though it never touches Pennsylvania, the Chesapeake Bay starts here. Flowing south through central Pennsylvania, the Susquehanna River provides 90 percent of the fresh water in the upper bay–and 50 percent for the entire bay. Pollution from both a growing population and large-scale animal farming along the river threatens the fragile ecosystem downstream, but Pennsylvania farmers are beginning to farm "green" to save the bay.

Fire Museum in an old Victorian firehouse at 1820 North Fourth Street (717–232–8915). Continuing the pyrotechnical theme is *The Firehouse,* a theme bar and restaurant 2 blocks from the capitol at 606 North Second Street (717–234–6064). The red hydrant behind the bar holds beer taps. Nearby is the capitol's answer to Philadelphia's Reading Terminal: the 1860s-era *Broad Street Market* (717–236–7923), with farm-fresh food, candies, preserves, and snacks. Open Tuesday through Saturday, eat here or carry a take-out picnic to the river along Front Street.

Four miles north of the city you'll find the gardens and greens of *Felicita,* an upscale resort with the usual dining and golf amenities. What sets this 650-acre property apart are the spectacular gardens created over thirty years by owners Richard and Alice Angino. Twenty-one gardens, with themes ranging from Alpine to Islamic to Japanese to Monet water lily, culminate in the grand Italianate, a spectacular setting best viewed from the four-level terrace. The gardens are private property, but if you visit in warm weather, they're generally open for $10 tours on Wednesday and Saturday morning. For garden tours or for resort reservations, call (888) 321–3713. Visit www.felicitaresort.com for more information.

While it's the southern border of the state that gets the most Civil War tourists, Civil War skirmishes reached right into Camp Hill, now part of the Harrisburg suburbs. Stop at the *National Civil War Museum,* which portrays personal experiences on both sides of the conflict. About 850 artifacts of 24,000 in the collection are on display to illuminate the lives of common soldiers, men and women on the home front, and African Americans in the conflict. It's open daily in warm weather from 10:00 A.M. to 5:00 P.M., noon to 5:00 P.M. Sunday; closed Mondays and Tuesdays from Labor Day to March 31. Appropriately, it's at One Lincoln Center at Reservoir Park. Admission is $8.00 for adults, $7.00 for seniors, and $6.00 for students. Call (717) 260–1861, or visit www.nationalcivil warmuseum.org.

The two giant cooling towers by the airport south of Harrisburg are the site of the country's worst-yet nuclear disaster, at *Three Mile Island.* The affected reactor was shut down immediately after its partial meltdown in March 1979; low levels of radiation were released. Take a photo (from a distance), and continue into Middletown. At *Alfred's Victorian,* the restaurant specialty is the Flaming Victorian Salad, which bears absolutely no relation to other kinds of leaking fuel. The best seats in the house are the tables in the old townhouse's turrets: table nine downstairs, twenty-three upstairs. The address is 38 North Union Street. For more information call (717) 944–5373, or visit www .alfredsvictorian.com.

A short drive down Interstate 83 from Harrisburg brings you to York, a biggish town (or a smallish city) whose history is everywhere. York, briefly the U.S. capital in the eighteenth century, is now a genteel county seat just north of the Maryland state line. The Articles of Confederation were signed here in 1777. But the northern edge of town gets lots of traffic these days, and not simply because of nearby strip malls. Here stand the muscle-flexing power of two macho monuments: the *Harley-Davidson Vehicle Operations and Tour Center* and the *USA Weightlifting Hall of Fame* at the York Barbell Company.

The brand-new visitor center at Harley-Davidson (1425 Eden Road) celebrates the lure of the open road—and the choppers that frequently cost more than four-wheeled cars. The well-designed exhibits and the factory tour are free. Over 60,000 visitors come by each year, double the number of those touring the town's colonial district. The factory tours are relatively quiet (you'll hear your guide through earphones) and are offered to guests over age twelve from 8:00 A.M. to 4:00 P.M. Monday through Friday. A play space at the center entertains younger kids. The gift shop—offering everything from leather jackets and caps to Harley-Davidson Yahtzee games—is open one hour earlier and later. Call (877) 883–1450, or roar over to www.harleydavidson.com.

Up the road, look for the larger-than-life weightlifter jerking his barbells high over I–83, five minutes from the Harley factory. A latter-day Atlas, he lunges forward, twirling continuously above the York Barbell Company. The USA Weightlifting Hall of Fame next door chronicles competitive strength from ancient Greece, through its late-nineteenth-century heyday when celebrity strongmen toured the world, to the present.

Really strong guys, at least in cartoons, favor leopard-skin leotards and handlebar mustaches. That's all due to Eugen Sandow and Louis Cyr, the trendsetters whose stunts awed Victorian fairgoers. The exhibit traces them and their descendants to the well-oiled era of Schwarzenegger and Steenrod (as in Vicki, a contemporary Hall of Famer). Most of the memorabilia in the Hall of Fame was acquired by York Barbell's founder, Bob Hoffman, who advocated weight training, health foods, and isometrics. Practicing what he preached, he lived to the age of eighty-seven. Free admission weekdays 8:00 A.M. to 6:00 P.M. and Saturday 10:00 A.M. to 5:00 P.M. at 3300 Board Road, exit 24 (old exit 11) off I–83; (800) 358–9675.

York County bills itself as "The Factory Tour Capital of the World." "Conveyor belts are great!" says its guidebook. You'll find Pfalzgraff, the pottery maker; Hope Acres Farm, where robots milk the cows; Snyders, the pretzel people; and more. A good place to sort out all the man-made possibilities is right at the Harley-Davidson Tour Center, where the county maintains an information office (888–858–9675 or visit www.yorkpa.org). One-stop shopping.

Among the kitschy delights of the Lincoln Highway is the *Shoe House,* just off Route 30 in Hellam, Adams County. It was built in 1948 by Mahlon Haines,

BEST ANNUAL EVENTS IN SOUTHEASTERN PENNSYLVANIA

Wake up early on New Year's Day and catch the *Mummers Parade,* the all-Philadelphia strut of 30,000 costumed "Mummers." Call (215) 599–0776 or visit www.gophila.com to find the current year's parade route and inquire about tickets for special viewing stands and indoor events. The best "seats," though, are standing on the corner.

Pigs. Tractors. Rodeos. Wool. The *Pennsylvania Farm Show* has it all. For ten days each January, the events at the Harrisburg Farm Show Complex attract human and animal competitors from all over the commonwealth. More than 350,000 people attend the show each year, making this century-old slice of Americana the largest indoor agricultural event in the United States. And it's free. For details call (717) 787–5373, or visit www.agriculture.state.pa.us.

Spring means flowers, but nowhere more so than at the *Philadelphia Flower Show*—the largest and most prestigious flower show in the world, with ten acres of lush gardens and lavish floral settings. It's held in March at the Pennsylvania Convention Center. There's an admission fee, paid even by the show's judges. Call the Pennsylvania Horticultural Society at (215) 988–8800 for dates and details.

The venerable *Penn Relays* are held at the University of Pennsylvania the last weekend of April. This track event attracts the country's fastest runners, from high schoolers to Olympic wanna-bes to the over-80 Masters. Reserved seating is available for Saturday events, which attract crowds of more than 40,000. Get the schedule online at www.thepennrelays.com, or by phone by calling (215) 898–6145.

The *Devon Horse Show and Country Fair,* the nation's largest outdoor horse show, creates traffic jams up and down Route 30 for a week at the end of May. It's at the Devon Fairgrounds, which you can reach at (610) 964–0550, or at www.thedevonhorseshow.org.

The first weekend in June celebrates wheels in Philadelphia: two wheels, not four. It's the *Wachovia Cycling Series USPRO Cycling Championship,* the nation's largest one-day professional cycling event. Call (215) 599–0776, or visit www.gophila.com for the route and the times.

Every June, Thomas the Tank Engine visits the *Strasburg Railroad,* located on Route 741 in Lancaster County. The forty-five-minute trip features Thomas, who also visits in December. For a full schedule call (717) 687–7522, or visit www.strasburgrailroad.com.

who made shoes, then boots, then a house for honeymooners shaped like a shoe. A really big shoe: 48 feet long and 25 feet high. You can tour the shoe May through September for $3.00; call (717) 840–8339 for hours and directions.

Hersheypark may be too crowded for you, but consider *Chocolate World* at the entrance to Hersheypark in Hershey, where all the world's sweet. A nine-

Her Majesty is at the *Renaissance Faire,* held weekends from late August through mid-October. Watch blacksmiths, taste "roasted turkey legges," and let storytellers mesmerize your children. Held at Mount Hope Estate and Winery, Route 72, 0.5 mile south of Pennsylvania Turnpike exit 266 (old exit 20) (Box 685, Cornwall 17016). Check out www.parenaissancefaire.com, or phone (717) 665-7021.

The *Philadelphia Folk Festival* features three days of traditional and contemporary folk music, dance, crafts, camping, campfire sing-alongs, storytelling, juggling, and special children's activities. The family-oriented event takes place on the Old Pool Farm near Schwenksville, in Montgomery County, the last weekend before Labor Day weekend. You can camp for the weekend or spend a day. Parking is available on-site, and children under age twelve are admitted free to all concert events. For tickets and information call (215) 242-0150 or (800) 556-3655, or visit www.folkfest.org.

Gettysburg hosts all kinds of soldiers' reunions. The Eisenhower National Historic Site, home of the Allied commander, observes *World War II Days* the third weekend of September, with reenactors, demonstrations, tanks, and talks. Call (717) 338-9114, or march to www.nps.gov/eise for details.

At Hersheypark you can celebrate the *Jewish Festival of Sukkot,* which occurs in late September or early October. The all-kosher event features hot dogs, potato knishes, and more, plus a day of rides to celebrate the harvest season. For details call the Central Pennsylvania Kosher Mart at (717) 392-5111. Sukkot proceeds go to the local Mikvah, a Jewish charity.

George Washington crossed the Delaware River on December 25, 1776, to launch his attack on the British in Trenton. The *Reenactment of Washington's Crossing* launches each Christmas Day from Washington Crossing Historic Park (1112 River Road, Washington Crossing) in Bucks County, 35 miles north of Philadelphia. The visitor center displays artifacts and provides details. Call the park at (215) 493-4076, or visit www.phmc .state.pa.us.

minute ride takes you through a simulated chocolate factory. It's interesting for adults and a treat for kids. Chocolate World is open from 9:00 A.M. to 5:00 P.M. Monday through Saturday (9:00 A.M. to 10:00 P.M. in summer) and 11:00 A.M. to 5:00 P.M. Sunday; closed Christmas. During some festivals, the hours may be extended. Call (717) 534-4903 or (800) 437-7439, or visit www.hersheypark

.com for details. You can't beat the price (it's free), and you get free candy treats at the end.

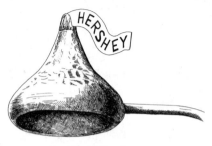

Hershey Kiss lamppost

The Moorish architecture of *Hotel Hershey* is worth a peek into the lobby, even if you can't afford its four-star prices. And the fabulous rose garden outside the hotel blooms freely (and is free for public viewing) well into November.

On Pennsylvania Dutch country barns and signs, you'll see lots of ornamental geometric suns, hearts, stars, and birds (here called distelfinks). These are hex signs, and their happy iconography bespeaks Old World traditions. Sun wheels connote warmth and fertility; tulips stand for faith; blue means protection, and red, emotions. Find an extensive collection at *Will-Char, the Hex Place* (3056 Route 30, East Paradise; 717–687–8329; www.hexsigns.com). The brilliant folk-art icons are also interpreted in quilts, and the *Old Country Store* (Route 340, Old Philadelphia Pike, Intercourse) has been called one of the nation's top-ten shops for this time-honored craft. The store honors the past with an upstairs museum; downstairs, there are coverlets, pillows, gifts, and quilting supplies. It's open Monday through Saturday 9:00 A.M. to 5:00 P.M., November through May, and until 6:30 P.M. the rest of the year. Call (800) 828–8218 or (717) 768–7101, or visit www.theoldcountrystore .com. Another sweet tradition, homemade jellies and jams, are on sale just down the road, at *Kitchen Kettle Village.* It's open year-round from 9:00 A.M. to 5:00 P.M., except Sundays; call (800) 732–3538 or (717) 768–8261. Don't drip any on the quilts.

Battlefield Territory

Don't miss *Gettysburg.* Union and Confederate soldiers fought the bloodiest battle of the Civil War here in 1863. The area is organized for tourism, with the absorbing history communicated in virtually every medium. *Gettysburg National Military Park* surrounds the city of Gettysburg. The visitor center is across from the entrance on Route 134. Exhibits explain the battle, and battlefield tours start from here. Its famous **Cyclorama**, a 360-degree painting, is being restored and will reopen in a new visitor center in late 2007. Visit Gettysburg online at www.nps.gov/gett, or call (717) 334-1124.

Saving Grace

Lancaster County boasts that it has the most productive nonirrigated farmland in the United States. There are more than 4,500 farms here, mostly small and family-owned. The pace of urban sprawl severely threatened these farms during the 1980s and 1990s—the *Philadelphia Inquirer* estimated the rate of loss at an acre an hour. To the rescue came the Lancaster Farmland Trust.

The Trust helps farm owners obtain conservation easements to preserve their lands for agricultural use forever. And it's stemming the tide of development: since 1994 there have been two county acres saved for every one lost to development. To date, 15 percent of the county's farmland has been preserved, the most successful of all such efforts nationwide.

War, they say, is hell. That's never more true than on a summer weekend at Gettysburg. The crowds are daunting. If at all possible, plan on a weekday visit, preferably in the off-season.

Make the most of your visit to this well-preserved battlefield by hiring a licensed tour guide. Gettysburg is the only battle site in the world where experts will accompany lay visitors on a two-hour tour—in your car, on foot, or otherwise. Each guide must pass a detailed oral exam. Take advantage of their proficiency, and stop by their office at the visitor center. Guides are available on a first-come, first-served basis, beginning at 8:00 A.M. daily. Rates are $40 for one to six people. Visit www.gettysburgtourguides.org for more information.

Gettysburg also offers bicycle, horseback, and Segway tours of the battle-field—an ideal way to cover ground and to bypass crowds on the battlefield roads—with guides who know their stuff.

Horseback tours are offered not by the National Park Service but by two local firms: the ***National Riding Stable*** at Artillery Ridge Camping Resort, 610 Taneytown Road (1.5 miles from the visitor center), (717) 334–1288; and ***Hickory Hollow Farm,*** 219 Crooked Creek Road, (717) 334–0349. Advance reservations are a must. Segs in the City offers two-hour battlefield safaris on Segway transporters, spring through fall, at $70 per person; visit www.segsinthecity.net, or call (800) SEGS–393.

Gettysbike offers morning, evening, and sunset tours that beat the heat. They'll rent you bikes, but you can also pedal on your own. Call (484) 880–6152, or visit in person at 240 Steinwehr Avenue or online at www.gettysbike.com.

If you want a film orientation before you pedal off, Gettysbike has teamed with the Patriot Point theater to screen *Gettysburg: The Battle in Motion* before your ride. Ticket prices vary, depending on whether you need to rent a bike and for how long. Another introduction to the battle puts you in the center of Pickett's Charge. *Fields of Freedom* plays every half-hour at Gateway Gettysburg, in the new, bigger-than-IMAX theater off Route 15 near the National Military Park at 20 Presidential Circle. Tickets are $9.00 for adults, $8.00 for students, and $7.00 for seniors. Call (717) 334–5575.

If you like your history sung, consider *For the Glory*, a Civil War musical performed eight times a week from June through September at the Majestic Theater, 25 Carlisle Street; tickets are $40 to $45. Call (717) 337–8200, or visit www.fortheglorythemusical.com.

At least two dozen attractions related to the Battle of Gettysburg and the Civil War clamor for your attention, including the ***American Civil War Museum*** (717–334–6245); the ***Jennie Wade House,*** home of Jennie Wade, the only civilian killed in the battle (717–334–4100); and the ***Gettysburg Battle Theatre*** (717–334–6100). The ***Hall of Presidents*** (717–334–5717) features wax reproductions of thirty-six presidents, who relate American history in their own words. For a complete listing of tourist territories, dining, camping, and lodging, stop by the ***Gettysburg Convention and Visitors Bureau*** at 102 Carlisle Street; call (717) 334–6274; or visit www.gettysburgcvb.org.

At Gettysburg the spirits of the past live on. Many of the 51,000 battlefield casualties were carried to homes and buildings in town, and legends of ghostly apparitions have persisted for decades. One place to get into the spirit, so to speak, is ***Farnsworth House*** (401 Baltimore Street). Occupied by sharpshooters during the battle, it has the bullet holes to prove it. In addition to selling Civil War memorabilia and books, the house also hosts candlelight evening ghost walks through town and presents the Civil War Mourning Theater, with dramatic and sometimes ghoulish monologues. A dinner theater on the premises offers period music. For details visit www.farnsworthhousedining.com, or call (717) 334–8838.

Also at Gettysburg the ***Eisenhower National Historic Site*** commemorates Dwight D. Eisenhower's military and presidential years. The only way to get there is on a tour that departs from the National Park Visitors Center. Your site visit includes the Eisenhowers' 230-acre farm and farmhouse, the only home the First Couple ever owned; a putting green and sandtrap given to the president by the Professional Golfers Association; a brick barbecue grill where he broiled 3-inch-thick steaks for guests; a skeet range; and the barn where Ike raised show cattle—but not the milk house where the Secret Service office was ensconced. The home first opened to the public in 1980, shortly after the presi-

Hall of Presidents

dent's widow, Mamie, died. Site manager Jim Roach describes it as "a period piece" characterizing the Fifties. "Eisenhower used this place for his style of personal diplomacy. On the porch he visited with Nikita Khrushchev in 1959, at the height of the Cold War, causing a slight thaw. De Gaulle, Churchill, and Adenauer visited this private place. Eisenhower invited them, he said, 'to get the measure of the man.' With all the trappings of office stripped away, world leaders came here and became real people." The trophies of Ike's life were not on display then, nor are they now. "If you visited when the Eisenhowers lived here—or now—you would never know that Eisenhower was the supreme commander of the Allied forces during World War II, let alone that he was president. The Eisenhowers were a couple who did not overwhelm you with their station in life." On the glassed-in porch stands an unfinished painting by Ike, who completed at least 260 others during the last twenty years of his life. The hours and the number of visitors allowed vary, so call first (717–338–9114), or visit www.nps.gov/eise/. The tour costs $5.50 per adult, $4.00 for youths thirteen through sixteen, $3.00 for children six through twelve.

Drive to 900 High Street, Hanover, and take a deep breath. Fresh air? No. Fresh Utz (the name rhymes with *huts*) potato chips. Here is the factory of ***Utz Quality Foods,*** and you're welcome to take a free self-guided tour Monday through Thursday 8:00 A.M. to 4:00 P.M. Call (717) 637–6644 or (800) 367–7629 for details.

As you head west on Route 30 from Gettysburg, you have an opportunity to see the largest herd of elephants in the country. The rolling farms hereabouts are nothing like the savanna, but you can find a plethora of pachyderms at *Mister Ed's Elephant Museum* in Orrtanna. Owner Ed Gotwalt curates a collection of 6,000 specimens, all his: political, plush, Hindu, and other specimens. Tusks and ivory carvings, too. Most of the items fall into the deliciously kitschy category. So do the old-fashioned penny candies and roasted peanuts on sale in the gift store. Open daily from 10:00 A.M. to 5:00 P.M., the shop—er, museum—is at 6019 Chambersburg Road. Call (717) 352–3792, or visit www.mistereds-elephantmuseum.com.

Hickory Bridge Farm B&B in Orrtanna offers nine rooms, including cottages, all with private baths. Two rooms have private whirlpools, too. Guest rooms are furnished with Pennsylvania Dutch antiques, and the cottages have wood-burning stoves. It's a genuine farmstead that boasts a red barn-turned-restaurant, a country museum with old farm equipment, a spring-fed swimming pond, and a trout stream surrounded by fifty acres of farmland. In the restaurant you're offered amazing quantities of Pennsylvania Dutch cooking in a designer-country setting, Friday and Saturday night and Sunday noon to 3:00 P.M. Call (717) 642–5261, or visit www.hickorybridgefarm.com for more information.

Places to Stay in Southeastern Pennsylvania

CHESTER HEIGHTS (CHADDS FORD)

Hamanassett Bed & Breakfast,
P.O. Box 366,
Chester Heights 19017;
(610) 459–3000;
www.hamanassett.com.
A Federalist-style mansion surrounded by Brandywine hunt country.

EPHRATA

Inns at Doneckers,
318 North State Street;
(800) 377–2206;
www.doneckers.com

GETTYSBURG

Brafferton Inn,
44 York Street;
(717) 337–3423;
www.brafferton.com

KEMPTON

Hawk Mountain Bed & Breakfast,
221 Stony Run Valley Road;
(610) 756–4224;
www.hawkmountainbb.com

LAMPETER

Australian Walkabout Inn Bed & Breakfast,
837 Village Road;
(717) 464–0707;
www.800padutch.com/
walkinn.html.
Ask for a pastry called an Australian tea-ring and, if you're brave, a dollop of Vegemite on your toast.

PHILADELPHIA

Thomas Bond House,
129 South Second Street;
(800) 845–BOND;
www.winston-salem-inn
.com/philadelphia.
In Independence National Historic Park, the home of a Revolutionary-era physician is now a restored bed-and-breakfast with views of the Delaware River.

Places to Eat in Southeastern Pennsylvania

CORNWALL

The Blue Bird Inn,
2387 Cornwall Road;
(717) 273–3000;
www.bluebirdinn.com.
Casual pub grub. Late-night entertainment on the tiki-torch deck attracts a young crowd on Friday and Saturday nights.

DENVER

Park Place Diner (formerly Zinn's),
Route 272, just north of exit 266 (old exit 21) on the Pennsylvania Turnpike;
(717) 336–2210

DOYLESTOWN

Paganini Trattoria,
81 West State Street;
(215) 348–5922;
www.paganiniristorante.com

HARRISBURG

North Street Zephyr Express,
231 North Street;
(717) 233–2009.
A tiny bistro 2 blocks from the Capitol complex, serving lunch and dinner.

LEBANON

Trattoria Fratelli,
502 East Lehman Street;
(717) 273–1443;
www.tratfrat.com.
Voted best in central Pennsylvania. Upscale, innovative Italian cuisine served Tuesday through Saturday. Try grilled chicken and polenta or crabmeat specials.

PHILADELPHIA

City Tavern,
138 South Second Street;
(215) 413–1443;
www.citytavern.com.
Located in Independence National Park, this public house was the unofficial meeting spot for the First Continental Congress. Authentic feel, with venison, cider, and ales.

Dante & Luigi's,
Tenth and Catherine Streets, South Philadelphia;
(215) 922–9501.
The oldest Italian restaurant in America.

DiNardo's,
312 Race Street;
(215) 925–5115.
Best known for hard-shell crabs.

Larry's Famous Steaks and Hoagies,
2459 North Fifty-fourth Street;
(215) 879–1776.
Across from the St. Joseph's University Field House. See why its cheesesteaks are called Bellyfillers.

Pat's King of Steaks,
1237 East Passyunk Avenue;
(215) 468–1546;
www.patskingofsteaks.com.
Cheesesteaks and hoagies.

Tavern on Green,
Twenty-first and Green Streets;
(215) 235–6767

Valley Green Inn,
Springfield Avenue and Wissahickon Creek;
(215) 247–1730;
www.valleygreeninn.com.
Built in 1850 on the site of a 1770s establishment, this hostelry serves superb food.

Villa di Roma,
936 Ninth Street;
(215) 592–1295.
Italian food in a tacky, brightly lit setting.

White Dog Cafe,
3420 Sansom Street;
(215) 386–9224;
www.whitedog.com.
A hip eatery and bar on the University of Pennsylvania campus.

READING

Antique Airplane Restaurant and Lounge,
4635 Perkiomen Avenue, Route 422 East;
(610) 779–2345

WEST CHESTER

Dilworthtown Inn,
1390 Old Wilmington Pike;
(610) 399–1390;
www.dilworthtown.com.
Dinner only.

South Central Pennsylvania: Valleys of the Susquehanna

As you head west into south central Pennsylvania, you'll see higher highs and lower lows. The mountains loom higher, the valleys get broader, and the attractions can throw you an unexpected curve. One of the biggest of the latter is the railroad wonder, **Horseshoe Curve.** As the early railroads expanded westward, the Pennsylvania Railroad ran into a major snag at Altoona: mountains. The grade in the Alleghenies was far too steep for a run straight up or down. To circumvent the situation and to connect two sides of Kittanning Point, engineers designed a huge, curving track, which opened to train traffic in 1854. Men used picks, shovels, and horses to carve the curve, which is still considered an engineering marvel. The length of the curve is 2,375 feet; the grade is 1.8 percent; the degree of curvature is 9 degrees, 25 minutes; and the central angle is 220 degrees.

When you come to this spot (using the Seventeenth Street exit off Interstate 99/220) where trains make a U-turn, ride the funicular or walk the 194 steps to the top; a sturdy fence protects your body from the trains but leaves your eyes and ears free to enjoy. To imagine what it's like, think of a football stadium fifty times larger than reality. You are sitting at one end near the goalpost, two rows down from the top tier. At the

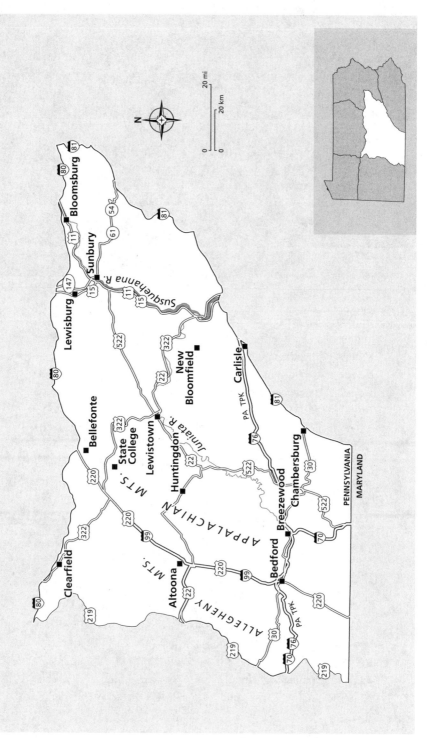

SOUTH CENTRAL PENNSYLVANIA

topmost level of the stadium, a train approaches from the far end. It chugs on by, wrapping around the curve—and around you—as the engineer waves and toots his whistle. The long train continues on the other side of the stadium so that at one point, you are surrounded by an endless iron snake. Eventually it disappears around another curve, but you can still hear it, and everyone near you is still smiling. If the weather's nice, you can have a picnic while waiting for a few more of the sixty passenger and freight trains that traverse the curve daily. The curve is open Monday through Saturday 10:00 A.M. to 6:00 P.M. and Sunday noon to 6:00 P.M., April through October. November through December, it is open weekends only. From January through the end of March, the curve is closed. An annual grounds pass to the curve costs $3.00, but for $6.50, you can buy a combination pass that also covers the round-trip ride on the curve's funicular railway and a ticket to the ***Altoona Railroaders Memorial Museum.*** This all-in-one admission can be purchased either at the curve or at the museum, 1300 Ninth Avenue. To get to the museum from I–99, take the Seventeenth Street exit, then turn right on Ninth Avenue. It's open daily April through October, Monday through Saturday 9:00 A.M. to 5:00 P.M. and Sunday from 11:00 A.M. to 5:00 P.M. For information on both sites, call (814) 946–0834 or visit www.railroadcity.com. Open only weekends in November and December; closed January 1 through March 31.

It costs only $1.00 to ride ***Leap the Dips,*** the historic wooden side-friction roller coaster in Altoona's ***Lakemont Park.*** The amusement reopened in 1999 after fourteen years in mothballs; the Leap the Dips Foundation spent a million bucks restoring the original cars and replacing the superstructure. To get to the park from Interstate 80, take Route 220 south; after Route 220 becomes I–99, exit at Frankstown Road. Call (814) 949–7275 or (800) 434–8006, or visit www.lakemontparkfun.com.

AUTHOR'S TOP TEN FAVORITES IN SOUTH CENTRAL PENNSYLVANIA

Carlisle	Millersburg Ferry
Coffee Pot	Penn State Trial Gardens
Gravity Hill	Pike to Bike Trail
Horseshoe Curve	Road Kill Cafe
Leap the Dips	Slinky Outlet Store

Alongside the park is the new home of the **Altoona Curve,** an AA Eastern League baseball team that also throws fastballs and sliders. This is "Bull Durham"–type baseball, laid-back and family-friendly. The State College Spikes of the New York–Penn League also play here. Check the schedule at (877) 99–CURVE or www.altoonacurve.com.

You'll find another historic landmark at 3205 Sixth Avenue. **Reighard's** claims to be America's oldest gasoline station, offering full service to motorists since 1909.

caboose with a view

The New Portage, Allegheny, and Gallitzin railroad tunnels were so strategically important that they were guarded during World War II. The bright-red caboose at tiny **Gallitzin Tunnels Park** tells their story. Call (814) 886–8871 to visit.

Just 12 miles west of Altoona on Route 22, visit the **Allegheny Portage Railroad,** now a National Historic Site. At this location in 1834, canal boats were loaded onto railcars, reducing the trip between Philadelphia and Pittsburgh from three weeks by wagon to four days by railroad and canal. At the visitor center you can take a brief history lesson. You can also walk forested trails along the railroad's route or, if you're so inclined, watch a costumed stonecutting demonstration. It's open from 9:00 A.M. to 5:00 P.M., closed major holidays. You'll get a week-long pass for $4.00. For more information write Allegheny Portage Railroad, 110 Federal Park Road, Gallitzin 16641; call (814) 886–6150; or visit www.nps.gov/alpo.

By now, you've got the idea: Railroad buffs love this area. Their hotel of choice is **The Station Inn** in Cresson. It's a little shaky. That's why they like it.

The Inn's front porch is the perch where enthusiasts can watch seventy trains rumble past each day on the Norfolk Southern line. The trains are just 150 feet from the door of the hotel, built in 1866. Its seven modest rooms are named for old railroads; the porch is where buffs trade anecdotes and lore. Contact the Inn, located at 827 Front Street, at (814) 866–4757, or visit www.stationinnpa.com.

If you head north on Route 220, then north on Route 360 and west on Route 322, you come to Clearfield, which originated as the Indian town of Chinklacamoose. A portion of the Old Town Historic District is listed on the National Register of Historic Places. Several stately Victorian homes offer an interesting self-guided walking tour extending 4 blocks along Front Street.

West of Altoona, along Route 22, visit the **Mt. Assisi Monastery** and the **Holy House of Father Gallitzin** in Loretto. Father Gallitzin was a Russian prince who gave up his title and inheritance; he became the first priest to receive all the orders in the United States, and he served the community of Loretto.

Catholics on a pilgrimage find it refreshing to stop there as well as at the Carmelite Monastery and St. Michael's Church. For more information and to schedule a visit to the gardens—open year-round, dawn to dusk—call (814) 472–3348, or write the Mt. Assisi Visitors Center, P.O. Box 188, Loretto 15940. The monastery is on the campus of nearby St. Francis University. While visiting, stop by its Southern Alleghenies Museum, one of four locations of this regional institution. The permanent collection of American art here includes works by Pennsylvanians Mary Cassatt, Thomas Sully, and John Kane.

Millions of adults and children around the world have tossed a *Slinky* down the stairs. Richard James invented the Slinky in 1943—by accident. He was trying to develop a spring that could help keep sensitive shipboard instruments steady at sea. He knocked some of these experimental springs off a shelf and was amused by the way they "walked" down, rather than just falling. You can still buy the toy in *Hollidaysburg* at the Slinky Outlet Store at 221 Allegheny Street.

trivia

Slinky comes from Pennsylvania. You can't visit the Slinky factory, but you can drive circles around it for effect. Slinky's home is James Industries, Beaver Street Extension, Hollidaysburg. Call (814) 695–5681 for details.

Heading northeast from Altoona, you discover the town of State College, home of *Pennsylvania State University* (not to be confused with the University of Pennsylvania, which is in Philadelphia). It's a member of the Big Ten football conference, so sports—playing, watching, and wearing blue-and-white outfits—is an important undergraduate major. Penn State was founded in 1855 as the Farmers' High School. It has grown. Beaver Stadium, the fourth-largest stadium in the country, is often packed beyond its 93,967-seat capacity.

Non-jocks can appreciate Penn State, too. One perennial—make that annual—favorite is the Department of Horticulture's *Trial Gardens,* where acres of colorful ornamental annual flowers are grown from seed. Ever wonder about those "All-American" varieties of salvia and impatiens at your local greenhouse? Penn State is an official selection site for that honor. The gardens, at Park Avenue and Bigler Road, are free and open from dawn to dusk. If you visit during the growing season, take a stroll to plan what you'll cultivate next summer. For details visit http://hortweb.cas.psu.edu/research/trial.html, or call the manager's office at (814) 863–7725.

Fourteen miles south of the main campus lies the university's *Shaver's Creek Environmental Center* (RR 1, Box 325, Charter Oak Road, Petersburg 16669). Located off Route 26 in the Stone Valley Recreation Area, it offers lots of painless education programs for kids and adults. The center has a cool

Raptor Center, where birds of prey like owls, hawks, and eagles can be studied up close and personal; a bat colony where more than 1,200 brown bats roost nightly; herb and flower gardens; and picnic areas. One popular annual event is the center's Easter egg hunt, which lets kids hunt for eggs painted to mimic those of great blue herons, turkey vultures, and robins. Book ahead at www .shaverscreek.org, or call (814) 863–2000.

Route 522 near Raystown Lake, a huge reservoir, runs along the ridgetop alongside one of Pennsylvania's prettiest streams: the Juniata River. The small village of Huntingdon is worth a detour onto Route 26. See a monument to the town's past and glimpse its future, in the students at Juniata College.

The Oneida Indians, who once lived in this region, had a custom of erecting a huge monolithic stone—think *2001:Space Odyssey*—outside their villages. These "standing stones" bore tribal symbols and history. When the first white settlers arrived in Huntingdon County in 1754, they reported a 14-foot standing stone near the Oneida village. Neighboring Tuscarora Indians somehow stole the stone. War erupted. Though the Oneida regained their stone, they moved west as settlers moved in, and the stone vanished. To commemorate Native American history, Huntingdon created a replica of the standing stone in the historic town center. It's still there, surrounded by well-kept century-old homes and the college. A peaceful cemetery crowns the hillside, its grave markers overlooking the town: a different kind of standing stone.

Valleys of the Susquehanna

trivia

The Statue of Liberty also lifts her lamp over the Susquehanna River near Dauphin Narrows. As you drive along Route 322, you'll see her 25-foot white replica on an abandoned pier in the middle of the river.

Due north of State College, although there are no direct roads, is Bellefonte, meaning "beautiful fountain." It's best known for its **Big Spring,** which gushes 11.5 million gallons of water each day. This diminutive town bred seven governors of Pennsylvania.

Boalsburg is home to the **Pennsylvania Military Museum,** honoring the women and men of Pennsylvania who served their country in war. From Benjamin Franklin's first military unit—the Associators—through the conflict in Vietnam, this museum tells the tale of these patriots. The museum is open Tuesday through Saturday 9:00 A.M. to 5:00 P.M., and Sunday from noon to 5:00 P.M. Admission is $4.00. For information call (814) 466–6263; write to P.O. Box 160A, Boalsburg 16827; or visit www.psu.edu.edu/dept/aerospace/museum.

Sail on. Sail on. Sail on and on to see relics and heirlooms of Christopher Columbus at the **Boal Mansion and Columbus Chapel,** just off Business Route 322 at 163 Boal Estate Drive in Boalsburg. The chapel, which was part of the Columbus family castle in Spain, contains the type of cross explorers planted on the shores of newly discovered territories. The Boal family brought the chapel to Boalsburg in 1909. Family scion Pierre Boal was a French flying ace in World War I and later served as a U.S. ambassador. That's why memorabilia from the early days of flight are also collected by the museum. You may visit daily except Monday, May through October. Guided tours ($10 per adult) are scheduled from 1:30 to 5:00 P.M. in spring and fall and 10:00 A.M. to 5:00 P.M. in summer. Call (814) 466–6210, or visit www.boalmuseum.com.

The people who live in Juniata and Mifflin Counties strive to uphold their heritage, their small-town way of life, and a standard of living not usually found in rural areas. Visiting here can be like taking a trip back in time, as you meet descendants of the early German settlers, including many Amish and Mennonite families. Any Wednesday during spring, summer, and fall, drop in on market day in Belleville (on Route 655, due west of Lewistown).

The stellar attraction in Mifflinburg is the **Buggy Museum** (598 Green Street), commemorating passenger carriages, not mosquitoes and bumblebees. The museum shows you where William A. Heiss manufactured horse-drawn vehicles from the late nineteenth to the early twentieth century, employing painters, blacksmiths, carpenters, and wheelwrights. Abruptly, the family shuttered the shop, and half a century passed before it was reopened, good as new. Visit the museum Thursday through Saturday 10:00 A.M. to 5:00 P.M. and Sunday 1:00 to 5:00 P.M., May through October. For more information call (570) 966–1355, or visit www.buggymuseum.org.

Take a deep breath while driving to Northumberland, which has a big spot in history for such a little place. It was the home of Joseph Priestley, who is remembered for his pioneering work in chemistry, most notably the discovery of oxygen. He was also the founder of the Unitarian church. Priestley's philosophic and scientific writings greatly influenced Thomas Jefferson, who based the curriculum of the University of Virginia on Priestley's ideas. Visit the scientist's laboratories at the **Joseph Priestley House** (472 Priestley Avenue), which is usually open Wednesday through Saturday from 9:00 A.M. to 5:00 P.M. and Sunday from noon to 5:00 P.M. It's closed Mondays and holidays except Memorial Day, Independence Day, and Labor Day. Call (570) 473–9474, or go to www.phmc.state.pa.us.

trivia

Lorenzo DaPonte, Mozart's librettist, lived for a time in Sunbury.

"A school for how to have fun" is how **Camp Woodward** describes itself. Simply put, it's an extreme-sports paradise, outfitted with runs and ramps galore for skateboarders, BMXers, and in-line skaters. Located 25 miles west of State College in Mifflinburg, Woodward supplements its kids' summer-camp business with weekend packages September through May, and they swear they even get some adult visitors without kids. (If you bring kids, fair warning: The camp requires you to stay and watch their every death-defying move.) Two B&Bs on the property fill quickly, especially during Penn State football season, so always book ahead. For room reservations call (814) 349–5520; for camps, call (814) 349–5633. Or do a double ollie to www.woodwardcamp.com.

Centralia, a tiny village off Route 61 in Columbia County, has the unique distinction of having been on fire since 1962. That's when an underground blaze erupted in a coal mine under the town. All sorts of engineering marvels were employed to put out the fire; none succeeded, and by 1991 nearly all of the town's residents had been evacuated. The wisps of smoke you see curling up through the ground are evidence that there's fire down below.

Most people driving along the Susquehanna River between Sunbury and Harrisburg take Routes 11 and 15 on the west side for speed; but on the east the less-traveled Route 147 gives you lovely glimpses of the river valley and the interesting towns that dot the banks. In Millersburg you can ride the **Millersburg Ferry,** one of the last surviving wooden, double-sternwheel paddleboats in the country. It runs a mile back and forth to Liverpool at one of the river's widest points. A National Historic Landmark, the first ferry began operation in 1825, a big step forward for passengers and freight haulers accustomed to using rowboats and pole boats. At the peak of river commerce, four boats made the trips.

Now only the *Falcon* and the *Roaring Bull V* ply the river, which at this spot rarely gets more than 3 feet deep. Each ferry accommodates four cars and fifty passengers. To find the pickup point, drive into Millersburg on Route 147 and follow the signs. Generally the ferries run daily mid-June through late August, Monday through Friday 11:00 A.M. to 5:00 P.M. and weekends 9:00 A.M. to 5:00 P.M. In May, early June, September, and October, ferries run weekends only. One car costs about $7.00. For more information call (717) 692–2442, fax (717) 692–2291, or write to the Millersburg Ferry Boat Association, P.O. Box 93, Millersburg 17061.

Across from the ferry landing, on the west side of the Susquehanna at Liverpool, lies **Hunters Valley Winery.** Located on a 150-year-old farm, the winery combines traditional wine-making methods with stainless-steel fermenters and fine filtration. The grapes come from vineyards that were planted in 1982. In many ways the growing conditions resemble those in parts of France, with full sun, good air circulation, excellent drainage, and temperatures moderated by the river and mountains. You may walk through the vineyards and picnic on the grounds Wednesday, Thursday, and Saturday 11:00 A.M. to 5:00 P.M.; Friday 11:00 A.M. to 7:00 P.M; and Sunday 1:00 to 5:00 P.M. Holiday hours vary. Call (717) 444–7211, or go to www.huntersvalleywines.com.

Southern Border

Head south to **Carlisle,** where I–81 connects with the Pennsylvania Turnpike and Route 15. All that concrete is thankfully on the outskirts of this comfortable Cumberland County seat.

Proud, prosperous, and preservation-conscious, the town's still-inhabited log cabins sport screened windows; the cannonball dents in the courthouse (relics of an 1863 pre-Gettysburg skirmish) are unrepaired. The colonial street plan is unchanged. The farmer's market has been held weekly for a couple of centuries. And how many towns of 19,000 have their own spacious historical society, complete with research library, gift shop, and guidebooks?

To call the town center the traditional town meeting place is an understatement. Five Indian paths converged here before white settlement. The pioneer settlers bent on killing western tribes mustered here in 1756. Constitutional and slave riots followed, a century apart; a hot-air balloon ascended in 1843. Geronimo paraded through in 1905, en route to Teddy Roosevelt's inauguration. And every event was carefully documented. The Historical Society provides a $5.00 guide for self-guided walking tours. The Society is housed in the beautiful red brick building at 21 North Pitt Street (717–249–7610), open Monday from 3:00 to 9:00 P.M.; Tuesday through Friday 10:00 A.M. to 4:00 P.M; and Saturday 10:00 A.M. to 3:00 P.M.

The historic district's blocks of stately churches and homes also have a modest hippie vibe, thanks in part to downtown Dickinson College. Instead of costumed interpreters, the streets buzz with skateboarders, guitarists, and pub patrons. The site where Ben Franklin stayed in 1753 is now Mandy's, a coffeehouse whose leisurely crowd spills onto the sidewalk. And as a college town, Carlisle also boasts plenty of pubs and good restaurants. The Market Cross Pub & Brewery at 113 North Hanover Street (717–258–1234; www.marketcrosspub.com) offers casual alehouse fare and an extensive list of you-know-whats.

Near Carlisle is some of the best fly-fishing in the world. The Letort Stream runs right through town. Another blue-ribbon favorite, Yellow Breeches Creek, gets its name from the British soldiers who crossed the creek during the American Revolution; their white trousers became stained from the yellow tint of the water. Many outfitters guide on this stream, and because so much of the

BEST ANNUAL EVENTS IN SOUTH CENTRAL PENNSYLVANIA

In January the Joseph Priestley House in Northumberland celebrates *Twelfth Day,* ringing in the New Year as English dissenters (like Unitarian scientist Priestley) did at the close of the eighteenth century. Call (570) 473–9474 for details.

The annual *Birding Cup* at Shaver's Creek Environmental Center is a twenty-four-hour race to count as many different species of birds as possible. Teams of birders compete during the first weekend in May to raise funds for the center's Raptor Center. Call (814) 863–2000, or fly to www.shaverscreek.org.

Memorial Day was born in Boalsburg in 1864 and declared a national holiday a few years later. The village celebrates annually with a *Day in Towne on Memorial Day.* From 9:00 A.M. to 5:00 P.M., it's crafts, food, music, and a reenactment of a Civil War event. At 6:00 P.M. everybody walks from the square to the cemetery, where cannons boom, a brass band and bagpipes play, scouts raise and lower the flag, and the VFW plays taps. If you're into Memorial Day, this is the Real Thing. Call (814) 466–6311 for more details.

Every summer Saturday morning brings dewy-fresh organic produce, baked goods, and more to the *Old Pomfret Farmers Market* in Carlisle. It's a tradition that dates back two centuries in this historic market town and county seat. From 8:00 A.M. to noon, shop at 16 West High Street (rear); call (717) 245–2648.

The first weekend in October the *Railfest* is held at the Railroaders Memorial Museum, Altoona; call (888) 425–8666 or (814) 946–0834; or visit www.railroadcity.com.

On the third weekend in October, McConnellsburg hosts the *Fulton Fall Folk Festival;* the annual *Grease, Steam & Rust Show* (featuring antique machinery); and the *Historical Society Open House,* all at once. Call (717) 485–4064, or visit www.fultoncountypa.com.

shoreline belongs to exclusive trout-fishing clubs, it's best to get expert advice on where you can safely throw your line. Contact Tom's Fly-Fishing Service in nearby New Cumberland at (717) 770–0796, or visit www.tomsflyfishing.com.

Civil War history awaits at *Chambersburg,* which is west on Route 30. The Confederates occupied the city three times during the Civil War. The last time, in 1864, 3,000 Confederate soldiers rode into town demanding $100,000 ransom in gold, which Chambersburg couldn't pay. The Confederates burned the town, putting two-thirds of its citizens out of their homes, then rode off to McConnellsburg. Mention it the next time a Southerner complains about Sherman burning Atlanta. In the 1960s Chambersburg won recognition for its

East Broad Top Railroad

efforts to preserve historic areas as part of city development plans. While the city could claim much history, actual historic buildings were in such short supply that saving them seemed especially important. Stop by the **Cumberland Valley Visitors Station** at exit 16 (old exit 6) off Interstate 81 (1235 Lincoln Way East; 717–261–1200).

From McConnellsburg, take Route 522 north 30 miles to the **East Broad Top Railroad,** a National Historic Landmark at Orbisonia. Some railroad buffs believe East Broad Top is the best train attraction in Pennsylvania. It is the last 3-foot-gauge (narrow-gauge) line in the East still operating from its original site. It was built in 1873 to move bituminous coal from the mines to Mt. Union, 11 miles north, where the "black diamonds" were dumped into standard-gauge Pennsylvania Railroad cars. The East Broad Top hauled coal until 1956. Today the 10-mile, hour-long, scenic, fun, and educational trip hauls railroad enthusiasts, excited kids, grinning grown-ups, photographers—and sound-recording zealots. People show up periodically, lugging audio equipment and stringing microphones along the track, to record the Doppler effect or to commit the train's distinctive chugs and choos to stereo for a film. You can stop for a picnic at the end of the line and come back on a later train. Trains leave at 11:00 A.M., 1:00 P.M., and 3:00 P.M., weekends only, June through October. The fee is $9.00 per adult. Write East Broad Top Railroad, P.O. Box 158, Rockhill Furnace 17249; call (814) 447–3011; or visit www.ebtrr.com.

trivia

Who knew? The fierce Molly Pitcher, an all-American girl who followed her man (or perhaps men) to Revolutionary War battle and actually got paid for it, is buried in Carlisle, where her statue brandishes a ramrod over the town graveyard.

The Complete History of Shanty Beans

Edenville is a town of 400 people, nestled up against North Mountain, near Chambersburg. There's one road in and one road out. A few times a year, the Edenville community center holds a fund-raising dinner, serving chicken, ham, and shanty beans. "About fifty years ago, three guys from Edenville were up on North Mountain hunting deer," says Allen Johnson. "It snowed, and they got stuck in a shack for four days. All they had to eat were lima beans, brown sugar, onions, and bacon. So Cham Clark, their cook, put all those ingredients together, and that's what they lived on. About twenty years ago, somebody got the bright idea to serve the beans—which they now call shanty beans—at the community center. Nope, they never got a deer."

Shielded from the interstates by the southern Alleghenies, **Bedford** is easy to miss. It's perched alongside the Raystown branch of the Juniata River along Route 30. But don't pass by this classic red brick county seat, enfolded by deep-forested mountains.

People have been passing through Bedford for centuries, starting with the Shawnee Indians, who blazed the first trail west. The British soldiers who followed hacked their way over the mountains on their way to kicking the French out of Pittsburgh. Bedford's buildings reflect these past transients. Forts and log cabins from the 1750s (a few with aluminum siding additions) still stand alongside Federal-era town houses. George Washington stayed in Bedford, while his troops, farther west, quelled the Whiskey Rebellion in 1794. The nineteenth century brought the grandeur of the now-deserted Bedford Springs Hotel. President James Buchanan received the first transatlantic cable at the fashionable spa, the object of repeated (and failed) redevelopment attempts.

Join the Friday afternoon historical walking tours with Dennis Tice (he's the droll director of the visitors bureau on Juliana Street). The free, easy, 4-block tour includes the 1828 courthouse (with the Ten Commandments by the front steps), the town squares, and the Espy House, where Washington stayed. "This place is operating now as what it was as far back as the 1700s," Tice tells groups at the tour's end at **Oralee's Golden Eagle Inn.** The basement-level tavern used to host muddy boots, smoke, and spurs. Now the three-story brick hotel and restaurant is beautifully restored, and owner Oralee Kieffer stores her surplus antiques in the basement. Write Oralee's Golden Eagle Country Inn and B&B at 131 East Pitt Street, Bedford 15522; call (814) 624–0800; or visit www.bedfordgoldeneagle.com.

Down the street is the Pitt Theater (showing only one movie a night), three antiques stores, the Fort Bedford Museum, and Old Bedford Village, a colonial-era re-creation. Also worth a quiet stroll is Bedford Memorial Park, a nicely restored 200-year-old cemetery.

Bedford County has fourteen covered bridges, and you can tour them on bike or by car. They are usually named for their original nineteenth-century builders, and most have been safely rebuilt in recent years. The Bedford County Visitors Bureau (800–765–3331; www.bedfordcounty.net) offers a Web link and a printed brochure with distances and details. It's open year-round Monday through Friday 9:00 A.M. to 5:00 P.M.; May through October, the bureau is also open Saturday 10:00 A.M. to 2:00 P.M. *Cycle the Southern Alleghenies* (www.cyclesa.com) offers online planning help for cycling tours, too; call them at (800) 458–3433.

Breezewood, the self-proclaimed "Town of Motels," is mainly a giant clover-leaf garnished with neon. But for cyclists, it's also a trailhead for a unique thrill ride: the *Pike to Bike Trail.*

The Superhighway Trail, or P2B as it's known hereabouts, became an appendix to the state's main east-west artery in 1968, when the Pennsylvania Turnpike was rerouted through bigger four-lane tunnels. Between the old ones, Sideling Hill and Rays Hill, the discarded stretch of road was relegated to highway researchers and underage boozers. But since the Southern Alleghenies Conservancy took it over in 2001, recreational cyclists—a few hundred each weekend—have reclaimed the roadway. Riding through the pitch-black tunnels (Rays Hill is 0.75 miles, Sideling Hill, 1.3) provides the thrill. In between there's Buchanan State Forest and not much else. Make sure to bring a bike light. For directions to the 8.5-mile trail, visit www.saconservancy.org. Look under "Our Projects."

To paddle the peaceful southern Juniata River, rent a canoe or kayak from Craig Mayer at *Adventure Marine* (P.O. Box 102, Bedford 15522; 814–735–2768; www.bedford.net/canoe), just outside of town. Canoes are $25 for the first two days; kayaks are $20. He'll be happy to let you have them as long as you want to paddle and camp.

On silent Route 4016 near New Paris, there's a country road that's downright spooky: *Gravity Hill.*

"Stay calm," read the directions in our county-issued brochure. "Keep cool. Put your car in neutral and take your foot off the brake." We did. And then the car began moving. Backwards. Up the hill. On cue, we screamed.

Whatever its explanation, Gravity Hill is one of those certifiably off-the-beaten-path attractions that you can't miss. And once you get there, you'll find a second Gravity Hill three-tenths of a mile past the first. Get the very specific directions from the Bedford County Visitors Bureau.

Seven miles west of Bedford on Route 30 is *Coral Caverns,* the only known coral-reef cavern, formed more than 300 million years ago when the area was covered by the Appalachian Sea. It's open for tours 10:00 A.M. to 5:00 P.M., weekends in June, September, and October and daily in July and August. Admission is $9.00 per adult. Call (814) 623–6882, or write P.O. Box 100, Manns Choice 15550, for details.

No cappuccino at the **Coffee Pot.** No latte. Not even cream and sugar. Just a way-larger-than-life-sized coffeepot built in 1925, an example of the "programmatic architecture" that dotted the Lincoln Highway, Route 30, aimed at luring tourists and travelers. The pot, located across the street from the entrance to the Bedford County Fairgrounds, has been closed for years. But things may be perking up. The Lincoln Highway Heritage Corridor is trying to preserve the, er, grounds and building for future java lovers. Call (724) 238–9030, or visit www.lhhc.org for more information.

When you hear the name **Road Kill Cafe,** you just have to go. The cafe is the nearest commercial establishment to **Grouseland Tours,** 10 miles south of Bedford in Clearville. Grouseland, featured on ESPN, offers lessons and guided mountain-biking tours; contact them at (814) 784–5000, or visit www.grouse land.com. The cafe offers home cooking and cabins ($25 for singles, $35 for doubles) and is run by Barb Snyder, whose homemade pies (as well as T-shirts with tasteful slogans like "You Kill It, We Grill It") have made the place a legend. The cafe (814–784–3257), on Crooked Run Road, is open Monday through Saturday 8:00 A.M. to 7:00 P.M. and Sunday from noon to 2:30 P.M.

Consider a side trip to Rainsburg on Route 326, a community established so long ago that a nineteenth-century historian wrote, "the memory of man runneth not to the contrary," regarding its existence. The small borough features the **Rainsburg Male and Female Seminary,** incorporated in 1853 to offer secondary education and train teachers. And while you're in the area, stop in Chaneysville, a small town also on Route 326, that sheltered fugitive slaves before the Civil War. For a wonderful look back in time, read David Bradley's excellent novel *The Chaneysville Incident.*

In New Baltimore, milepost 129 on the Pennsylvania Turnpike, a church sits *on* the highway. Formally St. John the Baptist, a Catholic sanctuary, the church usually is called the **Church on the Turnpike.** Whether you're traveling eastbound or westbound, you can stop your car right at the church and walk to mass. If you're driving you can take the Bedford or Somerset exit, both 20 miles away.

Places to Stay in South Central Pennsylvania

BEDFORD

Oralee's Golden Eagle Inn,
131 East Pitt Street;
(814) 624–0800;
www.bedfordgoldeneagle
.com

CARLISLE

The Carlisle House,
148 South Hanover Street;
(717) 249–0350;
www.thecarlislehouse.com

DuBOIS

The Inn at Narrows Creek,
44 Narrows Creek Lane;
(814) 371–9394;
fax (814) 375–7876;
www.narrowscreek.com

JEANERSTOWN

**Thee Olde Stagecoach
Bed & Breakfast,**
1760 Lincoln Highway;
(814) 629–7440;
www.oldestagecoachbandb
.com

SCHELLSBURG

**Covered Bridge Inn
Bed & Breakfast,**
749 Mill Road;
(814) 733–4093;
www.bedfordcounty.net/
cbi.htm

STATE COLLEGE

Atherton Hotel,
125 South Atherton Street;
(814) 231–2100 or
(800) 832–0132;
www.atherton.net

SUNBURY

Edison Hotel,
Market and South Fourth
Streets;
(570) 286–5605

Places to Eat in South Central Pennsylvania

CARLISLE

Piatto,
22 West Pomfret Street;
(717) 243–5020.
Regional Italian specialties in
a Civil War–era home or on
the porch. BYOB.

DANVILLE

Old Hardware Restaurant,
336 Mill Street;
(570) 275–6615

NEW BERLIN

Gabriel's Restaurant,
321 Market Street;
(570) 966–0321;
www.innatnewberlin.com

OSTERBURG

**Slick's Ivy Stone
Restaurant,**
8785 William Penn Road;
(814) 276–3131.
Open April through Decem-
ber; closed Monday.

Shamokin Dam,
Tedd's Landing,
Routes 11 and 15;
(570) 743–1591

Southwestern Pennsylvania: Pittsburgh Region

Golden Triangle

East is Philadelphia, and west is Pittsburgh, and never the twain shall meet. You'll be surprised how many folks in the former have only the vaguest idea where the latter is (it's 300 miles to the left). The Allegheny Mountains, it turns out, have been a pretty effective barrier to westward movement ever since the British first hacked their way into the wilderness 250 years ago. But easterners—in fact, any visitors—are bowled over by southwestern Pennsylvania's offerings, from high art to high fives (pro sports are big here), once they arrive.

Downtown Pittsburgh is often called the Golden Triangle, in reference to its location, where the Allegheny and Monongahela Rivers form the Ohio (next stop, via the Mississippi: the Gulf of Mexico). So much water, surrounded by high bluffs with lots of trees, reminds some folks of San Francisco, but with a winter.

All that's gold also glitters. Adding to the scenery is the dazzle of downtown architecture, including Philip Johnson's PPG Place (all glass, of course) and Michael Graves's O'Reilly Theater. Along the waterfront are architect Rafael Viñoly's swooping convention center and the contemporary Carnegie Science Center. A hard throw from the business district is PNC

SOUTHWESTERN PENNSYLVANIA

Park (named for the PNC Financial Services Group). It's the prettiest retro ballpark in America, next door to a brand-new pro-football stadium. The downtown bridges are painted gold, and the Steelers (football), Penguins (hockey), and Pirates (baseball) all have black-and-gold color schemes (colors that appear on the Pittsburgh city crest).

First, let's look back. From about 1870 to 1970, Pittsburgh led the nation in producing iron, steel, and glass and in mining bituminous coal. At the same time, Pittsburgh's environment rotted. Clouds rolled by on skies of black and gray, not blue, and nights sometimes glowed orange. Rivers flowed brown and green. Initial attempts at controlling smoke and floods were hampered by a couple of world wars and by a boom-and-bust economy. In 1941, the year Pittsburgh had the nation's highest rate of pneumonia, the mayor created a commission to eliminate smoke. Now, after decades of civic improvement, Pittsburgh has overcome its industry-induced pollution. And what a transformation: *Utne Reader* magazine recently called Pittsburgh "one of America's most underrated cities." It's a place you've got to see for yourself.

Don't neglect the Cultural District downtown, home to fabulously restored dowager theaters along Penn Avenue. Around the corner, on the side of the Byham Theater, you'll find the inside of an old steel mill—in a fabulous giant mural by Robert Haas. Next door is a subtle light sculpture by Robert Wilson,

triviatidbits

Between downtown stops, you can ride Pittsburgh's subway train, the T, for no charge.

The Three Sisters, Pittsburgh style, are the Clemente, Warhol, and Carson Street Bridges across the Allegheny River near downtown. Attribute their lyrical design to John Roebling, who also created the aqueducts in Lackawaxen, Pennsylvania, and the Brooklyn Bridge.

AUTHOR'S TOP TEN FAVORITES IN SOUTHWESTERN PENNSYLVANIA

Club Cafe	Kennywood Park
Confluence	Mattress Factory
Fallingwater	Ohiopyle
Jimmy Stewart Museum	Punxsutawney
Kayak Pittsburgh	St. Anthony's Chapel

Richardson Romanesque

Few architects have an architectural style named after them, but Henry Hobson Richardson is one of them. His Allegheny County Courthouse and Jail, begun in 1883, is a famous example of the architect's powerful style. Massive stonework, rounded arches, and towers are his signature, shown to great effect in his masterpiece in the heart of Pittsburgh. (Photos show his physique was much like his buildings.)

Called Richardson Romanesque because of its similarities to eleventh-century European architecture, the architect's style actually draws from a variety of sources. Richardson stressed theatrical sculptured shapes: deep-set windows, cavernous door openings, and bands of windows. (He devised an arched bridge over Ross Street, between the courthouse and the jail, to allow prisoners to be taken to trial directly from the jail. Hence the local nickname, the Bridge of Sighs.)

Richardson's work can been seen all over the East Coast, and once you see it, you'll always recognize his style. The courthouse is widely considered one of his finest works. He died at age forty-seven in 1886—just before its completion.

which is installed across the top of a building (look for the turning triangles). When you come to the corner of Eighth and Penn, facing a hulking Aztec-style pyramid, you've reached two more public art installations. Temporary ones often join the line-up. They're as much fun as the theatrical performances.

Around Town

If you ask for directions to "the Carnegie Museum" from downtown, you'll be branded a tourist for sure, because there are four. On the city's North Shore, find the *Carnegie Science Center* (One Allegheny Avenue; 412–237–3400; open daily). Kids love to visit its Earthquake Cafe, which really shakes them up. Ditto the nearby *Andy Warhol Museum,* with a cool style that appeals to both kids and adults (117 Sandusky Street; 412–237–8300; closed Monday). The *Carnegie Museum of Art* (4400 Forbes Avenue; 412–622–3131; closed Monday), 2 miles away in the Oakland section, is where old meets new: magnificent casts of architecture and sculpture from antiquity, plus fine impressionist and contemporary art collections. Drop-in tours are offered daily. Look for the bronze *Diplodocus,* nicknamed Dippy, outside the complex; he'll point you toward the *Carnegie Museum of Natural History* (4400 Forbes Avenue), with its nightmare-inducing *Tyrannosaurus rex* and other fossils. Dinosaur Hall will reopen in revamped form in late 2007. There are wonderful Egyptian and gem collections here, too. For exhibit information and hours for all four museums, visit www.carnegiemuseums.org.

The **Pittsburgh Zoo** (One Wild Place; 412–665–3640 or 800–474–4966; www.zoo .pgh.pa.us/) maintains more than 4,000 animals in habitats as diverse as an aquarium, an African savanna, and a reptile house. In the rain forest endangered species such as gorillas live safely. The zoo is open daily 10:00 A.M. to 5:00 P.M. Memorial Day through Labor Day and 9:00 A.M. to 4:00 P.M. the rest of the year. Closed Thanksgiving, Christmas, and New Year's Day. Admission fee varies with the season.

But, hey, you're here to get off the beaten path, so leave time for other stops. Pittsburgh's neighborhoods are the soul of the city. For funky grocery shopping visit **The Strip,** a flat, 20-block stretch along the Allegheny waterfront above the Convention Center. Start at the handsome **Senator John Heinz Pittsburgh Regional History Center** at 1212 Smallman Street, a converted nineteenth-century brick icehouse. From a steelworker's wake to the Homestead strike, it offers a working stiff's view of three centuries, starting when Pittsburgh was the country's western frontier. The center includes the Western Pennsylvania Sports Museum. This region's especially proud of its great NFL quarterback tradition. Here's where to pay tribute to Pittsburgh greats like Johnny Unitas, Jim Kelly, Dan Marino, Joe Montana, Joe Namath, and more. The museum is open daily 10:00 A.M. to 5:00 P.M. except major holidays; adult admission is $7.50. Call (412) 454–6000 or visit www.pghhistory.org for more information.

Continue east on Smallman Street, or on parallel Penn Avenue, for a bustling parade of restaurateurs (pinching melons and grabbing gourmet ingre-

eyeball art, anyone?

Go on a scavenger tour of downtown Pittsburgh's great public art with a new guidebook. More than eighty works, from the eyeball benches at Agnes Katz Plaza to the giant mayor on the steps of the City-County Building, are mapped in a booklet from the Greater Pittsburgh Arts Council. Pick up your free copy at 707 Penn Avenue.

Cover the Waterfront

Purposeful Pittsburgh used to use its riverbanks only for work: docks and steel mills. But now the city is celebrating its newly pristine shoreline with riverside trails. Joggers, bicyclers, and in-line skaters glide along the Eliza Furnace Trail (since it passes a county jail, it's usually called the Jail Trail). You can connect to the North Shore and skate to a Pirates game at PNC Park or bike across the Hot Metal Bridge (which used to carry buckets of molten steel) and head 10 miles south to the rural Great Allegheny Passage.

The Best Front Door in America

Your first words about Pittsburgh are likely to be "Oh, wow!" Called the "Best Front Door in America," the cityscape that bursts upon you as you emerge from the Fort Pitt Tunnel shimmers with rivers and riverboats, skyscrapers, towering hills, and golden bridges. Smoky city? No more.

When planners wanted to raise the guardrails on the Fort Pitt Bridge, local activists raised their voices. They argued that higher barriers would blind incoming motorists to Pittsburgh's signature view. The result: The state highway department bowed to the beautiful and agreed to keep the lower barriers.

---

dients) and hipsters (mingling at clubs like Have a Nice Day Cafe). The Strip's schizophrenia is part of its charm. Whether you need a whoopee cushion, fresh biscotti, aged cheese, or a full-size inflatable Steeler, this is the place to hit. At *Primanti's* (46 Eighteenth Street; 412–263–2142) get your daily fat quotient in one sitting, with french fries and coleslaw crammed inside your sandwich. For gorgeous gifts try the brick building grandly engraved as the Pennsylvania Railroad Fruit Auction and Sales Building, now the *Society for Contemporary Craft,* 2100 Smallman Street. (Check out the killer carved-wood handbags.) Call (412) 261–7003; fax (412) 261–1941; or visit www.contemporary craft.org; closed Sunday and Monday.

trivia

Novelist Michael Chabon set his *Mysteries of Pittsburgh* and *Wonderboys* here. Like his Pulitzer Prize–winning heroes, Kavalier and Clay, he grew up loving comic books (his favorite hangout was the comic emporium, Eide's Entertainment, on Liberty Avenue).

Mt. Washington is the riverside bluff that looms above the confluence, opposite downtown. A ride to the top on the inclines, the tiny vertical railways that have hauled Pittsburghers up and down the hill for more than a century, is an absolute must for visitors—and cheap, at $3.50 per round-trip.

Start the journey at water level, at *Station Square,* a grand railroad terminus-turned-entertainment center that's an easy subway hop from downtown. (This is also the boarding place for the *Gateway Clipper* fleet of paddleboats, which tour the rivers and ferry fans to Pirates and Steelers games.) Hop the *Monongahela Incline,* built in 1869, here (tip: it's pronounced IN-cline). Its partner, the red-sided *Duquesne Incline,* is a mile up East Carson Street. Both offer a steep and silent four-minute ride to the top.

The aptly named Grandview Avenue, along the crest of Mt. Washington, encourages gawkers with a promenade and viewing platforms. The street's restaurants are special-occasion destinations, mostly for their postcard view, so save your appetite for yet another bustling neighborhood below, the *South Side.*

trivia

Did you love *The Last of the Mohicans*? Each spring reenactors of the French and Indian War camp at Fort Pitt (now Pittsburgh's Point State Park), donning war paint, buckskins, and bonnets.

On the southern bank of the Mon, as locals call the Monongahela River, the South Side boasts that it has "both kinds of blue hair"—on the elderly residents of century-old row houses surrounding former steel mills, and atop youthful loft dwellers and students from Carnegie Mellon University and the University of Pittsburgh. On Saturday evening East Carson Street belongs to the latter, who flood the bars, coffeehouses, and grills.

trivia

Pittsburgh loves wedding soup, an Italian dish: chicken broth, tiny pastina noodles, spinach, and sausage meatballs. Divine.

If you're into magic, don't miss the *Cuckoo's Nest* (1513 East Carson Street; 412–481–4411), a shabby little storefront with juggling clubs, trick cards, wands, scarves, handcuffs—the works. Kids love this place.

Restaurants spring up along the Carson Street sidewalk like crabgrass. One neighborhood secret is the tiny *Dish Osteria and Bar* (128 South Seventh Street; 412–390–2012), with small appetizers (such as mixed marinated olives), great pasta, and fresh fish. Bring cash; no cards accepted. Other excellent spots, a bit more formal, are *Cafe Allegro* (51 South Twelfth Street; 412–481–7788)

George Washington Swam Here

Why is it called Washington's Landing? Easy. In December 1753 a young George Washington narrowly escaped drowning as he paddled across the Allegheny River where the Washington's Crossing Bridge now stands. Thankfully, he landed safely—in what's now called Lawrenceville.

Washington crisscrossed western Pennsylvania frequently, often in the company of Christopher Gist, a friend and guide. (You'll even find a marker showing his footsteps through Kennywood Park!) In fact, when he first set eyes on Pittsburgh, he made a note to himself: "fine place for a fort."

He was right.

pittsburgh
rocks

The view from the choir loft is impressive: a huge nave swelling with music, with wisps of smoke wafting from the sanctuary. The upturned faces of the young congregation seem transported. But then a snarling guitar chord rips rudely through the congregation, and the crowd at the former St. Ann's Church erupts. The liturgy being celebrated in this century-old house of worship isn't High Mass, but a gig at Pittsburgh's church of rock 'n' roll.

Let us play.

Esquire magazine raised a few eyebrows when it named Pittsburgh its number-one City That Rocks in 2004. But clubs like Mr. Small's, the desanctified Catholic church a few miles upriver from downtown in Millvale, the Brillo Box and Arsenal Lanes (yes, it's a bowling alley) in Lawrenceville, the Smiling Moose on the South Side, Gooski's on Polish Hill, and the Quiet Storm in Garfield attract the city's best local bands.

Rock comes downtown too, to clubs like the Cabaret at Theater Square, Dowe's on Ninth, and the Byham Theater, and moves outdoors with free concerts during the Three Rivers Arts Festival each June.

and *Le Pommier* (2104 East Carson Street, 412–431–1901; www.lepommier .com) for fine Italian and French cuisine, respectively.

Live—and loud—music is offered at the South Side's many bars, especially on weekends. But at *Club Cafe* (56 South Twelfth Street; 412–431–4950; www.club cafelive.com), you can find great big-name acts and good local bands on a tiny, starry stage, performing for a hundred folks at cozy tables. It's a sixties coffeehouse with a cyber-vibe.

Above the South Side lie the city's oddest streets: steep vertical steps that no cars could climb. To get to the top of the South Side Slopes, you'll need to bring a walking stick. And maybe a cardiologist. With nearly 700 steps just to the crest of the South Side Slopes, the workout is extreme, but it's the panoramic views that are killer.

The Slopes claim sixty-eight step streets, making this slice of the city feel like a European village: a blend of historic piety, cliffside houses, and quiet corkscrewed streets.

"When I walk the steps, I always get the sense of the mill workers from years ago," local steps historian Bob Regan tells me. "They walked down in the morning, and then, twelve hours later, they walked back up."

Start your climb on Eighteenth Street, pause for a breath at Pius Street, and continue to St. Paul's Monastery, a beautiful Bohemian church at the top. Each year, the community association sponsors a "Step Trek" tour of the neighborhood; go to www.southsideslopes.org for details.

From the base of the Slopes, follow Carson Street 10 more miles east and you'll arrive at **Kennywood Park** (Route 837 in West Mifflin; 412–461–0500; www.kennywood.com). This charming century-old amusement park is a National Historic Landmark. It's an institution so loved by Pittsburghers that they come back every summer, usually with a crowd: the company picnic, the school picnic, or on Nationality Days, a great local tradition (Italian Day, Croatian Day, etc.). Nationality Days date back to the immigrant steelworkers who flocked to this bank of the Mon. A few miles downstream is the site of U.S. Steel's Homestead Works, formerly the largest steel mill in the world and now a vast shopping and entertainment center.

thefourthriver

Three Rivers? Actually, four. The mighty fountain that gushes at the confluence in Point State Park draws water from a powerful underground aquifer that also supplies all of Pittsburgh's drinking water.

Kennywood's claim to fame is its roller coasters: the wooden Thunderbolt, ranked one of the best in the world by enthusiasts; the Phantom's Revenge, a coaster-in-the-dark; and many more. Hold on to the bar! Admission prices vary, depending on how much you want to ride. Open May through Labor Day.

Rising above Interstate 376 near Monroeville is a sight you might expect along the Ganges River, rather than the Monongahela: a huge, wedding-cake-style temple with Indian flourishes. It's the Sri Venkataswara Temple, one of only ten Hindu temples in the United States. It attracts worshipers from all over the East Coast. Remove your shoes and take a tour; it welcomes anyone who'd like to view the ornate building and appreciate its murals and statuary. It's located at 1230 South McCully Drive in Penn Hills; call ahead to (412) 373–3380. The Web site (www.svtemple.org) gives details and directions.

Head back to downtown Pittsburgh to the Point and plunge in. **Kayak Pittsburgh,** under the Clemente Bridge, offers kayaks and canoes for self-guided tours of the confluence May through October. One Federal Street; use the stairway next to statue of Roberto Clemente at PNC Park on the

They Came from Pittsburgh

Stephen Foster, composer; Billy Eckstine, musician; Rachel Carson, conservationist; George S. Kaufman and August Wilson, playwrights; Gene Kelly, actor and dancer; Willa Cather, author; Gertrude Stein, author; Shirley Jones, actress; Mary Cassatt, artist; Henry Mancini, composer; Perry Como, singer; and Michael Keaton, actor.

Cathedral of Learning

North Shore. Call (412) 969–9090 or (412) 255–0564, or visit www.ventureoutdoors.org. Kayak racks at PNC Park and the South Side let you "park" for an afternoon.

The forty-two-story *Cathedral of Learning,* a Gothic Revival skyscraper, dominates the University of Pittsburgh and the surrounding Oakland neighborhood. The Commons Room, on the first floor, is evocative of a medieval cathedral. Around its perimeter are the *Nationality Rooms* (157 Cathedral of Learning; 412–624–6000; www.univ-relations.pitt.edu/nat rooms). The classrooms are decorated in the style of twenty-six different nations. Pittsburghers are proud of them; visitors, especially international ones, are crazy about them. The *Stephen Foster Memorial* next door commemorates the country's first pop music composer (412–624–4100; www.pitt.edu/~amerimus/museum.htm).

Foster is buried with many other city notables, including Lillian Russell, in *Allegheny Cemetery* (4734 Butler Street; 412–682–1624) in Lawrenceville. Its grand spooky style is echoed in *Homewood Cemetery* (Forbes and Dallas Avenues; 412–421–1822) in Point Breeze. Ghost stories abound; take the tours to hear them.

Around Allegheny Cemetery, one of Pittsburgh's oldest neighborhoods is showing new life. *Lawrenceville,* running from Sixteenth to Sixty-second Streets along the Allegheny River, has turned Civil War–era Butler Street into a district of galleries, cafes, and design boutiques that remind some visitors of Brooklyn's Park Slope.

The shopping district anchored by the World War I doughboy statue at Penn and

trivia

Pittsburgh International Airport makes it a pleasure to land. The terminals' people-movers, Air Mall, fitness facilities, and restaurants earned it the rankings of "Best Airport in the U.S." and "Number 8 in the World" by publisher Condé Nast.

Butler Streets has plenty of antiques shops; try Scavengers at 3533 Butler (412–682–6781) or McDonough's at 3617 Butler (412–681–8858). For women's clothes, it's Divine at 3609 Butler (412–621–3040) and Sugar at 3703 Butler (412–681–5100). This laid-back group of friendly shop owners sponsors fun come-ons like an annual Christmas cookie tour and Easter egg hunts. Check out the Thunderbird Cafe (4023 Butler Street; 412–682–0177) for nightlife and Piccolo Forno (3801 Butler Street; 412–622–0111) for chic Italian eats. The Coca Café (3811 Butler Street; 412–621–3171) is located directly across from a historic landmark: The Arsenal School is named for the site where seventy-eight young workers, mainly women, were killed in an explosion at a Union munitions plant in 1862.

Schenley Park, behind the universities in Oakland, has amenities galore. A student favorite is the city's popular disc-golf course (where eighteen holes means tossing a Frisbee into eighteen baskets). The park's newest attraction is a shiny carousel, with ponies big enough for adults to ride. It's just off Forbes Avenue. The glass onion just over the hill is the *Phipps Conservatory,* a Victorian wonderland of exotic flowers and fountains. Take a guided tour on weekends. Admission ranges from $7.50 for adults to $4.50 for children. Open daily from 9:30 A.M. to 5:00 P.M., till 9:00 P.M. Friday. Overlooking the Steve Faloon Trail (voted one of America's top-twenty urban running trails by *Runner's World* magazine) is the visitor center, a charmingly restored coffeehouse with a balcony. Get details and directions at www.pittsburghparks.org or (412) 682–PARK.

Nearby *Clayton* (7227 Reynolds Street; 412–371–0600; www.frickart.com) is the grand former home of Henry Clay Frick, where you can see how Pittsburgh's

Some of the Movies Filmed in Greater Pittsburgh

1914	*The Perils of Pauline*	1993	*Striking Distance*
1951	*Angels in the Outfield*	1995	*Sudden Death*
1968	*Night of the Living Dead*	1996	*Diabolique*
1978	*The Deer Hunter*	1999	*Dogma*
1982	*Flashdance*	1999	*Inspector Gadget*
1990	*Silence of the Lambs*	2000	*Wonderboys*
1991	*Bob Roberts*	2002	*Mothman Prophecies*
1991	*Lorenzo's Oil*		

millionaires lived at the dawn of the twentieth century. Don't miss the working orchestrion, a room-size mechanical orchestra that was the home theater of its day. The greenhouse, art museum, and car museum are free. The cafe is award-winning gourmet; its afternoon teas are white-glove. House tours cost $10; open 10:00 A.M. to 5:00 P.M. except Monday.

In the historic Mexican War Streets section of the North Side is the *Mattress Factory* (500 Sampsonia Way; 412–231–3169; www.mattress.org), a fascinating display of contemporary art. The factory, which is, indeed, a converted factory, commissions, exhibits, and collects site-specific installations; it also provides living and working space for artists from around the world. Visionary contemporary artists such as James Turrell, Ann Hamilton, and Damien Hirst exhibit here; your fellow visitors are likely to be overseas art lovers who've come to Pittsburgh expressly because of the Mattress Factory's world-class reputation for cutting-edge programming. (Check out the basement.) Hours are Tuesday through Friday 10:00 A.M. to 5:00 P.M., Saturday 10:00 A.M. to 7:00 P.M., and Sunday 1:00 to 5:00 P.M. Admission is $8.00 for adults, except for Thursday, when it's half-price.

The motto of the *Pittsburgh Children's Museum* is "play with real stuff." So go ahead. Squirt water. Take things apart in The Garage. Get muddy in The Backyard. The award-winning renovation of this combination of two grand old buildings is a treat. Make a play date Monday through Saturday 10:00 A.M. to 5:00 P.M., Sunday noon to 5:00 P.M. Admission is $8.00 for adults, $7.00 for seniors and children.

Other North Side gems: *Photo Antiquities* (531 East Ohio Street; 412–231–7881; www.photoantiquities.org), a collection of rarities from the nineteenth century, including fine Civil War–era images (soldiers loved the newfangled invention). Closed Tuesday and Sunday. Hours vary. Admission is $6.50. And don't miss *St. Anthony's Chapel*, with its collection of 4,200 Catholic relics

Ride 'em Shovelers!

The annual Beaver County Snow Shovel Riding Championship in Ambridge is a classic community event, with minimal equipment required. "The key to winning," says organizer Jack Hilfinger, "is to remember that the shovel doesn't have to touch the ground." That means you can customize your ride with a snow tube, skis, or anything else that slides. The fun takes place the third Saturday of January, snow permitting.

from saints and popes. In the 1890s St. Anthony's was a sort of mini-Lourdes, where the faithful flocked to be blessed and healed by the church's pastor (who collected most of the bones, skulls, and other relics). Even in a city of churches, this one is completely unique. The ornate European-style chapel, at 1705 Harpster Street in Troy Hill, is open afternoons on Tuesday, Thursday, and Saturday (knock at the rectory next door) and offers tours each Sunday. Call (412) 323–9504 for details.

At the foot of Troy Hill, make a different kind of pilgrimage to the ***Pennsylvania Brewery*** (800 Vinial Street; 412–237–9402; www.pennbrew.com), which brews fine German-style beers and offers German-style food. Closed Sunday and major holidays.

Ohio River Valley

Heading north from Pittsburgh on Route 28, it's easy to miss ***Aspinwall***—but don't. This old-fashioned cutie of a riverside town has a real five-and-ten store (J&W Variety, 12 Brilliant Avenue; 412–782–2993), bookstores, gift shops, and great architecture.

Audubon at Beechwood, a property of the Western Pennsylvania Conservancy, has varied walking trails. Stop by the Audubon Society; the reserve is great for wildflowers, birds, and photography. Eight marked, named footpaths range in length and ease of terrain, so some are perfect for young'uns and people new at observing nature, while others appeal to more rigorous tastes. Goldenrod Footpath, for instance, has a gentle, easy slope; the Oak Forest path passes a deformed tree that shows how trees can respond to infections; and the Pine Hollow path smells best. The trails are open from sunup to sundown. Beechwood, formerly called Beechwood Farms Nature Reserve, includes a nature store and the Center for Native Plants, the region's only facility devoted solely to western Pennsylvania's 1,500 native plants. Volunteers and staff provide maps, information, and advice on where to walk, depending on your stamina. Weekly guided nature walks are scheduled year-round. To get to the reserve from Route 28, take the Fox Chapel Road exit north and go about a mile. Turn left on Squaw Run Road, then right on Dorseyville Road. Beechwood Farms is almost 2 miles on the left. For more information write 614 Dorseyville Road, Pittsburgh 15238; phone (412) 963–6100; or go to www.aswp.org.

On a warm evening there's no hotter ticket than the free concerts at *Hartwood Acres* (215 Saxonburg Boulevard). This county park cradles a band shell at the bottom of a ten-acre meadow and hosts summer concerts with national names. In the winter there are hayrides. Year-round there are tours of the original manor house. Call (412) 767-9200, or visit www.county allegheny.pa.us/parks for more information.

Talk about the sound of music: The *Bayernhof Museum* in Pittsburgh's North Hills turns up the volume. This converted suburban home, with a Bavarian theme that includes gnome statues and an indoor pool and grotto, houses a large collection of music boxes and other kitschy contraptions. Check out the serinettes (musical bird boxes), Wurlitzer band organs, player pianos, and more. It's at 225 St. Charles Place in a quiet residential neighborhood overlooking the Allegheny River. Tours (for those over twelve) are available by appointment; call ahead. The phone number is (412) 782–4231 or visit www .bayernhofmuseum.com.

In nearby Gibsonia lies one of southwestern Pennsylvania's best restaurants, the *Pines Tavern and Restaurant* (5018 Bakerstown Road; 724–625–3252). This is a five-star treat, well worth a drive from downtown.

You might dine at the Pines after a day in Springdale, where a modest tribute to one of America's first environmentalists exists in the *Rachel Carson Homestead.* Carson, who warned the public about the long-term effects of misusing pesticides in *Silent Spring,* learned to love nature on her family's farm. Now a museum, the homestead, which is open from 1:00 to 5:00 P.M. on warm-weather weekends, is close to the rugged 34-mile Rachel Carson Trail overlooking the Allegheny River. Write P.O. Box 46, Springdale 15144-0046; call (724) 274–5459; or visit www.rachelcarsonhomestead.org.

Allegheny anthracite lies under most of the mountains in western Pennsylvania. To get an up-close look at the history of coal mining, go underground at Tarentum's *Tour-Ed Mine* (748 Bull Creek Road; 724–224–4720; www.tour-ed mine.com). Take a tour 150 feet below the surface on a specially modified train. Don't worry; it's perfectly safe. The mine is just off exit 48 (old exit 5, Allegheny Valley) of the Pennsylvania Turnpike. It's open Memorial Day through Labor Day; limited hours through October. Admission is $7.00.

You can appreciate history on a trip to **Old Economy Village** at Ambridge, less than an hour northwest of Pittsburgh. Old Economy is the preserved third and final home of the Old Harmony Society. In 1804 nearly 800 farmers and craftsmen, members of the Harmonists, migrated to America from southwest Germany seeking religious and economic freedom. They spent ten years in Butler County, Pennsylvania, and ten years in Indiana before returning to the Keystone State to stay. Each time, at each locale, they named their community Harmony. The Harmonists based their simple, orthodox lifestyle on beliefs of the early Christian Church. Because they expected the Second Coming of Christ to happen at any moment, they adopted celibacy to purify themselves for Christ's thousand-year reign on earth. Religion came first in their lives—they celebrated the Last Supper six times a year—but their communal lifestyle was not austere. Harmonites ate well, adorned their furniture, played music, planted flower gardens, and made money for the community. The society developed economically and technologically. By 1825 they had built cotton and wool factories powered and heated by steam engines, a steam laundry, and a dairy. They constructed shops for blacksmiths, hatters, wagonmakers, and linen weavers. Their canny business sense produced fine furniture, sturdy buildings, beautiful grounds, and many beneficial investments in the nearby towns. The community lasted until 1905.

triviatidbits

Dancer Gene Kelly and composer Billy Strayhorn grew up in Pittsburgh's East Liberty neighborhood. They are remembered there at the Kelly-Strayhorn Theater, 5941 Penn Avenue.

The nickelodeon, the earliest form of public film exhibition, opened on Smithfield Street in Pittsburgh in 1905. The Harris Theater, which screens films around the corner, is named for the nickelodeon's inventor.

The Pittsburgh Pirates are the second-oldest professional athletic team in the country. Originally called the Alleghenies, they changed their name when other teams accused them of "pirating" players from their rosters.

Your hour-long tour takes in the community kitchen, the cabinet and blacksmith shops, granary, wine cellar, tailor shop, store, great house, and gardens. The tour guides know a lot about the religious beliefs and the history of the community. When an old object has been moved or when restoration somehow deviates from the original structure, the guides point it out and explain why. The village and its gift shop are open March through December, Tuesday through Saturday 9:00 A.M. to 5:00 P.M. and Sunday noon to 5:00 P.M. The village is closed Monday. Admission is $7.00 for adults, $6.00 for seniors.

For information about daily tours and special events, write Harmony Associates, Fourteenth and Church Streets, Ambridge 15003; call (724) 266–4500; or visit www.oldeconomyvillage.org. To get there follow I–79 to Sewickley, then go north on Route 65 along the Ohio River until you see the white picket fence.

If you're looking for an adventure that caters to the cowardly, consider hot-air ballooning over western Pennsylvania. Balloonist Tim Meteny flies daily in warm weather at dawn and dusk. You'll lift off from the tiny Beaver County Airport off Route 51 at the speed of the wind. That means the experience is gentle; the gondola barely sways as the green hills pass smoothly, 1,000 feet below. Schedule your adventure ($200 per person) in advance, but remember that weather conditions can rearrange your plans. Call (724) 336–2300.

Four miles and a few minutes north of Rochester, New Brighton offers the **Lapic Winery,** operated by Paul and Josephine Lapic. It's open Tuesday through Sunday 10:00 A.M. to 5:00 P.M. for wine-tasting and sales, except on major holidays. Call (724) 846–2031, or write to 902 Tulip Drive, New Brighton 15066.

trivia

Zelienople, in Butler County, has a sweet, old-fashioned Main Street and a peaceful stream alongside. But what's with the grandiose name? The town is named for Zelie Basse Passavant, wife of the town's founder. The locals affectionately call it Zelie.

As you head south from New Brighton, you're entering Whiskey Rebellion country. The **Oliver Miller Homestead,** in Allegheny County's South Park, is the home of one of the instigators, shot in August 1794, when he joined an angry mob that surrounded nearby **Woodville Plantation,** the home of General John Neville. Both sites, though modest, are open to the public. The Miller Homestead (724–941–6244), located on Corrigan Drive, South Park, is open Sunday spring through Christmas; admission is free. Woodville Plantation (412–221–0348; www.woodvilleplantation.org/house.html) is located on Route 50, Bridgeville, and is open May through September. Tours are offered Thursday and Sunday from 1:00 to 4:00 P.M.; admission is $5.00 per person, $10.00 per family.

Westsylvania

Slightly farther north you'll find **McConnell's Mill State Park,** which appeals to historians, geologists, rock climbers, birders, botanists, hunters, anglers, rafters, and, of course, picnickers. The park gets its name from a restored gristmill, which you can reach by parking in a lot near the top of the hill and following a footpath down. You may take a free guided tour of the mill in the summer or visit on your own. Through the park runs Slippery Rock Creek and its adjacent walking trail. Be sure to venture toward **Slippery Rock Gorge,** 20,000 years old and 400 feet deep. For details about tours, hunting, and fishing, phone (724) 368–8091. Take Interstate 79 to the Route 422 exit, and go almost 2 miles west on Route 422. A sign indicates a left turn for the park.

Want your own fishing cabin on a peaceful lake? At **Moraine State Park,** on the opposite (eastern) side of I–79 from McConnell's Mill, rent a nice one for a week (for $350), and fish Lake Arthur to your heart's content. The only powerboats allowed on the 3,200-acre lake are the putt-putt pontoon type, so it's blissfully quiet. Off Lakeview Beach, one of two sandy swimming areas, wind-surfers abound. To windsurf you'll need a state park launching permit from the Crescent Bay boat rental office. The Pleasant Valley Day Use Area on the south shore rents canoes and paddleboats. For more information call (724) 368–8891, or visit www.dcnr.state.pa.us/stateparks/parks/morain.htm.

trivia

Chipped ham, short for chip-chopped ham, is a local delicacy. It's pressed ham, sliced so thin you can see through it. Any self-respecting deli or grocery store in the Pittsburgh area carries it.

The town of Slippery Rock—home of the former Slippery Rock State Teachers College, now **Slippery Rock University**—resembles most college towns, with music stores and coffee shops. One resident said the addition of a McDonald's made the place "big time." Then came Burger King. If the town's name sounds familiar, it's because many football stadiums in the country announce the Slippery Rock scores at the end of their games. Enough people have been titillated by the name to generate some funny stories about its origin.

Between Erie and Pittsburgh, I–79 is largely rural, scenic, and lightly traveled. Roughly halfway between these cities, it's worth taking some time to go both east and west on Route 208. Near the intersection of I–79 and Interstate 80, the easterly road goes to Grove City, where signs direct you to **Wendell August Forge** (620 Madison Avenue). The forge is a self-contained industry in the middle of a quiet community, one of the few remaining forges in the country that still fabricates aluminum, pewter, bronze, and sterling-silver pieces by hand, without any production machinery.

Today the forge is operated by the Knecht family, who bought it in 1978. You can walk through part of the forge to witness the entire process and ask the craftspeople questions. All items produced at the forge are for sale in the showroom for prices ranging from a few dollars to a few thousand. No two pieces are alike. Call (724) 458–8360 or (800) 923–4438, or visit www.wendell august.com.

Going west on Route 208 from I–79 takes you to **Volant,** about 10 miles from Grove City, and, 4 miles farther, to **New Wilmington,** the historic home of Westminster College. This is the heart of a refreshingly noncommercial Amish area.

Volant is where tourists stop to buy quilts and sweets. But if you stand in front of the Tavern on the Square in New Wilmington, just across the road from a sagging barn, you'll glimpse a village where English and Amish cordially coexist.

The nicely restored tavern was once a stop on the Underground Railroad. It's just a few blocks from the handsome college, which overlooks Brittan Lake. The carillon in Old Main peals for special town events. Amish craftsmen bring their buggies to Wilson's Lumber to pick up supplies, so there are often as many horses on the street as there are cars. Stop for a cup of coffee at Mugsy's (that's all that's served here; the town is dry), and drink in the quiet.

As you pass the giant Prime Outlets at Grove City, where I–80 meets I–79, you'll swear the mall is being invaded by paratroopers. Wrong. Those parachutists are landing at an airfield just behind the shops, at **Skydive PA** (496 Old Ash Road, Mercer; 800–909–JUMP; www.skydivepa.com). Experienced instructors there, with a perfect safety record, will get you up and back to earth in just a day. Your jumping companions might be fraternity brothers, members of a wedding party, or an eighty-year-old grandma. Says owner Jeff Reckard, "The goal is to land safely with an open parachute over your head." (Duh.) Or stop for an hour, stretch out on the patio, and watch others land.

Golf, anyone? You might think that Atlanta and Palm Springs have the best golf courses. And, indeed, they might. But the nation's *first* golf course, or at least the oldest course in continuous use, is near where you are at this very moment: in Foxburg. One Joseph Mickle Fox learned the game of golf from a pro at St. Andrews, Scotland. He returned to his estate in Foxburg with golf clubs and balls made of gutta-percha. In 1887 Fox built a five-hole course for the enjoyment of his neighbors, with greens of sand and one-quart tomato cans serving as cups. Three holes were added, then one more, bringing the modern total to nine. Since its inception the course has seen continuous play and is now the **Foxburg Country Club.** Midweek fees are $10 for nine holes, $16 for eighteen holes (which means playing the nine holes twice); weekends and holidays, prices go up. Fore!

The nostalgic log clubhouse contains the **American Golf Hall of Fame** and the Tri-State P.G.A. Hall of Fame. The museum and library chronicle 400 years of golf. The museum, golf course, and clubhouse are open daily, April through October. For more information and tee times, call (724) 659–3196 during the season. The Foxburg Country Club is located just minutes south of I–80 (exit 6) on Route 58 in Foxburg.

Three miles from Foxburg, the wild and scenic Allegheny River runs through a spectacular and densely forested valley, where quaint Victorian homes lie just across the river in Emlenton (near I–80 exits 5 and 6). At the corner of Main and Second Streets stands America's first steam-powered gristmill. Built in 1875, the refurbished **Old Emlenton Mill** serves as a central point for the annual Christmas in Oil Country celebration.

Southwest Corner

Southwest of Pittsburgh, where the state borders West Virginia, Pennsylvania presents many winning, off-the-beaten-path discoveries. At the intersection of Interstate 70 and I–79 is the town of Washington, where you can visit the **LeMoyne House Historical Museum** (49 East Maiden Street), Pennsylvania's first National Historic Landmark of the Underground Railroad. In the house, built in 1812, you can learn about life before the Civil War. A nineteenth-century apothecary exhibit fills one room, and exhibits on local history change regularly. You might find a display on Victorians at home, for example, or nineteenth-century wedding gowns. Another interesting feature, way off the path most people want to follow, is the crematory LeMoyne built, the first in the Western Hemisphere; you can tour it the second Saturday of each month, May through September, 2:00 to 4:00 P.M.

Just outside, the garden contains medicinal herbs that LeMoyne used in his medical practice, plus culinary herbs and fragrant and flowering herbs for pleasure. Volunteers tend the garden, changing plants and shrubs frequently. You can take a self-guided tour of the garden and see, in addition to mint, foxglove, and brown-eyed Susans, a Native American grinding stone and mile markers from the old National Highway. And, lest you think old-timers were out of touch, look at the upping stone—a safe way for travelers to step off the stagecoach. Wouldn't you love one to access and exit your sport-utility vehicle? Tours run March through mid-December, Tuesday through Friday 11:00 A.M. to 4:00 P.M.; group tours only on Saturday. Admission is $4.00 per adult. Call (724) 225–6740, or visit www.wchspa.org for details. While you're at LeMoyne House, peek at the guns and uniforms in the **Southwest Pennsylvania Military Museum,** a repository of memorabilia from all of America's wars. The book and gift shop offers an array of history-inspired products. Appropriately, the Washington County Historical Society also operates from the LeMoyne House.

Also in Washington, tour **Bradford House** (175 South Main Street), once the home of David Bradford, a leader in the Whiskey Rebellion of 1794. The home is furnished in period antiques and is open by appointment only; call (724) 225–6740.

Albert Who?

At the three forks of the Missouri River, Lewis and Clark came to an agreement about names for them. They were to be the Jefferson, Madison, and Gallatin Rivers. Uh—Gallatin?

Albert Gallatin—the statesman, diplomat, financier, historian, ethnologist, industrialist, and farmer—is remembered today, at least by a few, at *Friendship Hill* (223 New Geneva Road; 724-725-9190), his frontier home near Point Marion. Overlooking the Monongahela, the estate (which Gallatin left in 1825) is a monument to the savvy financier, who paid for the Louisiana Purchase and oversaw the beginnings of a national transportation system. The next time you hear his name on *Jeopardy,* you'll be an expert. Check out the house, and stay till sunset to wander the trails. Open daily 9:00 A.M. to 5:00 P.M., except federal holidays; free admission.

A great place to take children is the **Meadowcroft Museum of Rural Life,** about 20 miles northwest of Washington. (Go north on Route 844, then west on Route 50.) People have lived and worked on the land at Meadowcroft for 14,000 years—longer than at any other documented site in North America. Archaeologists continue to excavate the Meadowcroft rock shelter, but it's also open to the public. Here you can see how Native Americans, frontier settlers, farmers, lumbermen, and coal miners shaped the history of western Pennsylvania. Step back in time and spin wool from the museum's flock of sheep, or watch a blacksmith forge red-hot iron. There are also a gift shop and cafe, outdoor picnic tables, and long, lovely wooded paths.

trivia

The Underground Railroad, the system used to help free Southern slaves, traversed Pennsylvania. See historic markers in Sugar Run, Rummerfield, Towanda, Ulster, and elsewhere.

Meadowcroft is open Memorial Day through Labor Day, Wednesday through Sunday 1:00 to 5:00 P.M.; special hours in May, September, and October. For information call (724) 587-3412; write to 401 Meadowcroft Road, Avella 15312; or visit www.meadowcroftmuseum.org.

If you're interested in unique towns for their own sake, travel southwest from Washington on Route 40, almost to the West Virginia border, to **Good Intent,** at the headwaters of Wheeling Creek's Robinson Fork. Nobody knows how the village got its name. In the early 1800s Peter Wolf built a gristmill here, but the mill pond filled up with silt, so he had to start over downstream. The town never got around to creating a main street. Two gristmills, two blacksmiths' shops, a tannery, a stage company, a harness and saddle shop, a post office, and a Baptist church have come and gone. Nobody teaches in the schoolhouse; somebody lives in it. The general store sells only stoves and is open only on Saturday. The town doesn't have a local government, but it has an unofficial mayor, who lives elsewhere. Folks who live here like it the way it is. They say that among the things Good Intent doesn't have are crime, legal contracts, and selfishness. That's what comes of Good Intent.

Here in Green County, a soggy summer day is always a cause for celebration. Back in 1978, locals noticed that it always seemed to rain on July 29. So, ever since then, the town has thrown an annual party on High Street, with food, music, crafts, and umbrellas. Get details on the **Waynesburg Rain Day** celebration at www.waynesburgchamber.com, or call the borough office at (724) 627–8111.

Three miles east of Waynesburg (take exit 3 off I–79) the **Greene County Historical Museum,** a mid-Victorian mansion, features period antiques, a country store, and collections of pottery, glass, quilts, and Indian and early-American artifacts—more than 10,000 items in all. The site, at 918 Rolling Meadows Road, once housed the county poor farm. Little is known about the operation of the poor farm except that after an extremely unfavorable review of the home by the *Atlantic Monthly* in 1886, a reform campaign was launched to improve the conditions. The museum is open May through August, Wednesday to Sunday, and in September and October, Thursday to Sunday. Admission is $2.50. Hours are Wednesday to Friday 9:00 A.M. to 3:00 P.M. and weekends from 11:00 A.M. to 4:00 P.M. Call (724) 627–3204, or visit www.greenepa.net/~museum/ for information.

A sculpted Mingo Indian seems ready to pounce on your car as you approach **Bushy Run Battlefield** (Route 993, Jeannette; 724–527–5584; www .bushyrunbattlefield.com). The statue marks the site of a fierce battle where Chief Pontiac's warriors fought 400 British soldiers at the end of the French and Indian War in August 1763. If the British hadn't won that crucial battle, we wouldn't need English. Check out the site's visitor center, open Wednesday through Sunday 9:00 A.M. to 5:00 P.M. (open weekends only in winter). Admission is $3.00.

The 104-mile Western Division of the Pennsylvania Mainline Canal ran through Saltsburg before connecting with Johnstown and Pittsburgh. Beginning in 1829, it was the town's lifeblood for nearly thirty years. Nearly two centuries later the village on the Kiskiminetas River remains mostly unchanged. To see it, shoot for Canal Days, held the first weekend of every June. Or paddle the local waterways in a kayak or canoe. And be sure to visit the **Rebecca B. Hadden Stone House Museum** (105 Point Street, Saltsburg; 724–639–9003; www .saltsburg.org/activities.htm). Hours vary; try to call ahead.

Jimmy Stewart Meets the Groundhog

Remember the movie *Groundhog Day,* in which Bill Murray plays a grumpy TV weatherman who has a really bad day—over and over and over again? Murray tries to learn from his mistakes—and turn the page on the calendar. Check out the scene for yourself in **Punxsutawney.**

In Punxsutawney (rhymes with chunks-a-SAW-me), Punxsutawney Phil, the groundhog, officially does or does not see his shadow at dawn on February 2, determining whether we will or will not have six more weeks of winter. The televised event takes place on Gobbler's Knob, a mythical, magical area, before an audience of media and more than 35,000 people. The town sits where Route 119 crosses Route 36. For more information call (814) 938–7700 or (800) 752–7445, or go to www.punxsutawney.com.

The groundhog tradition stems from beliefs associated with Candlemas Day and the days of early Christians in Europe. According to an old English song:

> *If Candlemas be fair and bright,*
> *Come, Winter, have another flight;*
>
> *If Candlemas brings clouds and rain,*
> *Go, Winter, and come not again.*

In Europe hedgehogs emerged in spring; in western Pennsylvania a groundhog had to do.

There's only one way to see Phil up close and personal on his big day: Get there early, around 2:30 A.M. That's when shuttle buses depart from six downtown locations for the music, fireworks, food, and mindless hilarity until 7:25 A.M., when Phil usually debuts. Visitors can't drive to the Knob and can't bring alcohol or illegal substances. But they can and do wear groundhog hats, suits, and T-shirts; carry banners ("Free Phil"); and cheer insanely when the Seer of Seers finally appears.

This is a once-in-a-lifetime must-do. But since the town has only one hotel, accommodations are scarce. The town sponsors overnight "crash pads" in public buildings, and there are a handful of motels within a half-hour drive. At the conclusion of the festivities, linger to enjoy church-sponsored pancake breakfasts and small-town charm.

Many of Punxsutawney's nostalgic Main Street building facades have been renovated, and beautiful tree-lined West Mahoning Street features Millionaires' Row, preserved from the days when Punxsutawney was a thriving coal, oil, and lumber town.

In the children's library of the Mahoning East Civic Center, downtown Punxsutawney, a window lets kids watch Punxsutawney Phil between his on-duty days. Who knows what Phil will predict next year? The shadow knows.

Even if groundhogs are the animals with the biggest reputation in metropolitan Punxsutawney, they're *not* the biggest animals. Bison are. At **Nature's Comeback Bison Ranch,** the Hineman family raises the large mammals. They may end up on your table, but they're happy, well-fed, free-range bison during their lifetime. "Many people are amazed at how playful bison actually are," says owner Brian Hineman. "They have been seen throwing logs that weigh over 500 pounds several feet in the air and bouncing around like little lambs. Bison can run up to 45 miles an hour—amazingly fast for their massive size." The breeder bull, who weighs over a ton, is called Hercules. To produce more healthful meat with lower fat content, Nature's Comeback feeds the bison only hay and grass. The meat, says Hineman, "tastes like your best cuts of beef without the waste of trimming the fat." The ranch, which has been in the family for over 150 years, will give you a warm-weather tour or sell you some tasty meat; call ahead (814–427–2544) to make a tour reservation at this off-the-beaten-path attraction. (Watch where you step as you get up close and personal with large animals.) You can write to Nature's Comeback Bison Ranch at 1436 Bower's Road, Punxsutawney 15767, or send an e-mail to hineman@key-net.net. Take I–80, exit 97 (old exit 16), 1 mile off Route 119 south.

upcloseand personalwithphil

My sons will never forget their first Groundhog Day in Punxsutawney. Unprepared for the crowds, we didn't reach the Knob in time for Phil's official pronouncement. But when we finally arrived, the mob had thinned out to reveal Phil himself—fat, sleek, and toothy. His top-hatted handler kindly let the kids pet the fifteen-pound Prognosticator—a thrill they remember fondly each February 2. They also remember that we found a five-dollar bill lying in the snow.

trivia

In 1868, in the Jacks (Oak Hall) School in Porter Township, Clarion County became the home of the Anti-Horse Thief Association. Although there is no record of a horse's being stolen for several decades, the Association holds an annual dinner. In 1956, when Dwight D. Eisenhower and Arthur Godfrey belonged, it cost $1.00 to become a life member.

A trip to nearby Smicksburg is an enjoyable drive, particularly at harvest time. Home of the largest Amish settlement in western Pennsylvania, Smicksburg has a lovely rolling landscape freckled with farms. Motorized vehicles share the winding roads with horses and buggies, and you find fine craftsmanship and craft shops at every turn. Because of the strong religious faith, many shops close on Sunday.

On Route 219, 4 miles north of Grampian, you will find **Bilger's Rocks,** a phenomenon of massive, ancient sandstone formations, called "rock city," covering some twenty acres. One 500-ton boulder rests on a smaller one in perfect balance. Visited for centuries, these giant sandstone formations tower 30 to 50 feet.

From groundhogs to bison to rabbits. Or at least invisible rabbits. Okay, *one* invisible rabbit. You know, Harvey, the bunny only Jimmy Stewart could see in the movie *Harvey*. Stewart's life and films are alive and well and entertaining everyone at the **Jimmy Stewart Museum** in Indiana, Pennsylvania. Sit back in a 1930s-style movie theater and watch *Mr. Smith Goes to Washington* and *It's a Wonderful Life*. The small museum occupies the third floor of the public library, and it's dedicated to the homeboy who catapulted from his family's hardware store to the heart of Tinseltown. Admission costs $5.00 per adult, and the museum is open from 10:00 A.M. to 5:00 P.M. Monday through Saturday and noon to 5:00 P.M. Sunday and holidays. January through March, it's closed Monday and Tuesday. The library is at 845 Philadelphia Street, and the mailing address is Box One, Indiana 15701. Call (724) 349–6112 or (800) 83–JIMMY (that's really 800–835–4669), or visit Harvey and the gang at www.jimmy.org.

The **Ghost Town Trail** threads through 16 miles of abandoned mining towns along the Black Lick Creek. At the midpoint of its run from Dilltown in Indiana County to Nanty Glo in Cambria County is **Eliza Furnace,** one of the best-preserved iron furnaces in the United States—and the source of haunted tales. Some say that owner David Ritter's wife ran off with a man named George Rodgers, or that Ritter's son fell into the furnace and was killed. Either way, he was so distraught that he hanged himself. His ghost can supposedly be seen hanging in the furnace's entrance.

coalinthemtharhills

As you pedal the Ghost Town Trail, look beside you: Near Vintondale you'll spy an exposed anthracite seam in a rock face alongside the trail, shining like dark icing in a stone layer cake. That's why Cambria County is still coal-mining country.

But don't let the tall tales keep you away. The Ghost Town bike trail features masses of rhododendrons in the spring (and some wild water colors where mine subsidence still fouls the creek). For directions call the Cambria County Conservation and Recreation Authority at (814) 472–2110; for details go to www.indianacountyparks.org.

Noah weathered a flood, but he heeded the warning. The town of Johnstown did not. Late in May 1889 it started raining. The neglected South Fork Dam, upriver from Johnstown, gave way May 31, and a wall of water moved 14 miles downstream, plucking chairs, doors, walls, and complete houses out of their rightful places. The water immersed and erased the industrialized city in ten minutes, killing more than 2,200 people. The ***Johnstown Flood Museum*** (304 Washington Street) re-creates this shocking episode—the catastrophe of death and homelessness, followed by the triumph of human spirit that allowed the town to rebuild. Every hour the museum shows *The Johnstown Flood,* which won the 1989 Academy Award for best short-subject documentary. One survivor expresses the drama: "My boyhood home was crushed like an eggshell before my eyes, and I saw it disappear." See the flood in 3-D, in books, and in souvenirs at the museum.

Around the time of the flood, thousands of immigrants from southern and eastern Europe, lured by ready jobs in its steel mills, came to Johnstown to build a better life. Experience their stories firsthand at the Frank & Sylvia Pasquerilla ***Heritage Discovery Center*** at 201 Sixth Avenue. You'll be handed an immigrant "identity card" that allows you to assume the role of one of eight characters, from a Bohemian farmhand to a Russian peasant, in the interactive exhibits.

Combined admission to the Heritage Discovery Center and the Flood Museum is $6.00. They're located a half-mile apart but are online together at www.jaha.org. Hours are daily, year-round, 10:00 A.M. to 5:00 P.M.; from June through August they stay open two hours later on Friday and Saturday.

Two years after the flood, the Cambria Iron Company (a predecessor of Bethlehem Steel Corporation) began building houses in the community of Westmont, 500 feet up Yoder Hill from downtown Johnstown. Since no roads existed, the company assembled a vertical commuter system, which remains today as the ***Inclined Plane,*** rising at a grade of 71 percent. The *Guinness Book of World Records* ranked it the steepest vehicular inclined plane in the world. Originally designed to carry people and their horses and wagons, it now accommodates people and their cars. In 1935 Bethlehem Steel sold the railway for a dollar to Westmont Borough, which now leases it to the Cambria County Tourist Council for $10 a year. The wheels, rails, and other parts came from standard railway equipment (and, in fact, the cars are duplicates of those that hauled cargo boats over the Allegheny Portage railroad). The Inclined Plane is composed of two sets of tracks implanted in the side of the hill; two cars run simultaneously, one going up and the other going down. The cables, three on each side, are 2 inches in diameter and 1,130 feet long. They can safely carry 337,000 pounds, or 167 tons. Here's the fun part: You may ride it. You can access the top from Route 56 or Route 403 and the bottom from Route 271. Above the funicular hangs an American flag that measures 30 feet by 60 feet. The plane operates from 11:00 A.M. to 11:00 P.M. during the winter and from 9:00 A.M. to 11:00 P.M. May through October. Round-trip tickets are $4.00 for adults and $2.50

for kids under twelve; parking at the entrance (on Route 56) is free. For more information call (814) 536–1816, or write 711 Edgehill Drive, Johnstown 15905.

At the top of the Inclined Plane is Westmont, originally called Tiptop. Take time to explore this appealing Victorian enclave, a bit of small-town America where you wish you grew up. Locals say the town has always been divided in two parts: the more affluent southern section with single-family homes, called the "dinner" side, and the less affluent northern section with twin homes and smaller singles, called the "supper" section. Westmont attracts naturalists, too: Lucerne Street contains the longest municipally owned stand of American elm trees east of the Mississippi (even small towns like a claim to fame). Although half of all American elms were killed by Dutch elm disease, this beautiful, stately "cathedral arch" of elms is maintained. The borough now has nine trees that qualify as historic elms, which means they measure at least 10 feet in circumference at chest height.

If you have a pioneer spirit, follow Route 219 south to Somerset and visit the *Somerset Historical Center,* which portrays rural life in southwestern Pennsylvania from the rugged pioneer struggles of the eighteenth century through the commercial agrarian enterprises of the mid-twentieth. At the center you can see utensils, machinery, and restored buildings from different periods of Pennsylvania history. Guided tours take place year-round from 9:00 A.M. to 5:00 P.M. Tuesday through Saturday and from noon to 5:00 P.M. Sunday. Hours vary, however, so call ahead at (814) 445–6077. The center closes on holidays and Monday, except Memorial Day, Independence Day, and Labor Day. Write to the historical center at 10649 Somerset Pike, Somerset 15501, or visit www.somersetcounty.com/historicalcenter/.

Shanksville, 6 miles from Somerset, will forever be remembered in world history as the first retaliatory strike in the war on terrorism. On September 11, 2001, United Airlines Flight 93 crashed here after passengers attempted to wrest the plane away from terrorists. Forty innocent people lost their lives. A permanent, formal memorial is planned near the site, which is a huge, empty gash in the earth, but many visitors have already left folk mementoes. To get to the site from Route 30, take Lambertville Road south for 1.7 miles to Skyline Drive and follow it 0.8 mile to the parking area. There's also a memorial Web site at www.flt93memorial.org.

To experience a different era of history, you can raft through the past on *Wilderness Voyageurs* historic float trips down the Youghiogheny River. In warm-weather months groups of six or more embark from Connellsville with guides clad in 1750s gear (you can wear a sweatshirt and sneakers—you won't get wet). On the two-and-a-half-hour float trip to tiny Dawson, the guides do all the work and offer fascinating lore about the river's role in the French and

Indian War, the Whiskey Rebellion, and the coal and coke industries. Reservations are required; cost is $26 per person. Call Wilderness Voyageurs at (800) 272–4141, or visit www.wilderness-voyageurs.com.

Laurel Highlands

Everyone who visits—or lives in—Pennsylvania should see *Fallingwater,* the summer retreat that architect Frank Lloyd Wright designed for the Pittsburgh department-store owner Edgar J. Kaufmann. The house, completed in 1939, was constructed of sandstone quarried on the property and built by local craftsmen. It's the only remaining Wright house where the original setting, furnishings, and artwork remain intact. Fallingwater reflects Wright's genius, which allows the house to merge with its environment outside and to echo nature in its stone and wood interior. The house, appearing to grow out of the boulders and rocks, extends over a natural waterfall of Bear Run. You can't see or hear the water from inside, but you can do both from any balcony or from a stairwell down from the living room. A gray sandstone four-story chimney at the core of the house anchors it into the stone cliff. Wright built a desk in every bedroom and placed all headboards on eastern walls so that no one would be awakened by the sun. Genius. The home retains a feeling of seclusion and oneness with the natural environment, even though many people visit. It's open for tours from mid-March through November, daily except Monday, 10:00 A.M. to 3:00 P.M. In December and early March it's open only weekends, and it's closed January and February. Reservations are required, especially during July, August, and October, the busiest months. Try to get there during midweek, and plan to wear comfortable walking shoes. For more information write P.O. Box R, Mill Run 15464, or call 724–329–8501. Fallingwater is on Route 381 between the villages of Mill Run and Ohiopyle (pronounce it Ohio-PILE) about two hours southeast of Pittsburgh via the Turnpike.

Fallingwater—the house that could be called *A River Runs Through It*—is maintained by the Western Pennsylvania Conservancy. At the end of your tour, guides invite you to watch a short film about the organization's activ-

Fallingwater

ities. The film is fascinating, and the work of the conservancy lifts your spirits. You may decide to join, even if you live out of state. Children under age six may not tour Fallingwater, but for $2.00 an hour they can stay in an on-site child care center. Forty-five-minute tours cost $12 midweek and $15 on weekends and holidays; they are scheduled from 10:00 A.M. to 4:00 P.M. For an in-depth two-hour tour, scheduled each morning at 8:30, the cost is $40 midweek and $50 on weekends. Saturday-only three-hour walking tours of the grounds are $50 per person.

West of Ohiopyle, 7 miles along a scenic mountain road, you can find another remarkable example of Wright's craft: ***Kentuck Knob,*** a smaller, simpler home that Wright designed for the Hagan family of Uniontown. (It was originally known as the I. N. Hagan House.) A dramatic yet serene place, the house is hexagonal, with hexagonal accents, all made of native fieldstone and tidewater red cypress. It hides in—rather than sits on—the mountain it occupies, so you're practically at the front door before you see it. The home has an open floor plan—with a heating system under the floor—and giant expanses of glass to enjoy the panorama of the Youghiogheny (rhymes with sock-a-SAY-knee) River Gorge and surrounding mountains. The name? Probably, says site manager Susan Waggoner, someone was heading for Kentucky and stopped here. A knob is a low, rounded hill. On the grounds behind the visitor center is an oversize apple core by artist Claes Oldenburg and other large-scale contemporary sculpture. In January and February you're invited to cross-country ski the grounds after your house tour. The house, opened to the public in 1996, is open for tours daily. December through February, hours are 11:00 A.M. to 3:00 P.M.; the rest of the year, it's open 9:00 A.M. to 4:00 P.M. Admission is $12 weekdays and $15 weekends. For reservations (suggested) at Kentuck Knob, write Box 305, Kentuck Road, Chalk Hill 15421, or call (724) 329–1901. Visit www.kentuck knob.com for more information.

Close by on Route 40 in Markleysburg you'll find a trucker's secret: the 24/7 home cooking at Glisan's (4625 National Pike; 724–329–4636). With country ham, fresh bread, and fifteen varieties of pies baked daily, it's worth a stop.

The Slides

I love the scenic waterfalls at Ohiopyle State Park—especially the Slides, where our family always ends the day with a ride down the slick limestone boulders. The stream varies from gentle to intense, depending on recent rainfall. If it's early in the summer, or there have been lots of recent showers, you'll move at top speed (and the water will be colder). Watch your step—Band-Aids may be required.

Now's a perfect time to stop for a walk or a picnic along the Youghiogheny River at **Ohiopyle State Park,** almost 18,500 acres of wilderness delight. The Youghiogheny Gorge, carved 1,700 feet into the Laurel Ridge by the river, takes your breath away. Totally contained within the state park is the borough of Ohiopyle, almost 2 whole blocks long. Eighty-three people live here, and commercial establishments include a grocery store with a small cafe, a gas station, and, in season, a Dairy Queen and a pizza parlor. A new addition is the town's first tavern, the **Falls City Restaurant and Pub** (112 Garrett Street; 724–329–3000; www.fallscitypub.com). Owner Eric Martin also owns Wilderness Voyageurs next door. The tavern is open daily from mid-May through September, Thursday through Monday.

"The name of the town, Ohiopyle, is subject to fact and fiction depending on who you're talking to," says Mark McCarty, mayor and manager of an outfitter. The state park's interpretation is something like "white frothing water," but if you study the early settlers' writings, it's more like "peaceful river." The water in this case is the Yough, Youghiogheny being an Indian word for "flowing in a roundabout course." Yes, it's off the beaten path, says Jim Greenbaum, manager of White Water Adventurers. "On the other hand, there are two interstate highways within a half hour of here." Ohiopyle has lured tourists since the early 1900s, when people came by train from Pittsburgh and Washington to swim in the river and hike on Fern Cliff. Once three large hotels dominated the borough. Then "the railroads went away," as Greenbaum puts it. In the early 1960s a new industry—white-water rafting—was born. The season for rafting runs March through October, with the bulk of tours scheduled from mid-May until mid-September.

The Middle Yough, says Greenbaum, is the easy section, great for kids over five or first-time adult rafters. The Lower Yough is rated intermediate, recom-

yurt, anyone?

Pennsylvania has eleven state parks that offer Mongolian-style accommodations in addition to cabins, and Ohiopyle has more yurts than any other park. The round-framed, fabric-covered structures have floors and even decks (but in typical nomadic fashion, no indoor plumbing).

The cost for Pennsylvania residents for a four- to five-person yurt is $27 per night Sunday through Thursday; $45 per night Friday and Saturday in the off-season ($32 and $60 for nonresidents); and $178 per week in summer ($212 for nonresidents). A six-person yurt is $33 ($40 for nonresidents) per night Sunday through Thursday; $55 ($66 for nonresidents) per night Friday and Saturday; and $221 ($263 for nonresidents) per week in summer. Otherwise, Western-style cabin rules apply: no pets, no alcohol, check-in at 3:00 P.M., check-out at 10:00 A.M. To reserve, go to www.visitPAparks.com or call (888) 727-2757.

mended for people age twelve and older. The Yough sections called Pure Scream-
ing Hell, Bastard, and Double Pencil Sharpener are recommended for rafters with
the most technical expertise—but then, so is Cheeseburger Falls. If you'd like to
try a rafting trip, call one of the four outfitters with state concessions:

White Water Adventurers, P.O. Box 31, Ohiopyle 15470. Phone (724)
329–8850 or (800) 992–7238; fax (724) 329–1488; www.wwaraft.com.

Laurel Highlands River Tours, P.O. Box 107, Ohiopyle 15470. Phone
(724) 329–8531 or (800) 472–3846; fax (724) 329–8532; e-mail: 4raftin@laurel
highlands.com.

Ohiopyle Trading Post, P.O. Box 94, Negley Street, Ohiopyle 15470.
Phone (724) 329–1450 or (888) 644–6795. You can also visit the Ohiopyle Trading Post online at www.ohiopyletradingpost.com.

Wilderness Voyageurs, 103 Garrett Street, Ohiopyle 15470. Phone (724)
329–1000 or (800) 272–4141; fax (724) 329–0809; e-mail: rafting@wilderness-voy
ageurs.com; Web site: www.wilderness-voyageurs.com.

The Great Allegheny Passage is a 100-mile-plus trail from the Pittsburgh
suburbs to Maryland. Biking fanatics have worked for a decade to clear this gorgeous path along the Youghiogheny and Casselman Rivers. The result is a flat,
scenic route right through to Cumberland, Maryland, where it links with the
185-mile Chesapeake and Ohio Canal towpath straight into Washington, D.C.
The trail still has a few gaps but took a leap forward with the opening of the
Big Savage tunnel, through a mountain on the Pennsylvania-Maryland border.
(The Western Maryland Railroad used to travel this right-of-way. Hence the
name rails-to-trails.) Meanwhile, you can explore as much or as little as you like.

If you like to recline while you reconnoiter, consider renting bikes from
Allegheny Recumbent Tours. Because the passage follows the level rail bed, it's
hill-free and easy to pedal. That makes these bikes with seat backs and low centers of gravity an ideal choice. Owner Jay Duchesne says they're safe for all ages
and abilities. Get details at www.recumbenttours.com or (888) 395–BIKE.

In addition to Ohiopyle, where the river outfitters also offer cheap bike
rentals, seek out the other charming villages along the trail. Confluence, some
12 miles south of Ohiopyle, has a great breakfast spot—*Sisters Cafe* ("sisterly
advice free of charge"; 482 Hughart Street; 814–395–5252), right next to Confluence Hardware (owned by the brothers-in-law). The *River's Edge Restaurant* (203 Yough Street; 814–395–5059) has a comfy Victorian porch for
lingering in the twilight, and next door is the *Parker House* (213 Yough
Street; 814–395–9616), a beautifully restored guest house, great for groups. In
Rockwood, another 18 miles south, you'll find a few more B&Bs and the
Opera House.

As you pedal along, you'll see a few anglers (trout fishing is big here), maybe a few black bears way down in the ravines, and lots of families also pedaling around Ohiopyle, especially on the weekends. Other than that, you'll have the Laurel Highlands to yourself—on the level.

For super-easy, one-click planning, including accommodations and meals, log on to www.atatrail.org, or contact the Allegheny Trail Alliance, 419 College Avenue, Greensburg 15601; (888) 282–2453.

If the sophistication of Frank Lloyd Wright's Fallingwater home makes you pine for an upscale night or two, consider **Nemacolin Woodlands Resort and Spa** in Farmington. With French food, French paintings, and a par-72 golf course, its motto could be "extravagance R us." Elegantly appointed guest rooms include marble baths and plush terry-cloth robes. Entertainment for kids, a shopping mall, a ski slope, a golf course, skeet shooting, stables, and a climbing wall are on the premises. The place is named for a Delaware Indian named Nemacolin who, in 1740, carved a trail through the Laurel Mountains between what is now Cumberland, Maryland, and Brownsville, Pennsylvania. When Congress established the National Highway in the mid-1800s, the highway incorporated Nemacolin's trail. For resort reservations log on to www.nemacolin.com, or call (724) 329–8555 or (800) 422–2736.

Near the popular ski resorts of Seven Springs and Hidden Valley lies the old-money charm of **Ligonier,** founded as a fort in the 1750s. Its "diamond" at the town's center has a Victorian bandstand and pleasant shopping—good restaurants, too. And just on the edge of town lies **Idlewild,** an amusement park with low prices, low temperatures, and a laid-back feel. Its biggest coaster isn't the Mauler, but the Wild Mouse. Even the shyest toddlers will love Idlewild's Storybook Forest, where they can meet the Billy Goats Gruff (played by real billies, but minus the trolls). Older kids can holler on the Tarzan vines and water chutes. A miniature railway runs over Loyalhanna Creek, and the towering trees keep pathways cool. Don't miss the restored pastel merry-go-round. Idlewild is open from Memorial Day to around Labor Day on Route 30, Ligonier. Admission prices vary. Call (724) 238–3666, or visit www.idlewild.com for details.

On Route 381 in nearby Cook Township lies **Powdermill Nature Reserve,** a field research station of the Carnegie Museum of Natural History. Here kids and adults can spy on wildflowers, trees, songbirds, butterflies, and salamanders with eyes and ears, magnifying glass, or camera. Youngsters can sign up for week-long nature classes during the summer, and individuals and families can attend other free programs. The nature reserve is open weekends April through October. In June, July, and August, the reserve is open most weekdays, too, usually

Beaver County Snow Shovel Riding Championship, held in Economy Park on the third Saturday in January, unless there's too little snow. Call (724) 846–5600 or (800) 342–8192.

There's only one place to be on February 2: Punxsutawney. The savvy little town has turned ***Groundhog Day*** into a multiday extravaganza with food fests, weddings performed by the mayor, music, and hilarity (when the holiday falls next to a weekend, look out).

In mid-May the ***National Road Festival*** celebrates the historic national road, US Route 40. Food, fun, and entertainment stretch for 90 miles along the National Road Heritage Park. Call (724) 437–9877, or check the Web site at www.nationalroadpa.org for details.

The ***Antique Flea Market*** is held in Somerset the second Saturday in August. Call (814) 445–6431 for details.

Saddle up yer bronco, or at least your sport-utility vehicle, and head to the ***North Washington Rodeo,*** on Route 38, 16 miles north of Butler, during the third week in August. Daily performances at 8:00 P.M. feature men doing saddle bronc, bareback, and calf-roping, and women running barrel races. There's always something at intermission for the kids and raffles for the grown-ups. You might win a registered colt or a steer that the rodeo organizers have purchased from the local 4-H group. For more information call (724) 287–6170, or you can gallop to http://nwvfd.com/rodeo.

Accordions. Trombones. Blues. Balkan bop. It's all at the ***Johnstown Folk Fest,*** held each Labor Day weekend. More than seventy hours of professional music are programmed each year. Everything takes place at the downtown festival park, bordering the stone bridge made famous by the infamous 1889 flood. Visit www.jaha.org for the line-up, or call (814) 539–1889.

During the second weekend in September, there's a ***Flax Scutching Festival*** at Monticue's Grove in Stahlstown. If the town's not off the beaten path enough for you, the event surely is. Here you can see how craftspeople used to take the flax plant and scutch it—in other words, break down the tough fibers to make linen. To learn more about scutching or the second-oldest flax-scutching festival in the world, call (724) 238–9244.

New Bethlehem initiated its annual ***Peanut Butter Festival*** in 1996 to promote the Smucker's peanut butter plant. If you think toast and jelly are naked without p.b., visit Gumtown Memorial Park on Water Street on a weekend in mid-September. Call the nutty people at the New Bethlehem Chamber of Commerce (814–275–3929) for details.

Get a cardio workout and a great view of downtown Pittsburgh during ***Step Trek,*** the South Side Slopes Association's open house along the steepest step streets in Pittsburgh. The early October event benefits the neighborhood association. For details call (412) 488–0486, or climb to www.steptrek.org.

The tiny Youghiogheny River town of Confluence proves it has more gourds than people each October at ***Pumpkinfest.*** There's a Pumpkinfest Queen, a tough-guy tractor pull, live bands, and more. Visit www.visitconfluence.org.

December 31, celebrate ***First Night*** (it's really Last Night, isn't it?) throughout downtown Pittsburgh. Call (877) 744–4744 or (412) 201–7380, or go to www.firstnightpgh.com for details.

Wednesday through Friday. For hours and program information, call (724) 593–6105, or visit www.powdermill.org.

All these hills, all these valleys: Sounds like a perfect place for mountain biking, and there are some gnarly opportunities on the **PW&S Trails** in Forbes State Forest. "When I ride here in the evening, I see grouse, deer, and bear," says Gates Watson, a local enthusiast. There are five loops here, carved from an old logging railroad; like ski trails, they vary in length and difficulty. For details call (724) 238–7560, or pick up a map at the Forbes State Forest office on Route 30 outside Laughlintown.

Route 669 leads you straight to (well, not really straight, but toward) **Mt. Davis** in the Forbes State Forest—at 3,213 feet above sea level, the highest elevation in the state. (So it's not the Rockies—wanna make something of it?) Providing an interesting speck of geological lore is the scattering of small, concentric stone rings caused by localized frost heaves. Each ring surrounds a spot in the soil that is a bit softer and looser than the adjacent ground. When the ground freezes, the soft spots rise and become minibumps. Surface rocks on these bumps, or humps, slide off; as this process repeats itself over thousands of years, the sliding rocks deposit themselves in ringlike formations. Cool! Not far away is the aptly named **High Point Lake.** Hiking trails and picnic sites abound.

Mt. Davis is actually a rock that sits atop **Negro Mountain.** A ten-page brochure about the area doesn't mention the origin of the name until page nine. "For 150 years after the first colonies were established," says the brochure, "Negro Mountain was untouched by white man" (and white women and African-American people of both sexes). The brochure says that the Indians claimed the land. In the mid-1700s British and French settlers developed a political and economic interest in the area. Various versions of the story agree that "a large, powerful black man valiantly distinguished himself in a battle with the Indians." He died—and was hastily buried in an unmarked grave—on the mountain, which was thus named for him, or at least for his race. Originally the mountain was a thousand feet higher, say geologists, and it is one of the area's oldest rock formations.

If you're into gallows humor, pop up Route 281, nearly to I–70, and go to the courthouse in Somerset. The building served as the county jail from 1856 to 1981, and the double hanging gallows is still intact. Who hanged together? Twins? Now the building holds county offices. What do you think they do to employees who are habitually late?

If you love art, glass, and what's now called art-glass, you'll enjoy the **Youghiogheny Station Glass and Gallery** (900 West Crawford Avenue, Connellsville), located in (surprise) the renovated, restored, and resplendent Youghiogheny train station in Connellsville. Amid the old ticket office, departure board, and lighting fixtures, you can explore a collection of Tiffany-style lamps and other decorative items, all for sale. The station, built in 1911, rates a spot on the National Register of Historic Places, and the collection rates a four-star listing on the must-see register of crafters' sojourns. The back room sells 120 colors of stained-glass sheets from the Youghiogheny Glass company. Hours are Thursday 10:00 A.M. to 6:00 P.M., Sunday noon to 4:00 P.M., and all other days 10:00 A.M. to 5:00 P.M. Call (724) 628–0332, or go to www.youghioghenyglass.com for more details or to learn about stained-glass classes. All aboard!

Places to Stay in Southwestern Pennsylvania

BEAVER FALLS

Beaver Valley Motel,
Route 18;
(724) 843–0630 or
(800) 400–8312

FARMINGTON

Stone House Bed & Breakfast,
3023 National Pike;
(724) 329–8876

HOLBROOK

Cole's Log Cabin Bed and Breakfast,
544 Hoovers Run Road;
(724) 451–8521

INDUSTRY

Willows Inn,
Route 68;
(724) 643–4500

PITTSBURGH

The Priory Hotel,
614 Pressley Street;
(412) 231–3338

Sunnyledge Boutique Hotel,
5124 Fifth Avenue;
(412) 683–5014

PUNXSUTAWNEY

Jackson Run Bed and Breakfast,
363 Jackson Run Road;
(814) 938–2315

Pantall Hotel,
135 East Mahoning Street;
(800) 872–6825

SLIPPERY ROCK

Applebutter Inn,
666 Centreville Pike;
(724) 794–1844

SOMERSET

Bayberry Inn,
611 North Center Avenue;
(814) 445–8471

VOLANT

Candleford Inn Bed and Breakfast,
Mercer Street;
(724) 533–4497

Places to Eat in Southwestern Pennsylvania

BEAVER

Lock 6 Landing,
610 Midland-Beaver Road;
(724) 728–6767.
Inside the former Ohio River lock and dam powerhouse.

Wooden Angel,
308 Leopard Lane;
(724) 774–7880.
Award-winning American wine cellar.

BEAVER FALLS

Giuseppe's Italian Restaurant,
Route 18;
(724) 843–5656

BROOKVILLE

The Meeting Place,
209 Main Street;
(814) 849–2557

CORAOPOLIS

Hyeholde Restaurant,
190 Hyeholde Drive;
(412) 264–3116

FARMINGTON

Stone House,
3023 National Pike;
(724) 329–8876.
Casual fine dining.

MERCER

Iron Bridge Inn,
1438 Perry Highway;
(724) 748–3626.
Famous for prime rib and
Sunday brunch.

NEW WILMINGTON

Tavern on the Square,
108 North Market Street;
(724) 946–2020.
Lunch and dinner in a former
stop on the Underground
Railroad. Open daily. BYOB.

PITTSBURGH

Ali Baba,
404 South Craig Street,
Oakland;
(412) 682–2829.
This traditional favorite of
the campus crowd offers a
Middle Eastern menu.

Isabella on Grandview,
1318 Grandview Avenue,
Mt. Washington;
(412) 431–5882.
Eclectic fine dining with a
view in a converted cliffside
Victorian.

Kaya,
2000 Smallman Street,
Strip District;
(412) 261–6565.
Upscale casual with tapas,
alligator on a stick, and
veggie dishes.

Laforet,
5701 Bryant Street,
Highland Park;
(412) 665–9000.
A chic blue-ribbon French
choice, with a four-course prix
fixe offering. Dinners Wednesday through Saturday.

Mezzanotte Cafe,
4621 Liberty Avenue,
Bloomfield;
(412) 688–8070.
In the heart of a funky Italian
neighborhood.

The Warhol Cafe,
Andy Warhol Museum,
117 Sandusky Street;
(412) 237–8300.
Open Tuesday through
Sunday 11:00 A.M. to 4:00
P.M. (Friday to 9:00 P.M.).
Seasonal light meals, wines,
and microbrews.

SCENERY HILL

Century Inn,
2175 East National Pike;
(724) 945–6600.
Casual dress in a 1794
building.

SLIPPERY ROCK

Wolf Creek School Cafe,
664 Centreville Pike;
(724) 794–1899.
Located in a restored one-
room schoolhouse. BYOB.

Northwestern Pennsylvania: National Forest

The Lake District

The tourist literature says the Erie area is "Erie-sistible." That's especially true for those who love long drives through the Commonwealth. Ohio, Lake Erie, and New York State form the western, northern, and eastern borders of Erie County, respectively, and getting to Erie from anywhere in Pennsylvania means driving through miles and miles and miles of scenic woodland and uninhabited terrain.

People here are fiercely proud of the pristine natural environment, from wildlife refuges to forest wilderness to rushing streams to the lake.

A few decades ago, Lake Erie was pronounced dead. But it wasn't really dead—the problem was actually too much of the wrong kinds of life. Nutrients such as phosphates and nitrates, especially plentiful in agricultural runoff, encouraged excessive growth of algae, which grew so fast that it choked out other forms of plants and fish. The process is called eutrophication. In water where no oxygen can reach the bottom, the only fish that can live are small panfish. As Lake Erie deteriorated, only the panfish survived. A massive combined effort by area manufacturing companies, local colleges, state

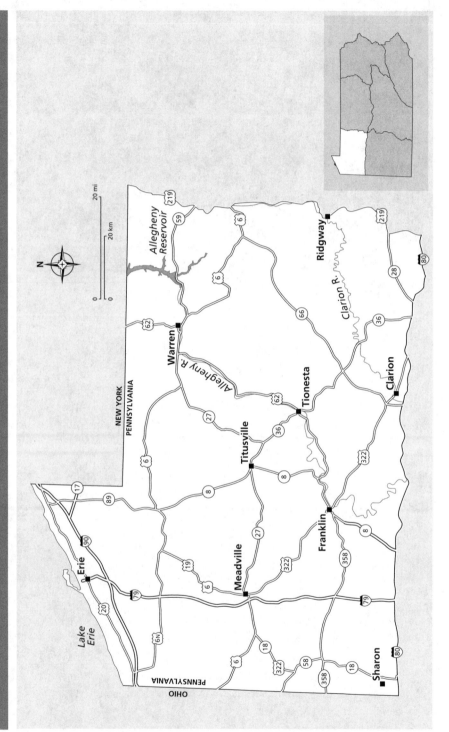

and federal governments, and concerned citizens turned things around. The City of Erie improved its sewage disposal system. The Department of Health now tests regularly for harmful bacteria. Industries treat their wastes so that they won't hurt the lake. Colleges run ecology projects, continuously monitoring the state of the water. At least one Erie councilman pilots his boat, at cost, for the monitoring teams. Game fish have returned. In fact, the city celebrated when the first coho salmon was caught after a long dry spell.

The resurgence of other species is no fish story. Every fall, hundreds of Pennsylvania anglers descend on the Lake Erie tributaries—Elk and Walnut Creeks and the mouths of Trout and Godfrey Runs—for the annual steelhead spawning runs. These whoppers are reputed to swim right up to the boat and can almost be scooped up by hand. They're most plentiful when the water temperature hovers around 55 degrees.

Part of the success story comes from the central role that Lake Erie plays in the lives of the people who live here. Hundreds of people go to the public dock in the city every day, if not to fish, at least to check out conditions. Adults who've lived here all their lives talk about having gone out fishing every morning before school or every evening after school. These stories help explain the spirit of the lakeshore. The passion is contagious. Among the most ardent anglers are the Erie Benedictine Sisters, whose main house is on East Lake Road. The sisters certainly talk about their vocations and ministries, about religious life, about helping the needy, and so on—but they're also wonderful folks to consult about fishing.

The best place to learn about Erie and the lake is ***Presque Isle State Park*** (rhymes with press-TILE). One of the most remarkable places in Pennsylvania, it offers enough outdoor recreation to keep you busy for weeks. It's a 3,200-acre peninsula extending from the City of Erie (just 4 miles west of downtown) into Lake Erie. Although in French Presque Isle means "almost an island," this area

AUTHOR'S TOP TEN FAVORITES IN NORTHWESTERN PENNSYLVANIA

Dan Rice Days in Girard	Indian God Rock
Erie Canal	Pithole
French Creek	Presque Isle
Glass Growers	Quaker Steak and Lube
Hickory Creek Wilderness	US Brig *Niagara*

has been a real island several times. Storm waves have broken through the neck of land, isolating the distant portion at least four times since 1819. One gap remained open for thirty-two years. Interestingly, the combined effects of erosion on one side and sand deposits on the other change the peninsula's shape and location noticeably, not in thousands of years, but in just a few. Geologists call it a recurving sand spit and estimate that the peninsula has moved about a half mile east in the past hundred years. The Stull Interpretive Center, located at the beginning of the park near Barracks Beach, displays maps showing the changes. If you avoid the peak summer swimming season, it's possible to walk for hours along the beaches and in the woods without seeing another human being.

The diverse nature of Presque Isle is astounding. It has six distinct ecological zones, each with a unique plant and animal community. Due to the peninsula's location along the Atlantic flyway (that's the celestial interstate system for migratory birds), more than 320 species of birds have been recorded here. They usually visit in April, while heading north, and again in November, because Presque Isle offers one of the best avian bed-and-breakfast systems around. At the tip of the peninsula, Gull Point is designated a restricted, protected, fragile ecosystem. You may not enter this area between April 1 and November 30. The interpretive center offers sophisticated displays and literature on migration and on species of flora and fauna as well as child-geared material on butterflies and ducks.

Children will probably want to head for the beaches, where the surf is usually high enough to be interesting without getting rough enough (in good weather) to be dangerous. Near Grave Yard Pond you can rent rowboats, canoes, and motorboats, but stay tuned to Channel 16 for boating conditions.

Presque Isle also offers bliss for bladers: a superb 9.6-mile recreation trail, beautifully leveled and paved, along the shoreline loop. Park at the first lot inside the park entrance off Route 832, strap on your in-line skates, and go.

Discoveries on Presque Isle

Jerry McWilliams has been birding on Presque Isle since he was five. As we hiked the secluded 1-mile trail to Gull Point, he talked excitedly about recent rare sightings: a white-morphed gyrfalcon from Greenland, the first ever seen at Presque Isle, and a boreal owl, a northern Canadian native not seen here since 1893. "They live in forests so deep that if they saw a human, they'd allow you to touch them. They don't know fear," explains McWilliams.

Presque Isle State Park, which is open from dawn to dusk, has almost as many phone numbers as it does species of gulls. For details about the Stull Interpretive Center, sports concessions, guided nature tours, movies, and lectures, phone (814) 833–0351. To reach the marina in season, call (814) 833–0176. To reach the lifeguard office in season, call (814) 833–0526. You can also surf to www.dcnr.state.pa.us, or write to the park at Box 8510, Erie 16505.

Lighthouse at Presque Isle State Park

Kids will also love **Waldameer Park and Water World,** the kind of old-fashioned amusement park that summer vacations are all about. It's located at 220 Peninsula Drive (the road into the park), and the phone number is (814) 838–3591. Waldameer's new competition is **Splash Lagoon,** a water park with laser tag, located off Interstate 90, exit 24 (old exit 6); call (866) 3–SPLASH.

Another way to cover the waterfront is aboard the **Lady Kate.** The 110-passenger cruiser makes frequent trips around Presque Isle from its moorings by the Perry Monument (on East Fisher Drive). From mid-June through Labor Day, there are five ninety-minute narrated tours each day, from 11:00 A.M. to sunset. From May 1 to mid-June and Labor Day through the end of September, there are three sailings a day on weekends only. Reservations are suggested. Fares for adults are $15.00; $9.00 for children five through twelve; children under five are free. Call (814) 836–0201 or (800) 988–5780.

For boating on a grander scale, visit the restored **US Brig** Niagara in Erie. The ship, captained by Oliver Hazard Perry during the War of 1812, commemorates the victory on September 10, 1813, when nine American ships triumphed over the British fleet on Lake Erie—the first time in naval history that a British squadron was defeated and captured. The *Niagara* and Perry gave the world the famous line: "We have met the enemy, and they are ours." (See the *Niagara* on special Pennsylvania license tags. They're tan and brown, and from a distance they look as faded as a pair of sixties bell bottoms.) The beautifully restored *Niagara* is one of only four remaining ships in the world from that era; the USS *Constitution* and *Constellation* and the HMS *Victory,* all built at the end of the eighteenth century, are the others. But the *Niagara* is the only one seaworthy enough for regular cruises (usually through the Great Lakes, but every four years, along the Atlantic Coast). During warm-weather months lucky land-

Three Erie Lighthouses

Presque Isle, residence of park superintendent. Exterior viewing daily 8:00 A.M. to sunset.

Erie Land Lighthouse, first built in 1818, replaced in 1856; no light since Christmas Eve 1899. Exterior viewing daily.

North Pier, located at the south entrance of the channel. Viewing daily.

lubbers are welcome aboard for day cruises—but you must apply in advance for this thrill. Demand far exceeds available space on the few Sundays and Mondays the *Niagara* boards guests (schedules change each season; consult the Web site www.brigniagara.org). To get on the day-cruise list, call (814) 452–2744, or write to Erie Maritime Museum, Homeport, Attn: Crew Coordinator/Daysail, 150 East Front Street, Suite 100, Erie 16507.

When the *Niagara* is berthed dockside at the Erie Maritime Museum, you can take one-hour tours (make reservations) above and below deck. In the days when its crew numbered 140, quarters on board were extremely tight, what with all those cannon, furled sails, and the manger of live animals. Watch your head below deck—the ceiling is 5 feet tall. By contrast, the tops of the masts tower twelve and ten stories above deck. Tours take place April through December, Monday through Saturday 9:00 A.M. to 5:00 P.M. and Sunday noon to 5:00 P.M. Winter hours are Thursday through Saturday 9:00 A.M. to 5:00 P.M. and Sunday noon to 5:00 P.M. Admission is $6.00 for adults when *Niagara* is in port, $4.00 to visit the museum when she's not. Call (814) 452–2744, or visit www.brigniagara.org.

Even if the *Niagara* has left port, the **Erie Maritime Museum** (the Commonwealth's newest) is well worth a visit. Inside a former power-generating plant, its creative exhibits give an overview of the War of 1812 and a glimpse of the human side of the conflict and its heroes. (Did you know that a quarter of Commodore Perry's men were African Americans?) A short video takes you through the famous battle of September 10, 1813.

But naval brigs aren't the only way around the Bayfront District. Buy a $5.00 pass for the **Presque Isle Water Taxi,** and you (and a bike or wheelchair) can hop from Dobbins Landing to Liberty Park and Presque Isle. The "taxis" run hourly during warm-weather months, with extra service on weekends. Call (800) 881–2502 for details.

For an action-oriented display visit the **Firefighters Historical Museum** (428 Chestnut Street), which is in the old #4 Erie Firehouse. It contains more than 1,300 items of fire department memorabilia, including old uniforms and equipment and an 1830 hand pump. The museum is open May through August, 10:00 A.M. to 5:00 P.M. Saturday and 1:00 to 5:00 P.M. Sunday. From September through October, the museum is open from 1:00 to 5:00 P.M. Saturday and Sunday. Admission costs vary. Call (814) 456–5969 for more information.

The **Watson-Curtze Mansion and Erie Planetarium** (356 West Sixth Street), housed in a twenty-four-room mansion from the late 1800s, has exhibits on regional and maritime history, including the Battle of Lake Erie. Other rooms contain decorative arts and period decor with outstanding woodwork and stained glass. The planetarium, in the carriage house, recreates the movements of the sun, planets, and stars. The museum is open Wednesday through Saturday 11:00 A.M. to 4:00 P.M. Additional hours are scheduled for the museum and planetarium in the summer; call (814) 871–5790 for details.

trivia

Strange but true. The only statue of George Washington wearing a British uniform is on High Street, next to the historic Eagle Hotel (now a restaurant and museum) in Waterford, not far from Erie. Call (814) 796–6990 to reach the restaurant.

Kids in Erie love the **ExpERIEnce Children's Museum** (420 French Street, 2 blocks from the waterfront), where they can paint their faces, dance on a stage, and learn what owls eat for dinner. Kids under two enter free, and others pay $4.50. The museum is open Wednesday through Saturday 10:00 A.M. to 4:00 P.M. and Sunday 1:00 to 4:00 P.M. In summer it's also open Tuesday. Call (814) 453–3743 or fax (814) 459–9735.

In the same complex, called Discovery Square, are two other museums. The **Erie County History Center** (419 State Street) focuses on county history. Phone the center at (814) 454–1813; fax (814) 452–1744; or e-mail echs@velocity.net.

That's Dinor to You

Don't ask me why diners in northwestern Pennsylvania are called "dinors." But they are, and one of the funkiest is the Park Dinor in Erie. *Diners of Pennsylvania,* the definitive study by Brian Butko and Kevin Patrick, calls it a classic—a tiny, trailer-shaped, 1948 Silk City model with room for two dozen diners (or dinors). Try the special Greek sauce, a spicy ground-meat gravy that tops everything from burgers to french fries. Located at 4019 Main Street, outside the General Electric factory entrance; open Monday through Saturday, 6:00 A.M. to 3:00 P.M.; call (814) 899–4390.

The ***Erie Art Museum*** (411 State Street) has a small permanent collection and changing exhibits of fine art. Phone (814) 459–5477, or visit www.erieart museum.org.

To see contemporary American jewelry, studio pottery, carvings, and textiles, stop at the ***Glass Growers*** (10 East Fifth Street; 814–453–3758). Upstairs are the creations of local and regional artists.

You've been through town, yet you haven't heard a word about the barges filled with lumber, coal, and hay. Where, oh where, is the ***Erie Canal,*** you wonder. It started on Elk Creek, a scant 20 miles down Route 5 from the city of Erie, and carried barges to the Hudson River, thus linking the Great Lakes and the Atlantic Ocean. The canal opened in 1844 and began to lose business to the railroads as early as the 1850s. When the aqueduct over Elk Creek collapsed in 1872, the canal closed. At least it survives in song. Beginning in 1918, commercial traffic began using the larger New York State Barge Canal.

Elk Creek flows through the town of Girard, which has a unique place in American history: Dan Rice lived there. Dan *who?* Dan Rice, the circus owner whose carnival spent summers in Girard. Dan Rice, whose flag-waving clown costume included a top hat and balloon pants. Dan Rice, whom Thomas Nast, an artist from *Harper's Weekly,* caricatured—and whose image became known as "Uncle Sam." *That* Dan Rice.

Wine Country

From Erie continue east on Route 5 to visit the local wine region, which stretches about 100 miles along the coast yet extends only 5 miles inland. Wine grapes flourish here because the lake creates a microclimate in which cold spring winds blow in from the lake, keeping the plants from budding too early and becoming vulnerable to frost. In the summer lake breezes cool the vineyards and keep the air circulating; in the fall the stored summer warmth from the lake delays frost. Because the lake once was much larger and has receded, the soils along the shore are especially fertile. Hence, fine wine. (Let's drink to that.)

In North East stop at the ***Hornby School Museum*** (10000 Colt Station Road, Route 430), a restored one-room schoolhouse, built in the 1870s. With a reservation you can arrange to experience the kind of lessons that would have been part of a typical school day. The school is open Sunday from May through October, 1:00 to 5:00 P.M. and by appointment. Call (814) 725–5680 for more information. It's free.

More fun than school, perhaps, ***Lake Shore Railway Museum*** (Wall and Robinson Streets) also has a lot to teach. Two children cried all the way there one morning because they hate museums, but at 5:00 P.M. attendants had to chase them out of the train cars to close up. The museum displays historical railroad items from the nineteenth and twentieth centuries, ranging from dining-car china to signaling devices. Outside the museum, which is in a station house by the tracks, you may tour a caboose and railroad cars on the siding—a Pullman sleeping car, diner, freight car, coach, and baggage car. The wooden caboose looks like one from the olden days, complete with a stove and cooking area. In front of the station is a steamless locomotive, built in Erie in 1937. The schedule of the museum varies with the season and includes some special holiday events, so call (814) 725–1911, or visit www.lsrhs.railway.museum for specific details.

trivia

So many fish are being fed at the Linesville Spillway, on Route 6 west of Meadville, that ducks can walk on the fishes' backs to compete for bread.

Mosey a half-hour south of North East and you're in the land of biodiversity, home to French Creek and a national wildlife refuge. **French Creek,** named by George Washington for the former residents of this region between Meadville and Franklin, has recently been rediscovered as a stream of astounding diversity. The creek's glacial history and outstanding water quality make it a haven for all kinds of creatures, including peaceable humans.

French Creek and the Allegheny River used to flow north, as part of the St. Lawrence River system. However, the glaciers of the last ice age, which ended about 15,000 years ago, forced the creek to run south. As a result, 117-mile French Creek eventually began emptying into the Allegheny River. Today the creek retains species from the northern waterway as well as the Allegheny. It's home to eighty kinds of fish (an angler's dream), two dozen types of mussels, and a giant, very shy, rarely seen salamander—the hellbender, which some locals call a "mudpuppy." The hellbender can grow up to 29 inches long and live up to twenty-nine years.

Canoeing is the perfect way to savor the beauty of the area, and there are plenty of launching spots. The **French Creek Project** offers exhibits and maps at the project's headquarters (at the corner of Routes 6 and 19 east of Edinboro). The French Creek Project is headquartered at Allegheny College, but the project office, open Monday through Friday 9:00 A.M. to 5:00 P.M. is 20 miles north along the creek; call (814) 332–2946, or visit http://Frenchcreek .allegheny.edu.

As you drive toward the **Erie National Wildlife Refuge**—located in a marsh near Guys Mills, south of the lake—be on the lookout for bald eagles,

petroglyphs on the allegheny

For over 300 years people have pondered the engraved graffiti on *Indian God Rock,* 9 miles south of Belmar along the Allegheny River. In 1889 a local newsman proposed that the strange runes were actually made by Norse explorers. More recent experts said that the animals, weapons, and other shapes were definitely made by Native Americans sometime before 1650. To protect the boulder from further vandalism—many eighteenth and nineteenth century visitors had added their names—the rock was placed on the National Register of Historic Places in 1984. There's a viewing platform near the 22-foot-high stone so you can look but not touch. If you're hiking or biking, take the Sandy Creek Trail.

which find good hunting in the wetlands. This federal site, one of two in the state, offers nearly 9,000 acres for hiking, hunting, fishing, and, of course, bird-watching. A new indoor bird observation area gives you binoculars, bird books, and even microphones to eavesdrop on 237 different species. Enter the refuge 10 miles east of Meadville on Highway 198. The visitor center is open weekdays from 8:00 A.M. to 4:30 P.M. Write to 11296 Wood Duck Lane, Guys Mills 16327; call (814) 789–3585; or visit http://erie.fws.gov.

Did you know that John Brown slept here? The abolitionist rabble-rouser lived in New Richmond, 13 miles north of Meadville, from 1826 to 1835, long before his Harpers Ferry raid. You can't see the tannery where he worked, but you can visit the small *John Brown Farm Museum* near his home (if and only if you call ahead) April 15 to October 15 or in winter, and view interpretive displays at the tannery site. The site is located at the intersection of Routes 77 and 1033. For information call (814) 967–2099.

Oil Country

Sharon is a very small town with some giant-sized attractions. In *Reyer's,* it has the world's largest shoe store; in *Daffin's Chocolate Kingdom,* the world's largest candy store; and in *Quaker Steak and Lube,* the self-proclaimed best hot wings in the U.S.A.

Whether your teenager needs size 16 sneakers or your mom needs AAAAA width, Reyer's, with 150,000 pairs of shoes, can fit their feet. It's been in business for 120 years at 40 South Water Avenue (800–245–1550). The store is open daily till 5:00 P.M.; shop online at www.reyers.com. Daffin's (496 East State Street; 724–342–2892) boasts a chocolate menagerie that includes a 400-pound turtle and a 125-pound reindeer. It's open Monday through Friday from 9:00 A.M. to 9:00 P.M., Sunday from 11:00 A.M. to 5:00 P.M.

BEST ANNUAL EVENTS IN NORTHWESTERN PENNSYLVANIA

Each April when Earth Day rolls around, **Creekfest** celebrates the biodiversity of the French Creek with awards for those who protect it, a big-name evening concert, and an art exhibit. For details contact the French Creek Project at (814) 332–2946, or visit http://frenchcreek.allegheny.edu.

In late July check out **Discover Presque Isle Days,** run by the Presque Isle Partnership. Call (814) 838–5138.

A stilt-walking Uncle Sam leads the parade at the annual **Dan Rice Days** in Girard. Held the first Saturday in August, the festival includes games, food, crafts, and such—and Uncle Sam, fashioned after local legend Dan Rice. Call (814) 774–3535 for more details.

Mid-August you can participate in **Erie Celebrate** on Perry Square in Erie. Call (814) 870–1593.

During the last full weekend of September in Tidioute (rhymes with "pretty suit"), you can participate in the **Pennsylvania State Championship Fishing Tournament.** Call the Warren County Tourism/Northern Alleghenies Vacation Region at (800) 624–7802 for rules and regulations.

If you've always wanted to do some grape-stomping, the town of North East will give you the chance each fall at its **Wine Country Harvest Festival.** You can also sample wines by the glass and try a few champagnes—a local specialty. For details call (814) 725–4262, or visit www.lakeside.net/ne.

Kids love the gremlins and goblins at the **Zoo Boo,** a scary evening event held for several weeks prior to Halloween. Call the Erie Zoo at (814) 864–4091.

Quaker Steak and Lube is, of course, a play on both the Quaker State and locally made Quaker State Motor Oil, and it carries the automotive theme to fantastic extremes, with real cars as overhead art. People come for the wings, but you can get all sorts of pub-style choices too. Insert your oil joke here. It's open from lunch to at least midnight seven days a week at 101 Chestnut Avenue; call (800) HOT–WING.

If you remember the Lettermen, you'll be pleased to know that the **Vocal Group Hall of Fame** is right here in the hometown of Tony Butala, one of their founding members. Tony is now working to reopen the Columbia Theater at 82 West State for hall of fame performances; the museum next door is expected to open soon. Get details at (724) 983–2025, or visit www.vghf.org.

In the grand Richardson Romanesque style (seen also in downtown Pittsburgh) is the **Buhl Mansion Guesthouse and Spa** at 422 East State Street. Built in 1890 for a wealthy local couple, it's been restored to glory by owners Donna and Jim Winner (he invented the anti-theft device The Club®). Visit www.buhlmansion.com, or call (724) 346–3046.

Let Meadville lure you off the interstate (off Interstate 79, to be precise). **_Allegheny College,_** one of the oldest colleges west of the Alleghenies, has a good collection of Abraham Lincoln memorabilia in the Pelletier Library. Ida Tarbell, one of the college's first female students, majored in biology because she hoped to find God with what she could learn through a microscope. After graduating, she became one of the muckrakers famous at the turn of the twentieth century, journalists who tried to expose the abuses of businesses and the corruption of politics. Tarbell wrote an extensive biography of the Lincolns and later donated the papers to her alma mater. The library also has many interesting papers, books, and artifacts related to Tarbell. Two college buildings, Bentley Hall and Ruter Hall, are listed on the National Register of Historic Places.

Meadville's downtown includes more than a dozen historic buildings that should interest those who care about old architecture. You can pick up a free self-guided tour to bygone Meadville at the **_Market House_** (910 Market Street). The Crawford County Tourist Association office is on the second floor. On the ground floor a farmers' market flourishes, as it has for more than a hundred years. You can eat at the lunch counter and shop for produce, flowers, baked goods, handicrafts, cheese, ceramics, and collectibles in the marketplace. Market House is open year-round.

Approximately 30 miles east of Meadville, you can get a glimpse of the early influence of oil, before Texans thought of liquid gold. Start at Titusville with the **_Drake Well Park and Museum_** (814–827–2797; www.drakewell.org), site of the world's first successful oil well and an 1860s boomtown. The well is topped by a replica of the derrick. An old-fashioned museum details the early oil days and shows films about how the first well came to be drilled. (One vintage film stars Vincent Price. Now that's scary.) In the library are thousands of photographs plus papers of Ida Tarbell related to her famous exposé of the Standard Oil Company. Though the museum won't hold their interest, kids may enjoy dipping into "the pits." These are slight depressions in the ground, near the banks of Oil Creek, where Indians scooped oil off the surface

Drake Well Park and Museum

of the water—tipping off white settlers to what lay 38 feet below. The oil still seeps to the surface in warm weather. The museum is open from 9:00 A.M. to 5:00 P.M. every day, except November 1 to the end of April, when it is closed all day Monday and until noon Sunday. Closed on major holidays. Admission is $4.00 per adult.

A short drive southeast on Route 27, then south on Route 227, brings you to Plumer. Go 1.5 miles farther south to the ghost town of **Pitbole,** which was an oil boomtown in the late 1860s and was abandoned when the oil business fell off. A visitor center contains a pictorial history and artifacts of the town. By far the most interesting activity is wandering the site where people and businesses used to thrive and where nothing remains but cellar holes, wells, and the depressions that used to be streets. You can pick up a walking-tour brochure at the visitor center, open from the first Saturday in June through Labor Day, Wednesday noon to 5:00 P.M. and Thursday through Sunday 10:00 A.M. to 5:00 P.M. Hours are subject to change, and modest fees are charged. Call (814) 589–7912 for more information.

Another way to see oil country and its history is to ride the **Oil Creek and Titusville Railroad,** sponsored by the Oil Creek Railway Historical Society. The two-hour trip runs from Titusville to Rynd Farm, 4 miles north of Oil City, passing through the sites of several boomtowns and some lovely countryside. You can board a train at the Drake Well Museum, at the Perry Street Station in Titusville, or at Rynd Farm. The schedule of northbound and southbound trains is complicated, may change without notice, and includes additional trains scheduled for special celebration weeks in the summer; moreover, you need advance tickets to guarantee a place on the train. To learn what the schedule will be when you plan to visit, write to the railroad at 409 South Perry Street, Titusville 16354, or call (814) 676–1733. Tickets are $12 per adult.

If you'd like to make part of the same trip on bicycle, try the 10-mile paved trail along Oil Creek from Petroleum Center to Drake Well Park. The trail is open from 8:00 A.M. to dark.

Enjoy a more amusing kind of history at the **DeBence Antique Music World Museum** (1261 Liberty Street), not far away on Route 8, Franklin. The museum has more than a hundred antique music machines from the Gay Nineties and the Roaring Twenties. Hear the nickelodeons, band organs, orchestrions, and music boxes. The museum is open March 15 through October 31, Tuesday through Saturday 11:00 A.M. to 4:00 P.M. and Sunday 12:30 to 4:00 P.M.; November 1 through December 23, it's open Friday through Sunday. Call (814) 432–8350, or visit www.debencemusicworld.com for details. Admission is $8.00 per adult. Sounds great!

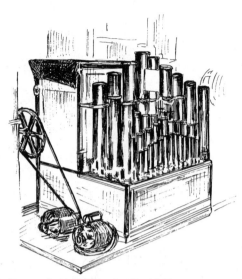

DeBence Antique Music World Museum

The town of Franklin dates to 1753, when the French established Fort Machault here. Seven years later the British built Fort Venango. But, as with so much of this part of Pennsylvania, striking oil was what really gave life to the community. Take the time to check out the local history displays in the *Hoge-Osmer House* (corner of South Park and Elk Streets) and at the *Venango County Courthouse* (Twelfth and Liberty Streets). If you're on Twelfth Street on Wednesday or Saturday, you can browse through the local farmers' market. Wander around town, or request a self-guided walking tour at the Franklin Area Chamber of Commerce (1259 Liberty Street). For further information phone (814) 432–5823, or go to www.franklin-pa.org.

Rolling along the River

One not-to-be-missed country road is Route 62, which hugs the bank of the Allegheny River between Warren to the north and Tionesta and Franklin to the south. Those three towns, plus the vacation cabins scattered along the shoreline, are just about the only signs of human habitation you'll see as you drive through the forest, passing magnificent vistas as the river widens and contracts. Any time of year is the right time to try Route 62.

Allegheny National Forest

The 500,000-acre *Allegheny National Forest* is one of fifteen national forests in the eastern United States and the only national forest in Pennsylvania. Hardwoods—black cherry, yellow poplar, white ash, red maple, and sugar maple—make up most of the timber. More than 65 million board feet of timber, especially black cherry, are harvested each year. The black cherry is used for fine furniture; much of the rest is used for pulpwood. *Hearts Content,* one comparatively small area of the forestland, has some of the oldest tracts of virgin beech and hemlock trees in the eastern United States.

You can access the forest from many points along Route 6 and Route 62 for some truly off-the-beaten-path travel. Just past East Hickory, at Endeavor, turn right on Route 666, heading into the forest.

From here, turn around and drive back about a quarter mile, where you see a dirt Forest Service road just before Mayburg. Turn left here, on Robbs Creek Road, also known as Forest Road 116. Drive on to Hearts Road (though the signs often disappear), and turn left again. In about 2 miles you'll come to *Hearts Content Recreation Area* in the Allegheny National Forest. From Hearts Content you can hike, camp, and picnic—you know, to your heart's content. Whatever you do, you must take the scenic walk marked by signs. It is short and easy, and it seems to invite meditation. Streams make light music. The old deciduous trees arch high above, letting through just enough blue sky and sunlight to nurture the carpet of ferns, which reach your knees. Pines and hemlocks, nature's original incense, perfume the air. The forest floor, softened with pine needles and leaves, absorbs enough sound to make the surroundings seem as quiet as a cathedral. A six-year-old child walking through the area for the first time captured its mystery by asking, "Are we inside or outside?"

The *Hickory Creek Wilderness,* all 8,570 acres of it, is next to the campground. No motorized equipment is allowed. An 11-mile hiking loop takes you through rolling terrain. You will probably see deer, small wildlife, and all kinds of birds.

strangebuttrue

Off the beaten path defines Forest County, Pennsylvania's least-populated county, which boasts no traffic lights, no four-lane highways, no radio stations, and no daily newspapers.

You can find a smaller—much smaller—peaceful, tranquil natural area in *Clear Creek State Park* by heading north from Sigel on Route 36, then north on Route 949. Call (814) 752–2368 to reach the park office. Scenically located in Jefferson County's Clear Creek Valley, the park encompasses 1,200 acres, with another 10,000 acres of natural resources in adjacent Kittanning State Forest. A highlight of the park is the outstanding self-guided Ox Shoe Trail, which depicts logging practices of earlier years. The area is noted for its abundant wildlife, its hunting and fishing, and the breathtaking beauty of its mountain laurel, which blooms from mid-June to early July, peaking in late June. See if you—or your kids—can identify some mountain laurel, the state flower. The plant grows from 3 to 6 feet high on rocky, wooded slopes. Look for petals that form a nearly perfect pink or white pentagon.

trivia

The town of Corydon, near Warren, was submerged when the Kinzua Dam was built in 1965. But during a drought late in 1998, roads, bridges, and the foundations of buildings began peeking above the surface. Take a tour.

You're quite near **Cook Forest State Park,** which, in 1994, earned a *National Geographic* listing as one of the nation's top-fifty state parks. One of the finest stands of virgin timber in the eastern part of the United States is located here, and the area has been designated a National Natural Landmark. The trees in this ancient forest are hundreds of years old, measuring up to 5 feet in diameter and towering nearly 200 feet. During a recent old-growth forest conference, three of the tallest trees in the East were identified here in Cook Forest. The old Cook sawmill, home to the Sawmill Center for the Arts, features summer theater, festivals, and craft markets and draws artisans to instruct classes in traditional arts and crafts. Much of the area exists almost as it was in the days of William Penn, when it was known as the Black Forest. Cecil B. DeMille used the park in his film *Unconquered,* starring Gary Cooper.

Silver Stallion Stables, just north of the Cooksburg Bridge, offers one- and two-hour trail jaunts daily in the summer for riders as young as six years old (summer forest temperatures hover from the mid-sixties to mid-seventies). No matter how dumb you might feel in the saddle, the stables' owners, Mark and Lori Mills, say, don't worry, the horses are smart. "We're particular to Appaloosa and paint, for their intelligence, their stamina, and their beauty," he notes. Riders with disabilities or other special needs are welcome. Average prices are $20 per hour at Silver Stallion (814–927–6636).

Cook Forest Scenic Rides and Dude Ranch, off Clarion-Miola Road, offers "dude packages" with lodging, meals, and rides. Prices start at $99 per person for two dudes. Call (814) 226–5985 for details.

In these parts you may hear a clarion call to slow down and smell the roses— or look at the leaves. **Clarion,** calling itself the autumn-leaf capital of the known world, boasts the rugged beauty of untamed natural resources and the nostalgia of an old-fashioned Main Street. It is unmistakably off the beaten path. Stop in the Free Library, on Main Street next to the post office, in downtown Clarion to pick up a booklet outlining a historical and architectural tour of the town, noting forty structures of interest. Enjoy the old-fashioned streetlights and nostalgic building facades as you stroll downtown. A parasol would be nice.

Places to Stay in Northwestern Pennsylvania

CAMBRIDGE SPRINGS

The Riverside Inn,
1 Fountain Avenue;
(800) 964-5173;
www.riversideinn.com.
This famous nineteenth-century inn on the banks of French Creek is open April through December.

CLARION

Clarion House Bed & Breakfast,
77 South Seventh Avenue;
(814) 226-4996 or
(800) 416-3297;
www.chouse.com

COOKSBURG

Gateway Lodge,
Cook Forest, Box 125,
Route 36;
(814) 744-8017;
www.gatewaylodge.com

ERIE

Spencer House Bed & Breakfast,
519 West Sixth Street;
(814) 454-5984

NORTH EAST

Grape Arbor Bed & Breakfast,
51 East Main Street;
(814) 725-0048;
www.grapearborbandb.com

SHARON

Tara,
2844 Lake Road, Clark;
(724) 962-3535 or
(800) 782-2803;
www.tara-inn.com.
Dedicated to "the greatest movie of all time, *Gone With the Wind*," with rooms with names like "Rhett's Room" and "Belle's Boudoir." Tours by costumed guides, dining rooms, a spa, and a lake.

WATTSBURG

Timbermist,
11050 Backus Road;
(814) 739-9004 or
(888) 739-9004;
www.timbermist.com

Places to Eat in Northwestern Pennsylvania

ERIE

Smuggler's Wharf,
3 State Street;
(814) 459-4273.
On Lake Erie.

SHARON

Quaker Steak & Lube,
101 Chestnut Street;
(724) 981-7221 or
(800) 468-9464.
Located in a former gas station. Your dining companions are a 1936 Chevrolet on a grease rack and a Corvette suspended from the ceiling. Hot wings and cool cars.

TIONESTA

Five Forks Restaurant,
Route 62, 1.5 miles
south of Tionesta;
(814) 755-2455.
Overlooking the Allegheny River.

TITUSVILLE

Four Sons Brewery and Restaurant,
113 South Franklin Street;
(814) 827-1141.
Microbrews and casual fare.

North Central Pennsylvania: Allegheny National Forest

Getting Your Kicks on Route 6

One of the best ways to see what Pennsylvanians call the "northern tier" is by jumping on **Route 6** and following it east through Warren, McKean, Potter, and Tioga Counties. This pleasant, flat two-laner stretches all the way to Pike County, home of the Delaware Water Gap. Running through the Brokenstraw Valley, with mountains on either side, the road is an easy (and in some cases, the only) way to get through this neck of the woods, connecting most of the county seats. It's also one of the state's designated bike routes.

With such dense forests, it's no surprise that fall is a popular time to visit the area. But the upper Allegheny River offers plenty of summer fun, too, and on a crystal-clear winter morning, the vistas from a snowmobile are glorious. And you're welcome anytime.

National Geographic called Route 6 "one of America's most scenic drives." (But don't neglect Route 59, which links the Kinzua Bridge State Park with Kinzua Dam and Allegheny Reservoir, offering scenic views at every turn.) Route 6 even has its own Web site to help you get your kicks: www.paroute6.com.

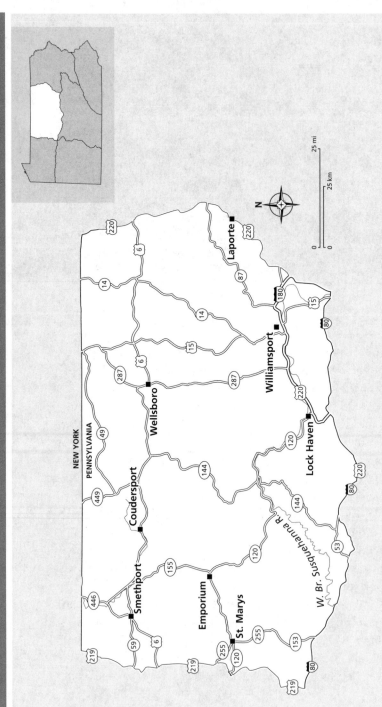

Wild Country

Start your wild-country trek with a fiery sightseeing experience—by visiting the **Zippo/Case Visitors Center** (1932 Zippo Drive) in Bradford, off Route 219 just below the New York border. Zippo is the company that first made windproof lighters. (Legend has it that zippers had recently been invented, and the inventor liked the name, so he copied it.) Your visit includes the museum, which opened in 1994, the repair clinic, and the gift shop (though not the factory). Since Zippos include a lifetime guarantee, and since the repair shop receives about 400 lighters daily, there's always something to watch. The center is open Sunday noon to 4:00 P.M. between Memorial Day and Christmas; other days, noon to 5:00 P.M. Look for streetlights shaped like giant lighters. Call (814) 368–1932 or (888) 442–1932, or light up www.zippo.com.

Nearby **Glendorn** is the opposite of utilitarian. It's a plush inn and four-star restaurant that's the grandest hostelry around, with room rates starting around $500 a night. For that price, you get elegance to the max. The Relais and Chateaux–approved property, nestled in the mountains outside of Bradford, offers skeet, tennis, and other outdoor activities year-round. Choose the Big House or the cabins; they're equally luxurious. Owner Holbert Lawson is a member of the Dorn family, which built this retreat in the 1920s. It's at 1000 Glendorn Drive in Bradford. Call (800) 843–8568, or reserve rooms or meals online at www.glendorn.com.

For a completely different dining experience, you might drive through the Bradford McDonald's on Main Street. There may have been billions of burgers served at the chain worldwide, but this is the only location that serves them with a side of real oil. Cline Oil #1 in the parking lot pumps dozens of gallons

AUTHOR'S TOP TEN FAVORITES IN NORTH CENTRAL PENNSYLVANIA

Elk	Smethport
Elk Burgers	Wellsboro
Frenchville	Woolrich Factory Store
Grand Canyon of Pennsylvania	World Series of Little League Baseball
Lookout Tower (which we climbed at Valley Forge)	World's End State Park

each day, just as it has since the 1870s. You'll see other private wells dotting front yards throughout the region.

Pop up to **Singer's Country Store** (814–368–6151) at the crossroads that is Custer City, at the intersection of Routes 219 and 770 West. For about 60 cents you can pluck a fresh pickle out of the briny barrel and chat about the countryside with the owner, Mary Dach.

trivia

In Austin, just south of Route 6 on Route 872, a dam broke in 1911, leveling two towns and killing eighty-nine people. The site is listed on the National Register of Historic Places.

From Custer City you can slip south on Route 46 to **Smethport,** a picture-perfect country town and county seat. Main Street boasts a solid core of restored Victorian homes and pleasant sidewalks for strolling. The McKean County Courthouse exudes stability, right down to the Civil War statue out front: He's a Bucktail, the local regiment of volunteers who formed the core of the Union Army's Forty-second Pennsylvania Regiment. The fact that every soldier decorated his cap with a deer's tail gives you a hint about the local wildlife.

Main Street is home to a mini-millionaires' row of superb mansions. It's also home to the Smethport Diner, also known as the Route 6 Diner, and the Hub, a gas/convenience store named in honor of the Hubbers, the local high school nickname.

With over a century and a half of history, Smethport is home to the Mc-Kean County Historical Museum (814–887–5142) in the 1872 jail, open a few afternoons each week right behind the courthouse. Residents have also created the wonderfully named Planet Smethport Web site (www.smethporthistory.org). You can tour local landmarks by clicking up and down streets and learn (lots) about former residents. It's almost like peeking through their windows.

forthebirds

Enjoy Tioga-Hammond and Cowanesque Lakes, where wildlife is protected and recreational opportunities abound. Check out the osprey habitat.

Head east on Route 6, through Coudersport. Across from Denton Hill State Park at Galeton, you reach the **Pennsylvania Lumber Museum,** an outdoor gallery that depicts the history and technology of Pennsylvania's prosperous lumbering activities. Two of the world's largest sawmills were located in Austin (24 miles southwest of the museum) and Galeton (11 miles southeast). The museum displays more than 3,000 artifacts related to the logging industry. Walk among the old buildings of the logging camp, the sawmill, and a logging pond, all surrounded by

Pennsylvania Town Names We Like

Thirsty? Follow Interstate 80 to get to Stillwater (exit 36) and Swiftwater (exit 44).

Monarchy. Who says Americans don't believe in the monarchy? We have a King of Prussia, now home to one of the country's largest megamalls, plus towns named Queen, Princeton, and Duke Center.

Upper class. Visit communities named Upper Darby, Upper Merion, Upper Black Eddy, Upper St. Clair, and Upper Strasburg. Plus Upland, Topton, Highland, and Highspire.

What's in a name? Philadelphia International Airport is in Essington, Harrisburg Airport is in Middletown, and Pittsburgh International is in Coraopolis.

Law firm name we'd like to see. Clayton, Drayton, and Creighton.

Appalachian Mountain wilderness. The visit re-creates the tough life of "wood hicks" in the days of lumbering. The men worked six days a week, from 5:00 A.M. to 9:00 P.M. (no, that's not a typo!), with time off for extended periods of downpour, though rarely for cold or snow. In about 1910 the workweek was reduced to six ten-hour days, and in 1920 to five eight-hour days. Lice and dirt were everywhere. Bathing facilities were nowhere.

Even though the workers' conditions weren't pristine, the forests and trees were, and the giant white pines were in great demand. Wood hicks felled the trees, tied them onto rafts, and floated them down the Susquehanna River and into the Chesapeake Bay, where they were exported to England to be made into ships. The Lumber Museum, administered by the Pennsylvania Historical and Museum Commission, is open 9:00 A.M. to 5:00 P.M. daily, April through November (except on fall holidays). Admission is $4.00 per adult. Phone (814) 435–2652; fax (814) 435–6361; write P.O. Box 239, 5660 Route 6, Galeton 16922; or visit www.lumbermuseum.org for more information.

The most dramatic aspect of this section of the state is the mountainous and wooded **Pine Creek Gorge,** commonly known as the **Grand Canyon of Pennsylvania.** The gorge, comprising mostly state parks and wilderness, is 50 miles long and 1,000 feet deep, covering 300,000 acres of state forest. You can access the canyon by driving south on Route 660, midway between Galeton and Wellsboro.

Before the pharaohs built the pyramids, the headwaters of Pine Creek, near Ansonia, flowed to the northeast. Then came glaciers. As the glacial ice melted, it left a dam of gravel, sand, and clay, which blocked the creek's path. This natural dam forced Pine Creek to reverse direction and flow south. Thus

The Tower That Traveled

The *Lookout Tower* in Leonard Harrison State Park affords views for 100 miles with the naked eye. The tower originally stood atop Mount Joy, in Valley Forge, where George Washington and his troops spent the winter of 1776 and 1777. Built in 1906, the tower was a birders' haven until 1988, when surrounding trees grew too tall for its use as an observation tower. At that time, it traveled 240 miles to its current home. Visit the tower daily, sunrise to sunset, weather permitting. Climb 125 steps to reach the top.

formed the Grand Canyon, with land formations dating back more than 350 million years. In 1968 the National Park Service declared a 12-mile section a National Natural Landmark.

At two state parks—*Leonard Harrison State Park* on the east rim of the canyon and *Colton Point State Park* on the west (570–724–3061 reaches both park offices)—you can stop at lookouts and pick up short hiking trails that don't require safari gear. Leonard Harrison State Park has a nature center (open summer and fall) and a relatively easy trail along the rim that gives you an orientation to the canyon. If you follow Turkey Path about a mile down to Pine Creek, you'll encounter more ambitious hikes that take in creeks and waterfalls. The area is noted for ferns, songbirds, and superb scenery in any season. In Colton Point State Park you can hike an easy mile-long loop through a hardwood forest rich in wildflowers and fragrant mountain laurel, the state flower.

trivia

Pennsylvania leads the nation in producing mushrooms and potato chips.

One of the state's most spectacular rails-to-trails projects is the *Pine Creek Trail,* which runs 42 miles from Ansonia to Waterville. This level crushed-limestone path, closed to motor traffic, lets you explore by bike or by foot. If you're a hardbody, you might want to bike in with a tent and backpack and camp overnight at Harrison State Park; if not, there are ten trailheads where you can exit the trail, and there are motels and inns at both ends where you can actually sleep in a bed. Hot water, too. For a map or information, contact the Tioga County Visitors Bureau at (888) 846–4228; www.visittiogapa.com; or the Lycoming County Tourist Promotion Agency at (800) 358–9900; www.vacationpa.com.

Wellsboro, the Tioga County seat, is a beautiful little town, with old trees and gaslights lining the streets. In the public square, called the Green, a fountain splashes over a statue of Wynken, Blynken, and Nod in their wooden shoe. When Wellsboro was incorporated in 1830, it had 250 residents. In the 1990 census, it had grown to 3,400, with another 5,000 within a 5-mile radius and 5,000 more within 10 miles.

Lots of cars in town sport bike racks, a clue to the popularity of the nearby trail, and Country Ski and Sports (81 Main Street; 570–724–3858) rents bikes right in town.

One person who fell in love with Wellsboro's slow pace is Nelle Rounsaville, who came here after twenty years as a flight attendant. "It's just a wonderful Victorian town," she says fondly. She started small, with a cozy Charles Street B&B on the town square that she dubbed *La Petite Auberge.* Then she bought the *Wellsboro Diner,* a classic 1939 eatery down the block. Then she bought the larger *La Belle Auberge* on Main Street. (Make reservations at the inns at www.nellesinns.com, or call Nelle at 866–250–8117.) Aside from being entirely made of porcelain, the Wellsboro Diner has another claim to fame: It was the subject of a "Zippy the Pinhead" cartoon by Bill Griffith. It serves breakfast all day, has daily specials, and is open daily until 8:00 P.M. at 19 Main Street. Call (570) 724–3992, or check the menu online at www.wellsborodiner.com.

You can request an area map from the Wellsboro Chamber of Commerce, 114 Main Street, Wellsboro 16901. Phone (570) 724–1926; fax (570) 724–5084; or go to www.wellsboropa.com.

The End of the World

Another near-wilderness park is *World's End State Park,* as remote as it sounds. To get there take Route 220 to Eagles Mere, which is about midpoint between Route 6 and I–80, then go west on Route 154. Part of the lure of World's End is its primitive quality and its ideal position for picnicking, fishing, swimming, and boating. The park phone number is (570) 924–3287.

The town of *Eagles Mere* is the cosmopolitan village you turn to after exploring World's End. Eagles Mere, which used to call itself "the town that time forgot," is so earnest and simple that it might have inspired Norman Rockwell. In the 1800s wealthy folk from Philadelphia's Main

trivia

Bald eagles were once so rare that they were considered an endangered species. In 1980 Pennsylvania counted only three. Thanks to the national ban on DDT (in 1972) and the state Game Commission's introduction of eagles from Saskatchewan, Canada, by spring 1998 eagles were spotted in twenty-seven nests. Eagle populations grow slowly, because pairs rear only one to three young each year, and it takes five years for the young to mature.

Line visited the 2,100-foot-high mountain area, fell in love with the clean air and clear water, and set about causing development to happen. They built Victorian "cottages," similar to the gargantuan dwellings of the same name in Newport, Rhode Island. In 1892, with ninety rental cottages, the town had a summer population of 2,500. Since the roads were not paved, boardwalks covered the streets to protect the ladies' white dresses from dirt. In 1898 workers who helped move a building earned 15 cents per hour. A week at the Eagles Mere Hotel cost $7.00; the Lakeside Hotel charged $2.50 a day. A broom cost a dime; a bottle of ink, a nickel; and a gallon of gasoline, 20 cents. Expect to pay somewhat more today.

While the geology is a nature photographer's utopia, one human-made element also stands out. It's the *Slide,* a toboggan run built in 1904. When the first intrepid rider, sitting on a big iron shovel, tested the grooved, planed, wooden course, he whizzed so fast that he burned the seat off his pants. Today the slide is a 120-ton, 1,200-foot-long channel of ice, down which you can ride in relative safety—if you first pay a few bucks and sign a waiver—at 45 miles per hour.

To relax after this thrilling plummet, treat yourself to dinner at the *Eagles Mere Inn,* the last remaining full-service inn from the nineteenth century. Its cozy guest rooms make you yearn for the days before cell phones. In the dining room, where lace covers the tables, hosts Susan and Peter Glaubitz provide a menu that changes daily but always reflects Peter's substantial background as a chef. One night you might try Cajun steak; another, baby French hen in cranberry merlot sauce; and a third, trout stuffed with sole and shiitake mousseline.

trivia

In 1892 the first lighted nighttime football game was played at Mansfield University, Mansfield.

If you prefer vegetarian or other special diets, call ahead (570) 525–3273 or (800) 426–3273, or visit www.eaglesmereinn.com, and they'll try to honor your request. Write to the inn at Mary Avenue, Box 356, Eagles Mere 17731.

Like hot dogs? Like peanuts and Cracker Jacks? Every August, *Williamsport* hosts the Little League World Series, attracting thousands of spectators and some of the best twelve-year-old baseball players in the world. The thwack (or, perhaps, the ping) of the bat and the shouts of the kids remind you why the sport is the national pastime. The *Little League Museum* (570–326–3607; www.littleleague.org) honors Tom Selleck, Dan Quayle, George Will, Bill Bradley, Kareem Abdul-Jabbar, Nolan Ryan, and Mike Schmidt, to name a few. Admission costs $5.00 per adult. Summer hours are Monday through Saturday 10:00 A.M. to 7:00 P.M. and Sunday noon to 7:00 P.M. The rest of the year it's closed Tuesday and Wednesday; Monday, Thursday, and Friday it's open 10:00 A.M. to 5:00 P.M.; Saturday noon to 5:00 P.M.; and Sunday noon to 4:00 P.M.

Closed Thanksgiving, Christmas, and New Year's Day. It's located on Route 15, Williamsport.

Just north of Route 220, between Lock Haven and Williamsport, is the town of Woolrich. If the name sounds familiar, look inside the neckband of your hunting jacket. The company of **Woolrich,** in the town of Woolrich, makes sportswear and outerwear under both its own brand and that of other companies, including L. L. Bean and Lands' End. John Rich built his first woolen mill on Plum Run in 1830, and the rest, as they say, is red buffalo plaid. The actors in *The Horse Whisperer* wore Woolrich garb. Visit the original factory outlet store in Woolrich (570–769–7401 or 800–995–1299), or at outlet malls in Grove City, Lancaster, and Reading. Visit the Woolrich Company Store from 9:00 A.M. to 6:00 P.M. Monday through Thursday, 9:00 A.M. to 9:00 P.M. Friday and Saturday (January through August to 6:00 P.M. Saturday), and noon to 5:00 P.M. Sunday.

In **Laporte,** the bustling little historical society can help you find local relatives. "Genealogy is very important in small towns," explains museum curator Melanie Norton. "Here we have 6,000 people, if everyone and their dog stays home. There are so many shared family names and so many shirt-tail relations." The museum can help you sift through 150 years of records on births, deaths, marriages, and other details. The complex includes the main brick structure, the Baldwin House (with authentic details like garden plants, outhouse, and playhouse intact), and two barns. The museum can also point you to **Celestia,** a mountaintop settlement a mile and a half out of town. That's where a fervent 1850s Christian named Peter Armstrong and his followers planned a town, with a lot reserved for God himself. The museum shows his original street grid and offers

triviatidbits

So what if Abe Lincoln didn't sleep in Wellsboro. That's no reason not to claim his presence. Or presents. At 140 Main Street is the Lincoln Door House. Abraham Lincoln gave the door—now bright red—to Dr. and Mrs. J. H. Shearer when they bought the house in 1858. Mrs. Shearer and Mrs. Lincoln were friends in Springfield, Illinois.

Guidebooks say the name Tioga comes from an old Indian word, but they disagree on what that word meant. Some say it meant "the meeting of two rivers," and others say it meant "gateway" or "place to enter." Either way, Tioga County is a hunter's paradise, serving as home to many species of white-tailed deer, bear, cottontail rabbits, wild turkey, ruffed grouse, and ducks.

Between 1628 and 1762 three kings of England issued four separate charters giving land in today's Tioga County to three different states— once to Pennsylvania, once to Massachusetts, and twice to Connecticut. The Continental Congress resolved state ownership in 1780. It's part of the Keystone State. For now.

Elk Lore

May is the most popular month for elk to have babies.

Female elk, or cows, usually hang out with the other ladies, disappearing for privacy a few days before childbirth. Mommy and baby remain solitary for about three weeks.

In late summer the bull elk's antlers are usually white and ivory; they darken later as the animal rubs against shrubs and trees covered with juices and sap.

Elk antlers, which can grow a half-inch a day, are among the fastest-growing animal tissues.

Elk, like many humans, dislike thunderstorms.

During the rutting season males mate with as many cows as possible, act dangerous to scare off other males, and feed and rest very little. They may lose a hundred pounds in a month. That's serious rutting.

a brochure for a self-guided tour. The **Sullivan County Historical Society Museum** is open mid-June through Labor Day, Thursday through Saturday from 1:00 to 5:00 P.M. But whenever you see the "open" sign in the window on Meylert Street next to the county courthouse, says Melanie, just come on by. Admission is free. Call (570) 946–5020 or e-mail sullymuseum@chilitech.net.

One treasure in this neck of the northern woods is the 23,000-acre **Bucktail State Park,** which extends southeast—and downstream—from Emporium to Lock Haven. Route 120, a good road between the mountains, essentially parallels the park, as does the Susquehanna River for half the distance. This pleasant, scenic drive takes you through state forests, parks, and wilderness areas. If you're in the mood for a more active experience, hike a trail or choose a private clearing for a view and a picnic. Almost always, you can count on being alone. Incidentally, the park's name comes only indirectly from deer; the name actually commemorates Civil War volunteers, like the ones from Smethport.

A state-designated Scenic Byway also takes the Bucktail name. Take Route 120 from Ridgway to Lock Haven for views of hang gliders, elk, and more. This 100-mile stretch through the Sproul and Elk State Forests is another old Indian trail turned highway. Native Americans called it the Sinnemahoning Trail, and used it to travel between the west branch of the Susquehanna and the Allegheny River. Map it at www.visitpa.com/visitpa/byways.pa.

West of Emporium is St. Marys, a town with a frothy claim to fame—**Straub Brewery** (303 Sorg Street). Straub's is one of the smallest independent breweries left in the United States. "Of course, that depends on how you define 'small,' " says owner Terry Straub. "A microbrewery makes fewer than 15,000 barrels per

Every sunny day you can catch a perfect sunrise from **Colton Point State Park.** Enjoy the sunset from **Leonard Harrison State Park.** Both times, you luxuriate in a view of the Grand Canyon of Pennsylvania.

Each February Ridgway hosts the **Chainsaw Carvers Rendezvous,** where you can view the creation of ice and wood sculptures. Many of the results are auctioned off; all proceeds go to charity. Call (814) 772–0400, or buzz off to www.chainsawcarver.de/.

Mary Wells Days, a founder's day celebration, takes place over Memorial Day in Wellsboro. Call (570) 724–1926 for details.

The first weekend in June, you can watch the **Susquehannock Trail Pro** auto racing rally in Wellsboro. Call (570) 724–1926.

The third weekend in June, Wellsboro holds the **Pennsylvania State Laurel Festival.** The parade is on Saturday. Call (570) 724–1926 for information.

Celebrate **Fourth of July** weekend in Mansfield. Call the Mansfield Chamber of Commerce at (570) 662–3442. Or celebrate the Fourth in Galeton, where thousands of visitors watch the fireworks in the natural amphitheater. Call (888) 768–8372.

Watch the **Little League Baseball World Series** in Williamsport during the last full week of August that does not include the Saturday before Labor Day. You'll see the eight top U.S. teams (from the East, Central, West, and South regions) compete against the eight best international teams (from Canada, Latin America, the Far East, and Europe).

Seats are free, and the only day you need a ticket is the Saturday of the championship, since the stadium holds only about 5,000 people. The stadium is built into a hillside, so the other 30,000 or 40,000 spectators without tickets spend the day picnicking on the hill and watching from afar. For tickets write *in January* to the Little League Museum, P.O. Box 3485, Williamsport 17701. Mark the envelope "World Series Tickets." Go, Babe! For more information call (570) 326–3607.

Country line dancing, elk bugle imitations, and elk burgers are all part of the fun at **Elk Expo** each September at Winslow Hill (at the peak of fall foliage season). Contact Northwest Pennsylvania's Great Outdoors Visitors Bureau, (800) 348–9393; www.pagreatoutdoors.com.

1890s Weekend is held the last weekend in September in Mansfield. Call the Mansfield Chamber of Commerce at (570) 662–3442.

During the first weekend in October, you can come home to the **Homecoming Harvest** in Wellsboro. Expect sidewalk sales, craft and food vendors, and antiques. Call (570) 724–1926 for details.

The first Saturday in December, catch the **Dickens of a Christmas** in Wellsboro. For details call (570) 724–1926.

Best Baked Goods?

If you live in Montgomery, Alabama; Madras, Oregon; or anywhere in between, Pennsylvania has an effect on your cookies. The packages of saltines, chocolate-chip cookies, and buttered biscuits that you buy near home may be marked REG. PENNA. DEPT. AGRICULTURE even if they were made in Madrid, Spain, or Minneapolis, Minnesota. Why? Because the Pennsylvania Department of Agriculture has the strictest standards in the country for packaged baked goods. The department inspects all Pennsylvania bakeries and requires copies of inspection reports for out-of-state and out-of-country bakeries that want to sell to Pennsylvanians. REG. PENNA. DEPT. AGRICULTURE indicates to oatmeal-cookie lovers everywhere that the package comes from a sanitary, safe facility.

year and sells it only on the premises. We average over 36,000 barrels a year, and we distribute it in Pennsylvania and Ohio. So it's okay to call us 'one of the smallest.'" Bottoms up. Straub produces beer made of water, malt, grains, and hops; no sugar, syrup, or additives. The *Connoisseur's Guide to Beer* named Straub's one of the five best-tasting beers in the country. The company distributes only within a 150-mile radius, which means that to taste the beer, you must either visit the area or convince a friend to send you a six-pack. St. Marys is where Routes 255 and 120 intersect. Hours are Monday through Friday 9:00 A.M. to noon for free tours and free tastings from Straub's "eternal tap." Be a good guest—wash out your own glass at the sink. To be sure you catch the brewery in operation, call (814) 834–2875 and hope to be placed on hold: The recording plays the sound of a tinkling brook, a subtle reminder of the all-fresh ingredients. Visit the Web site at www.straubbeer.com.

trivia

Pennsylvania has the nation's fourth-largest highway system— more than 44,000 miles of highways under state control. And the Keystone State has the eighth-highest count of highway miles— nearly 119,000 miles. Bottom line: It's real easy to get around.

If you want to see something strikingly singular, head to Route 555, and keep your eyes peeled for elk. The 700-head herd of wild, free-roaming elk is one of the largest in the East. The St. Marys airport and the village of Benezette are prime viewing spots.

Elk are huge in Pennsylvania these days. Actually, they're always huge— bulls weigh nearly a ton, with antlers up to 5 feet long. But this state is big on the prospect of big game, and the herd roaming Elk County provides a target of opportunity for both tourists who stay at a safe distance and hunters who dream of getting close enough for a shot. Elk don't outnumber people here—yet. But their population boom over the past twenty years has brought a steady increase in fall visitors. (In summer, elk, like humans, try to stay in the shade.)

Above the tiny village of Benezette (population 237), the state-built viewing area at **Winslow Hill** overlooks meadows and magnificent hillsides. When fall colors explode through the Allegheny Mountains, the elk graze, gallop, and occasionally clash during the annual rut. The unearthly mating call of the bull elk is called a bugle. It sounds like a cross between a hyena's cry and a rusty hinge, and it is eerie and absolutely unmistakable. Making their most predictable appearances at dawn and dusk, the elk are the subject of a video at the Winslow Hill amphitheater that boasts of the state's success in reintroducing the animals.

Elk were hunted here until 1931, when they became protected by law. By the mid-1970s, their numbers had dwindled to only thirty-eight.

trivia

Pennsylvania was the first state to issue "vanity," or personalized, license plates—in 1931.

Ski Areas off the Beaten Path

Of the twenty-five areas listed in the *White Book of Skiing,* here are the seven smallest, each with less than 500 feet vertical drop.

Blue Marsh,
Bernville;
(610) 488–7412;
www.skibluemarsh.com

Crystal Lake,
Hughesville;
(570) 584–2698;
www.crystallakeskicenter.com

Mountain View,
Cambridge Springs;
(814) 734–1641;
www.skimtview.org

Mount Tone,
Lake Como;
(800) 747–2754;
www.mttone.com

Mystic Mountain,
Farmington;
(724) 329–8555 or (800) 422–2736;
www.nemacolin.com

Split Rock Resort,
Lake Harmony;
(800) 255–ROCK;
www.splitrockresort.com

Tussey Mountain,
Boalsburg;
(814) 466–6266 or (800) 733–2754;
www.tusseymountain.com

In the intervening years, north-central Pennsylvania dug deep into its hills for coal and lumber (HOUSE COAL: HARD OR SOFT signs still line the main road). But when those economic engines sputtered, a new one emerged. It turned out to be the elk. Coal strip mines, replanted with tasty grasses, provided a habitat that allowed elk to thrive. Ditto clearcut forest, streams, and farms, all of which dot the local hills. The state lent encouragement by sowing food plots and cleaning polluted streams. The resulting rebound gave Elk County its signature attraction.

It may seem a contradiction that the state now allows fall hunts to thin the herd, but hunters are thrilled at the prospect. (The viewing area around Winslow Hill is, of course, a no-hunting zone.) When the state announced its first lottery for thirty elk licenses in 2001, nearly 51,000 people leapt at the chance. The winning chances (one elk per license) are announced at Elk Expo, a fall weekend festival. For details contact Northwest Pennsylvania's Great Outdoors Visitors Bureau at (800) 348–9393; www.pagreatoutdoors.com.

Frenchville used to be a place where you could go to *parler français,* but no longer. Mary Kay Royer, a seventh-generation Frenchviller, tells the story. Early in the 1800s a Philadelphia lawyer acquired a tract of land in upstate Pennsylvania. He advertised it in French newspapers at the bargain rate of twelve acres free with each fifty paid. And he found buyers. "You'll notice," says Royer, "that everyone came from within about 20 miles of one another, from Normandy and Picardy in France." Men pioneered, she says, apparently walking overland from the ports of Baltimore and New York. When they signed their purchase agreements, they didn't understand that they were buying isolated land inaccessible by normal transport. Clearfield, which was just developing, was the closest town, and Bellefonte was next closest—yet neither of those was (or is) a thriving metropolis. Eventually the men sent home for their families.

In this isolated area, settled in 1832, people farmed, mined, and worked on the developing railroads. They stuck together, speaking French among themselves and mastering the smidgen of English necessary to communicate with outsiders. Even the inscriptions on tombstones are in French, though misspelled and grammatically incorrect. As new inventions came along—automobile, radio, television—the villagers incorporated English words into their speech. The few people in Frenchville who are still fluent in French speak a classically pure French, without an American accent and *sans* the slang of contemporary French streets. But few French-speakers remain. Royer's father spoke French at home as a child but was prohibited from speaking it once he got to school, as were others of his generation. He's lost the French he once knew. Royer's parents grew up in Frenchville—"almost everybody is related somehow. And we don't get many newcomers. You can live here ten years and still be the new person on the block."

The village of several hundred people hides in a pocket of hills and rugged woodlands in Clearfield County. The trip over pitted blacktop roads winds through the remains of played-out strip mines, some of them growing scraggly conifers planted as part of reclamation projects. The heart of the community, as always, is St. Mary's Church, a parish established in 1840. Its first home was a log cabin, where the cemetery now stands. The current building, of native hand-cut stone, was occupied in 1870, the year the town's picnic originated. It was a ceremony of thanks for the construction of the church, and it continues annually, during the third weekend in July, in recognition of that heritage. For more information about Frenchville, St. Mary's, or the Frenchville picnic, e-mail rectory@iqnetsys.net, or phone the rectory at (814) 263–4354.

Places to Stay in North Central Pennsylvania

COUDERSPORT

Potato City Country Inn,
3084 East Second Street;
(814) 274–7133;
fax (814) 274–7135;
www.potatocity.com

RIDGWAY

Towers Victorian Inn,
330 South Street;
(814) 772–7657;
www.ncentral.com/~towers

ST. MARYS

Towne House Inn,
138 Center Street;
(814) 781–1556;
www.pagreatoutdoors.com/townehouse/

WELLSBORO

Coach Stop Inn,
Route 6 West;
(570) 724–5361 or
(800) 829–4130;
fax (570) 724–7773;
www.thecoachstopinn.com

Penn Wells Lodge and Hotel,
62 Main Street;
(570) 724–2111;
www.pennwells.com.
Modern facilities or an old-fashioned country inn.

Places to Eat in North Central Pennsylvania

BRADFORD TOWNSHIP

Glendorn,
1000 Glendorn Drive;
(814) 362–6511;
www.glendorn.com.
Gourmet dining at a 1,200-acre estate that welcomes overnight guests.

ST. MARYS

Station Inn,
322 Depot Street;
(814) 834–1010

WELLSBORO

Antlers,
Route 6 West;
(814) 435–6300

Log Cabin,
Route 6;
(814) 435–8808

Steak House,
27 Main Street;
(570) 724–9092.
Dinner only; closed Sunday.

WILLIAMSPORT

Bullfrog Brewery,
231 West Fourth Street;
(570) 326–4700;
www.bullfrogbrewery.com

Northeastern Pennsylvania: Pocono Mountains and Endless Mountains

You could start a visit to northeastern Pennsylvania in **Promised Land State Park**. But really, wouldn't it be more appropriate to end it there? And it won't take forty years to wind your way through this region of mountains and gorges, with breathtaking panoramas above and plenty of anthracite below. The region's two major roads, Interstate 80 and 81, can get you from point to point fairly easily. When you reach water—the Susquehanna, Lehigh, or Delaware Rivers—stop and enjoy the view.

Hard-Coal Country

To understand northeastern Pennsylvania, you need to understand coal mining. Legend says that in 1791 in the quiet village of Summit Hill, in western Carbon County, Pennsylvania, a major discovery altered American history. While tracking game, a hardy backwoodsman named Philip Ginder accidentally kicked a piece of shiny black rock. He pocketed the stone and took it to Revolutionary War veteran Colonel Jacob Weiss, who took it to his colleagues in Philadelphia. Turns out, Ginder had discovered anthracite coal, often called "black diamonds" because of its value in the marketplace.

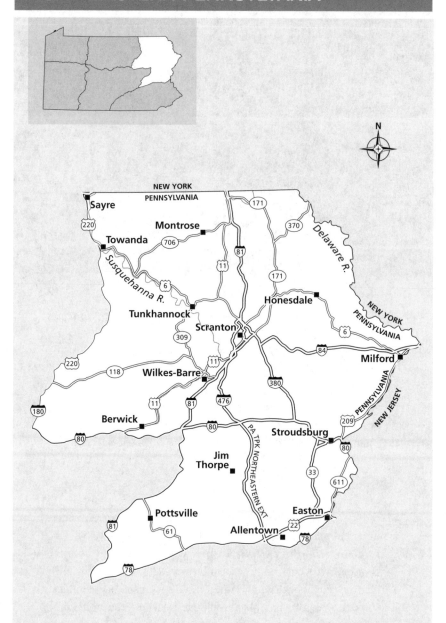

N

NEW YORK
PENNSYLVANIA

Sayre

220

Montrose

Towanda

706

171

370

Delaware R.

81

11

6

Susquehanna R.

171

Honesdale

Tunkhannock

Scranton

309

11

309

NEW YORK
PENNSYLVANIA

6

84

Milford

220

118

Wilkes-Barre

380

PENNSYLVANIA

NEW JERSEY

180

11

81

476

Berwick

80

PA. TPK NORTHEASTERN EXT.

209

Stroudsburg

80

Jim
Thorpe

33

611

81

Pottsville

61

Allentown

22

Easton

78

78

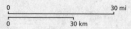

0   30 mi

0   30 km

As you probably learned in elementary school, coal is a fuel substance composed of plant material. You can inspect primitive forms of coal if you fail to rake leaves in your backyard for a few thousand years. The two primary types of coal are anthracite, or hard coal, and bituminous, or soft coal. Anthracite is more valuable because it has more carbon content and less moisture, thus it burns cleaner.

In the coal region some stretches of roadway through the hills are lovely, though the landscape has been marred by mining. The working mines aren't especially aesthetically pleasing, but the area is historically rich in details that let us see how people there used to live and work.

Nowhere is the legacy of coal mining more obvious than in Scranton. In downtown Scranton, on Cedar Avenue between Lackawanna Avenue and Moosic Street, the *Pennsylvania Anthracite Heritage Museum* describes the lives and work of the ethnic communities in the region. Exhibits survey activities related to canals, railroads, silk mills, factories, and, of course, coal. The museum is on Bald Mountain Road in McDade Park. Take the North Scranton Expressway to the Keyser Avenue exit. Follow Keyser Avenue and signs to McDade Park. The museum is open year-round, 9:00 A.M. to 5:00 P.M. Monday through Saturday and noon to 5:00 P.M. Sunday; closed major holidays. Admission is $4.00 per adult. Call (570) 963–4804 for details.

Also for viewing at the museum complex are the *Scranton Iron Furnaces,* open daily from 8:00 A.M. to dusk. These four huge blast-furnace stacks, built by the Scranton brothers between 1841 and 1857, are remnants of the iron industry around which Scranton grew, with coal mining and railroads falling into place as companion industries. Admission is free.

AUTHOR'S TOP TEN FAVORITES IN NORTHEASTERN PENNSYLVANIA

Blue Mountain Sports	Jim Thorpe
Boulder Field at Hickory Run State Park	Mountainhome Diner
	Roebling Bridge
Delaware Water Gap National Recreation Area	Ryah House
French Azilum	Upper Mill
Inn at Jim Thorpe	

McDade Park has picnic tables and barbecues, so you can grab a bite before going on to the **Lackawanna Coal Mine** tour, which begins next to the Heritage Museum. The tour takes you down into an abandoned slope mine to see what the miners did and what conditions were like. An electrical-powered coal car lowers you from the loading platform to the mine interior. The big yellow car and hoist were designed especially for this purpose.

Inside the mine a retired miner or teacher takes you on a 600-foot tour along a wooden walkway, explaining the sights and answering questions. In the spacious underground area, mannequins in mining clothes and a life-size stuffed mule seem to say "Hi." Although the mine isn't really dirty, it *is* underground, and coal can leave its marks, so consider blue jeans and walking shoes. The hour-long tours leave hourly, more frequently during busy times. More exhibits and artifacts are housed aboveground in a building called Shifting Shanty. From April through November, tours begin at 10:00 A.M.; the last tour leaves at 4:00 P.M. Admission is $7.00. Call (570) 963–6463 or (800) 238–7245, or visit www.nvds.com/coalmine.html.

Within walking distance of the mine is the **Steamtown National Historic Site,** the only place in the national park system that tells the story of steam railroading. The Steamtown Yard is open to the public. Visit the museum, which showcases coal-fired steam locomotives, restored cabooses, freight cars, and railroad coaches, offering a nostalgic journey to a period in American history when industry was on the move. The sights, sounds, smells, and even tastes of that era are brought to life in the presence of some of the most powerful machines ever built. It's located in the original Delaware, Lackawanna & Western Railroad Yard, which operated continuously from 1851 to 1963. The site boasts active locomotive and restoration shops, and a complex that includes a visitor center, history and technology museums, a 250-seat theater, and an operating roundhouse and turntable—the device that was invented to let trains turn around and start over again in the other direction. It's open daily except Thanksgiving, Christmas, and New Year's Day. While you're here, ride the steam train, a scenic, two-hour, 26-mile round-trip to Moscow and back. (That's Moscow, Pennsylvania.) Reserve ahead for the trains, which run from late May until late October. The park is open daily from 9:00 A.M. to 5:00 P.M. (9:00 A.M. to 6:00 P.M. during the excursion season). Adults pay $6.00 for the museum and $15.00 for the train. Although the entrance to the park is on Lackawanna Avenue, the mailing address is 150 South Washington Avenue, Scranton 18503. For more details visit www.nps.gov/stea/; call (570) 340–5200 or (888) 693–9391; TDD (telecommunications device for the deaf) (570) 340–5207.

Magician Harry Houdini performed in Scranton, where the **Houdini Museum** (1433 North Main) honors his memory. Ehrich (or Erik) Weiss (or

Weisz)—who, abracadabra, became Harry Houdini—was born in 1874 in Budapest and moved to the United States when he was four. He lived for years in Appleton, Wisconsin, of which he later said: "The greatest escape I ever made was when I left Appleton." In 1918, at the Hippodrome in New York City, Houdini first made an elephant disappear on stage. He performed underwater stunts, for which he practiced by holding his breath in the bathtub. In the museum you'll see Houdini's explanation of how he escaped from the incredible predicaments in which he put himself: "My brain is the key that sets me free." Since his parents spoke Yiddish, Hungarian, and German, his brain was probably also the key that taught him English.

The Houdini Museum also catalogs the history of Scranton and its coal and railroading industries. One exhibit, for instance, says that the Lackawanna Railroad created the image of Phoebe Snow, a delicate woman in a white dress, to foster the idea that riding coal-run trains was a clean event, hence the white dress. "Nothing could be further from the truth," it says. The old steam engines blew soot onto passengers riding the trains with open windows on warm days. Call (570) 342–5555, or go to www.houdini.org.

Near Scranton is the ***Dorflinger-Suydam Wildlife Sanctuary,*** a 600-acre nature preserve and unique museum. The Dorflinger family manufactured glass until the 1920s, and eight U.S. presidents owned some of it. Today the museum of cut glass is open mid-May through October, 10:00 A.M. to 4:00 P.M. Wednesday through Saturday and 1:00 to 4:00 P.M. Sunday. On summer weekends the Wildflower Music Festival hosts open-air concerts. It's located on Route 6, midway between Hawley and Honesdale; the town is called White Mills, and the location is the intersection of Long Ridge Road and Elizabeth Street. Write to P.O. Box 356, White Mills 18473; call (570) 253–1185; or go to www.dorflinger.org for more information.

Harry Houdini, Skeptic

Despite the annual Halloween seances in which people have tried to communicate with the ghost of Harry Houdini, the magician's spirit has been a no-show—perhaps not surprising for a man who delighted in exposing charlatans and fake mediums. After ten years of trying, Houdini's wife, Bess, wasn't concerned. She wrote to friends that Houdini's permanent eternal silence "struck a mighty worldwide blow at superstition."

Ricketts Glen

Knowledgeable outdoorspeople consider **Ricketts Glen** the most spectacular of Pennsylvania's state parks. Its more than 13,000 acres of mountains, streams, waterfalls, and lakes spread through Sullivan, Columbia, and Luzerne Counties. The glen has twenty-two named waterfalls and a virgin hemlock forest with trees more than 500 years old. The only activity permitted in the natural area is walking. No picnics, campfires, camping, mountain biking, whining, or picking wildflowers. Just hiking. You'll find bass, a swimming beach, and a summer-only concession stand on Lake Jean. The park has 23 miles of hiking trails, some strictly for the physically fit and some shorter loops that are less strenuous. The Falls Trail along the gorge gives you a view of all the falls in the glen and is breathtakingly close to the edge. It is possible to find deserted hiking trails almost any time and wander into the woods feeling that you're the only person in the forest primeval.

The hills are alive with the sound of RVs. You can rent cabins at Ricketts Glen (though not in the natural areas), and the park has good camping for recreational vehicles and tents. Reservations are mandatory for overnight visits, especially during high season, which often lasts through October. Drive to Ricketts Glen via Route 487 or Route 118 north, depending on which side of the park you wish to enter. The grade is so steep that large vehicles should take Route 220, then turn north on Route 487 at Dushore. The park phone number is (570) 477–5675.

Working Valleys

From Scranton you can get to Hazleton quickly on I–81 or cross over to Route 11 and drive down along the Susquehanna River. From about Wilkes-Barre the drive becomes especially hilly in the narrow river valley. Almost any time you tire of it, you can pick up a short road back to the interstate to Hazleton, another formerly thriving coal burgh that was founded in 1837. Whether you follow the highway or your own way, you'll pass some little river towns—not the picturesque, renovated towns of slick decorating magazines, but real working towns inhabited by laboring folks. You may still see women wearing babushkas (head scarves), kids scuffing their shoes on the sidewalks, and town merchants sitting in front of their stores during idle moments.

Yuengling Brewery, in Pottsville, started brewing in 1829. During Prohibition the factory switched to nonalcoholic items—ice cream and dairy products. Four daughters in the fifth generation of Yuenglings (pronounced ying-LING) now run the firm.

The writer John O'Hara, who lived at 606 Mahatongo Street from 1916 to 1928, set some of his major works in Pottsville.

Nine miles east of Hazleton, the **Eckley Miners' Village** gives you a chance to visit a spot that is part historic site and part living community. It is authentic, not because it has been re-created, but because it has never changed—the black silt heaps, open strip mines, and slag are ever present. Eckley was a company town from its settlement in 1854 until 1971 and is now administered by the Pennsylvania Historical and Museum Commission. Its population of retired miners, widows, and children has dwindled to about fifteen. The village, covering a hundred acres, is off Route 940. Follow the signs to the site, which is open Monday through Saturday 9:00 A.M. to 5:00 P.M. and noon to 5:00 P.M. Sunday. It is closed holidays except Memorial Day, Independence Day, and Labor Day. Admission is $4.00 per adult. For more information write to the village at RR 2, Box 236, Weatherly 18255; call (570) 636–2070; or go to www.phmc.state.pa.us/bhsm/toh/eckley/eckley.asp.

Another coal locale is the **Pioneer Tunnel Coal Mine** in Ashland. The tunnel follows an anthracite vein that is nearly 200 feet thick in some places (huge by mining standards). You can take a half-hour tour ($8.00 per adult) in an open coal car pulled by a battery-powered mine motor. Another half-hour train tour ($5.50 per adult) goes around the outside of the mountain, not through tunnels. A steam locomotive, called a *lokie,* pulls the train past an open pit mine that was dug close to the surface with steam shovels and a "bootleg hole" where poachers dug out coal. To get to the Pioneer Mine, take Route 61 into Ashland, where it becomes Center Street. Turn left (south) on Twentieth Street and continue for 3 blocks. The mine is open from Memorial Day to Labor Day, 10:00 A.M. to 6:00 P.M. daily. Call (570) 875–3850, or go to www.pioneertunnel.com for hours in April, May, September, and October; closed the rest of the year.

Walk across Higher-Ups Park to the **Anthracite Museum,** featuring a collection of tools, machinery, and photographs showing how anthracite, or hard coal, has been mined from the early pick-and-shovel days to contemporary surface-mining operations. The museum is open from June 1 through August 29, 10:00 A.M. to 6:00 P.M. Wednesday through Sunday; closed the rest of the year. Admission is $3.50. For more information call (570) 875–4708, or write to the museum at Pine and Seventeenth Streets, Ashland 17921.

trivia

The town of Jim Thorpe has gone through several incarnations. At its founding it was known as Coalville. In 1815 it changed its name to Mauch Chunk, the local Native American term for Bear Mountain. Now it's named for one of the United States' greatest athletes.

Check out Nesquahoning, a mining town on Route 209, southeast of Hazleton. Nesquahoning is built on hills so steep that nothing seems level. Driving slowly, you can peek through a barbershop window to glimpse an elderly gentleman getting a haircut. In front of the homes, flowers spill from their beds over cement walls toward the sidewalk. In backyards women hang laundry to dry on clotheslines. Then you're through town, and signs usher you down the mountain into Jim Thorpe.

Little Switzerland

Until about 1950 Mauch Chunk was another Pennsylvania mining town whose economy fluctuated with the coal market, where miners lived in uncertainty and millionaires lived in mansions. Trying to survive, citizens of Mauch (rhymes with "hawk") Chunk and East Mauch Chunk donated a nickel a week to an economic development fund. In 1954 the towns merged and became *Jim Thorpe.* If you love small towns, you'll love Jim Thorpe.

Mauch Chunk's history is synonymous with coal mining and railway transport. Josiah White, a self-taught civil engineer and founder of the Lehigh Coal & Navigation Company, designed and invented a device to schlep his coal to his canal. He contrived the switchback railroad, which followed the Delaware Canal to Philadelphia and the Morris Canal to New York City, and

"Thanks, King"

Controversy in the Olympics didn't start with murder in Munich or bribery in Salt Lake City. In 1912 in Stockholm, Sweden, Jim Thorpe, a Native American from Oklahoma, won gold medals in the pentathlon and decathlon. King Gustav V, presenting the medals to the twenty-four-year-old, said, "You, sir, are the greatest athlete in the world," to which Thorpe replied, "Thanks, King." When the International Olympic Committee (IOC) learned that Thorpe had earlier played semipro baseball, earning $2.00 a game, it demanded that he return his trophies, which he did. He later played baseball for the New York Giants, Cincinnati Reds, and Boston Braves and football for the New York Giants and other teams. After retiring from professional sports, Thorpe played bit parts in several Hollywood movies. When he died of cancer, penniless, in 1953, Oklahoma refused to build him a monument, so his widow started looking for a place where her hero husband could be buried with honor. She found Mauch Chunk and East Mauch Chunk, which voted to consolidate their communities as Jim Thorpe Borough. In 1982 the IOC reinstated Thorpe's amateur status and gave his family replicas of his gold medals. Thorpe's grave is on Route 903.

Bike the Gorge

Want to enjoy world-class white water without getting wet? Bike the Lehigh Valley Gorge Trail, a 25-mile level path from Jim Thorpe to White Haven. This traffic-free rails-to-trails experience hugs the Lehigh River shoreline the whole way. Roaring rapids, breathtaking scenery. River outfitters at the trailheads in White Haven, Rockport, and Jim Thorpe can supply fat-tire bikes and shuttle services. Get the details at www.800poconos.com or (800) 762–6667.

which jokers refer to as the first roller coaster. The 9-mile Gravity Road was completed in 1827; ten wagons, each carrying one and a half tons of coal, traveled down Summit Hill powered entirely by gravity. Mules pulled the empty cars up the incline, then got a free ride down. After the demand for coal diminished, the train was used by tourists.

trivia

In Mauch Chunk, now Jim Thorpe, miners in 1913 earned 23 cents an hour.

Driving down the highway into the heart of Jim Thorpe, you quickly realize why locals call their home Little Switzerland. Park in a public lot (or at a meter, where a quarter still buys an hour) to explore the narrow, winding streets on foot. This area at the foot of the hills is Hazard Square. It quickly becomes obvious how it got its name. Drive and walk defensively.

On the square, in the *Jim Thorpe Railroad Station,* you can buy tickets for rides on diesel-powered locomotive trains through the mountains to Old Penn Haven, round-trip, in spring and summer. During the autumn foliage season, trips of nearly three hours to Haucks and back leave twice a day. Tickets for the short trip are under $6.00, for the longer trip about $11.00. For complete schedules and rates, contact the Lehigh Gorge Scenic Railway at www.lgsry .com or (570) 325–8485.

Across the square from the station, you see the *Hooven Mercantile Company.* On the first floor, specialty shops laid out in emporium fashion, without partitions, feature coal jewelry, dolls, decorated eggs, and various other craft items and supplies. Upstairs is the *Old Mauch Chunk Scale Model Railroad HO Display,* a train-lover's exposition with thirteen model trains that pull cars over more than a thousand feet of track. Hours vary seasonally, so call ahead (570–325–2248). Admission is $3.00 per adult.

Drive up the hill on Route 209 to tour the *Asa Packer Mansion,* providing a dramatic contrast to the cabins of Eckley Miner's Village near Hazleton.

Engineering, a Team Sport

Lehigh University, founded by Asa Packer in 1865, prides itself on its excellent engineering department, so much so that its sports teams were nicknamed The Engineers. But in 1996, the school mascot became the Mountain Hawk. The school still uses the nicknames "Brown and White" and "Engineers" about teams of the past but uses the winged nickname in the present. Lehigh has the longest-running rivalry in college football with Lafayette College, in nearby Easton; the teams have clashed annually for 140 years.

Asa Packer is said to have worked his way from humble beginnings to become the founder and president of Lehigh Valley Railroad, founder of Lehigh University, and a philanthropist on a grand scale. In 1860 European craftsmen built the Victorian home, lavishly decorated and furnished in mid-nineteenth-century opulence. It stands today as it did when the Packers celebrated their fiftieth wedding anniversary, preserved rather than restored. Among the outstanding pieces is the first-prize gas chandelier of the 1876 Centennial Exposition in Philadelphia. Producers of the film *Gone With the Wind* wanted to use the chandelier. "Frankly, my dear, no way," was the response, so the movie moguls made a perfect copy. You'll find collections of carved walnut furniture, paintings, sculpture, crystal, and china. Hours are 11:00 A.M. to 4:15 P.M. daily, June through October; weekends only, April, May, November, and December. Modest admission fee. Write to P.O. Box 108, Jim Thorpe 18229, or call (570) 325–3229 for more details.

strange as it sounds

Of the twenty-six millionaires living in the United States before World War II, thirteen had homes in Mauch Chunk.

Asa gave his son, Harry, the brick-and-stone Second Empire–style mansion next door as a wedding gift. This house is lavish, too, with hand-decorated ceilings and Victorian antiques, including some pieces that belonged to the Packer family. The **Harry Packer Mansion** (Packer Hill) operates as a bed-and-breakfast inn, with thirteen rooms. The mansion has mystery weekends and sometimes turns over the entire establishment to special celebrations, so be sure to call ahead. Write to P.O. Box 458, Jim Thorpe 18229, visit www.murdermansion.com, or call (570) 325–8566.

One block south of Broadway, Race Street winds along the path once taken by a millrace and passes old buildings, more specialty shops, and the stretch of stone facades called Stone Row, built by Asa Packer in 1848. Today longtime residents and shopkeepers live side by side with newly arrived artists and writers.

Don't miss **St. Mark's Episcopal Church** at 21 Race Street, considered one of the most notable late Gothic Revival churches in Pennsylvania. It was built in 1869 by Richard Upjohn, the architect who was responsible for the Third Trinity Church of New York City. St. Mark's is laid out in the form of a Latin cross, with an altar of white Italian marble, Minton tile floors, and two Tiffany windows. The reredos (which is the partition behind the altar), made of Caen stone, is a memorial to Asa Packer. Half-hour tours are held daily by appointment. A $3.00 donation per adult is requested. Call (570) 325–2241, or visit www.stmarkandjohn.org for more information.

While Jim Thorpe is a historian's heaven, it's also a sportsperson's paradise. The 100-mile-long Lehigh River runs right past it. Hiking and biking trails attract athletes from hundreds of miles away. Of the several outfitters in Jim Thorpe, you can't do better than **Blue Mountain Sports** (34 Susquehanna Street). Of course, owners Tom and Elissa Marsden sell clothes and equipment and rent kayaks and mountain bikes, but they do more: They know and love the area, and they talk, as long as you wish, about the best paths and routes for your particular preferences. Visit their Web site at www.bikejimthorpe.com, or call (570) 325–4421 or (800) 599–4421.

For more information about the town, call the tourist center toll-free at (888) 546–8467, or visit www.visitjimthorpe.com.

Just outside of Jim Thorpe, overlooking Route 209 at the base of Mount Pisgah, is a memorial plaque on a large rock where the village of Northern Liberties used to be. In 1861 virtually all the village males between the ages

Bitter Memories: The Molly Maguires

In the late 1870s a group of men were hanged in the Mauch Chunk Jail (now the Old Jail Museum in Jim Thorpe) for murdering two mine bosses. The men were members of a group called the Molly Maguires, Irish immigrants who fled the famine and found a dismal existence in the mines of northeastern Pennsylvania. Poor pay and rotten working conditions led to a strike, which led to management's hiring a spy, which led to long-term controversy. Before the trial, which the coal companies financed, all newspaper reports called the men killers. See Sean Connery and Richard Harris in the movie *The Molly Maguires,* and decide for yourself the guilt or innocence of the executed men.

of sixteen and twenty-six volunteered to serve the Union in the Civil War; their wholesale death effectively destroyed the village by killing off its reproductive population. All that remains is the plaque memorializing the soldiers.

Consider **Country Junction** a transition from the old world into the new. Country Junction may or may not be the world's largest general store, as it claims, but once you sing a few tunes with the life-size statues of the Blues Brothers and have a conversation with the parrot, you won't care. It's a hoot, this rural version of a shopping mall. Buy a wall plaque that says I FISH, THEREFORE I LIE. Pick up potted plants, plaid pillows, or purple paint. Look at lawn ornaments, lumber, and lightbulbs. Country Junction is open seven days a week; Route 209 in Lehighton, 4 miles west of I–476. Call (610) 377–5050.

peeps!

Peeps, the fluffy, nutrient-free marshmallow candy chicks that nest in Easter baskets all over the country, are produced by the Rodda Candy Company in Bethlehem. The company makes 1.5 million of the little guys each year. Emory University researchers subjected Peeps to a number of experiments several years back, testing their resilience in ovens, vacuum chambers, liquid nitrogen, and more. See the results online at www.peepresearch.org.

Head down Route 209 to Route 33 for a respite from anthracite memories in two famous towns: Nazareth and Bethlehem. These namesakes of biblical cities are blessed with charm.

In Nazareth a folk landmark strikes a chord: the **Martin Guitar Company.** David Crosby and Joan Baez are two of the many famous musicians who insist on this brand, made locally since 1839. (Elvis Presley loved Martins, too.) The firm also used to manufacture banjos, ukuleles, and mandolins but now concentrates on its premier acoustic product. Take a free one-hour guided tour weekdays starting at 1:00 P.M. The factory, museum, and store are located at 510 Sycamore Street (a great all-American name). Call (610) 759–2837, or visit www.martin guitar.com.

In Bethlehem, a thriving city of 72,000 that shares a metro area with Allentown, you'll find living history. Settled by Protestant Moravians in 1741, the city is still home to many members of that faith, which predated Anglicanism by a hundred years. Its famous multipointed star, called Moravian, is today a symbol of the town.

Shoppers love Bethlehem's Main Street, a nineteenth-century gem with welcoming sidewalks and Victorian storefronts. Its famous **Moravian Bookshop,** founded in 1745, claims to be the oldest bookstore in the world; some of its proceeds still go to support church charities. Over the years it has grown to encompass food items, a delicatessen, gifts (including Moravian stars of all sorts), and music. It's open seven days a week at 428 Main Street (610–866–5481), or shop online at www.moravianstar.com.

Shining just down the block, at 564 Main Street, is the **Sun Inn,** the place to see and be seen for nearly 250 years. It hosted Revolutionary War heroes in the 1770s; in 1792 fifty-one chiefs and warriors of the Six Nations Confederation, including Red Jacket, Corn Planter, and Osiquette, lodged at the inn on their way to Philadelphia to meet President Washington. Guided tours and fine dining are offered daily Tuesday through Saturday (there's a gift shop, too). For reservations call (610) 974–9451, or visit www.suninnbethlehem.org.

In an eighteenth-century log home, the **Moravian Museum** (66 West Church Street; 610–867–0173) offers twelve exhibit rooms. It's run by the Historic Bethlehem Partnership, which also operates five other period properties in town. For details check www.historicbethlehem.org.

How much is that doggie in the window? At **Pott's Doggie Shop** (known fondly as Pottsie's), 114 West Fairview Street (610–865–6644), a great hot dog costs just over a buck. Get all-American takeout here.

As you might guess, Christmas celebrations are a big draw in this town—with stars everywhere, Christmas markets, arts events, and music by the city's famous Bach Choir. Get the full holiday lineup from the convention and visitor bureau at (800) 747–0561, or visit www.lehighvalleypa.org.

The Poconos

The Pocono Mountains, northern foothills of the Appalachian Range, are diminutive when compared with the Rockies—but they're right here, within easy reach of the Boston-to-Washington (Bos-Wash) corridor and its multitudes. The highest Pocono—the impressively named Mount Ararat, in Preston, Wayne County—towers 2,654 feet above sea level. Not high enough to give you altitude sickness, it can, however, promote a natural high. Best known for honeymoon hideaways, the Poconos also offer welcome respite from flatland woes. City dwellers, mostly from Pennsylvania, New Jersey, and New York, find that looking up at the tall evergreen and deciduous trees, looking out over serene ponds and lakes, and looking inward with pleasure bring immense peace and relaxation. Even those who jokingly call the Poconos "the Pinocchios" aren't lying when they say how much they enjoy the local mountains.

To see some of the lesser-known parts of the Poconos, take Route 33 out of Nazareth and join Route 209 at Sciota. In its time Route 209 was a major highway, important enough for its construction to displace homes, cemeteries, and prize stands of sugar maples. This route has lost much tourist traffic to interstates; here and there you still see a failed group of tourist cabins predating today's motels or an abandoned gas station with weeds growing through the macadam. These properties might be good investments for people who can afford to wait for a return, because I–80 often resembles a parking area for trucks hauling double trailers up the mountains. One can imagine traffic returning to Route 209 in sheer desperation. By today's standards it's narrow and slow due to the steep hills and curves, but the surface is in fairly good condition, trucks pull over to let traffic pass, and most of the countryside is lovely. Even where it's not beautiful, it's interesting. Traveling south, this highway skirts Lehighton.

In Lehighton most folks speak in Pennsylvania Dutch accents; many have lived here all their lives, as have their parents, grandparents, and even great-grandparents.

Continue north on Route 209, then turn right (south) on Old Route 115. Turn left on Lower Cherry Valley Road, and follow the signs into the ***Cherry Valley Vineyards,*** a friendly little winery run by the Sorrenti family. (From Route 33 take the Saylorsburg exit, then Old Route 115 south, and follow the signs.) The Sorrentis produce a limited amount of chardonnay that they say has a "dry, delicate, incredibly wonderful balance" plus a dry champagne and several fruity, semidry wines. The winery is open seven days a week from 10:00 A.M. to 6:00 P.M. for tastings and sales. Tours, which include information about the wine's fermentation, filtering, and bottling processes, are led weekends from 1:00 to 5:00 P.M., March through December. For more information write to the vineyard at RR 5, Box 5100, Saylorsburg 18353; call (570) 992–2255; or visit www.cherryvalleyvineyards.com.

A quick jog back on Route 33 north takes you to Snydersville, which isn't much more than a gas station, a school bus stop, and antiques dealers in old homes. The names and proprietors may change, but this remains a good area for antiquing—the dealers are knowledgeable but not in the thick of the tourist stream.

At Snydersville pick up Business Route 209 (paralleling the four-lane Route 209) going south. Turn right on Hickory Valley Road and follow the signs to ***Quiet Valley Living Historical Farm.*** (If you start in Stroudsburg, take Business Route 209 north, turn left on Hickory Valley Road, and follow the signs.) Alice and Wendell Wicks, with their daughter and son-in-law, Sue and Gary Oiler, saw the possibilities for this centuries-old Pennsylvania German farm. The Wicks and the Oilers have invested work, time, and money in researching, repairing, and collecting furnishings and farm equipment. In 1963 they opened Quiet Valley as a living museum, showing how the original Pennsylvania Dutch family lived on this virtually self-sufficient homestead from about 1770 to 1913. The families restored the existing buildings to full function and reconstructed others that would have been there; for a while the Oilers lived in the top floor of the home. "We don't own it anymore," says Sue Oiler. "It's now a private, nonprofit organization. My home is in the middle of a nonprofit farm. In my head I know it's not really mine, but in my heart I care for it and love it as if it were."

Using costumed area residents as role-players, Quiet Valley takes you through the daily routines and seasonal activities of the colonial family. One of the most interesting parts of the tour is the earthen-floored cellar kitchen in the main building. At first the settling family lived entirely in this room, with only the clay-hearth fireplace for heat and cooking. A costumed guide uses the cooking utensils and talks about her "life" as a colonial woman. Outside, kids can pet the animals and jump in the hay, even if they end up a little dirty and itchy. After the tour, consider picnicking in the grove. Quiet Valley is open Tuesday through Saturday, June 20 to Labor Day, 10:00 A.M. to 5:30 P.M. weekdays and 1:00 to 5:30 P.M. Sunday. The last tour begins at 4:00 P.M. Cost is $7.00 per adult. For more information write to Quiet Valley Living Historical Farm, 1000 Turkey Hill Road, Stroudsburg 18360; visit www.quietvalley.org; or call (570) 992–6161.

The Poconos offer options for every imaginable enthusiasm—as well as some unimaginable ones. For most of us, auto racing is a spectator sport, but the 2.5-mile race course **Pocono Raceway** is also home to the **Bertil Roos Racing School.** Go equipped with a driver's license, sneakers, and gloves, and experience handling a standard shift. The raceway provides instruction, race cars, racetracks, colorful driving suits, and helmets. Your instructor will show you when to brake, when to accelerate, how to handle

pennhenge

While "new megalith" may seem like an oxymoron, the ones erected in the late 1970s at **Columcille** (2155 Fox Gap Road, Bangor) are worth a look.

Trying to emulate the peaceful and mystical vibe of the Scottish isle of Iona, the pair of idealists who created this park named it for St. Columba (Colum Cille). The sixth-century founder of a monastic community, he protected the legacy of Celtic Christianity. The Pennsylvania park mimics its giant menhirs and stone circle and includes a meditation pond and an Infinity Gate. As Columcille's Web site explains, it "suggests to all who enter that these are portals into a world of myth and mystery where the veil is thin between the worlds." All quarried locally, the stones are mind-bendingly old: 400 million years at their core.

Catch the ancient energy daily from dawn to dusk at Columcille Megalith Park and Celtic Art Center. It's located 3 miles from Quiet Valley Historical Farm. For more information call (610) 588–1174.

From Tanneries to Tannersville

Whether or not you stop in Tannersville, you'll certainly drive through it. While you're waiting for the traffic light to change, a bit of deep background: Early on, the Lenni-Lenape Indians lived in this valley in the foothills of the Poconos. In about 1750 John Larned bought the land and built a log tavern and two gristmills. Twenty-nine years later General Sullivan and his army, en route to the Wyoming Valley, spent the night in tents next to the tavern. In 1834 Jacob Singmaster built a large tannery, which became the village's main industry and inspired the name change from Larneds to Tannersville. Fire destroyed several tanneries, but innumerable candle shops keep the heat on.

corners, and, presumably, how to pray for safety. Call Roos March through October at (800) 722–3669, or zoom to www.racenow.com. The office is on Route 115 in Blakeslee.

Consider popping into the **Pocono Cheesecake Factory** (Route 611, Swiftwater), where chefs prepare up to a hundred cheesecakes daily. Watch through the giant window as almonds, raspberries, chocolate chips, and liqueurs blend into the dessert of your choice. A drooling visitor recently estimated that she could count 700 springform pans, and she worried who was going to clean them. As you choose between your wallet and your waistline, read the sign: LIFE IS UNCERTAIN. EAT DESSERT FIRST. Call (570) 839–6844 for prices, hours, and calorie counts.

Heading north on Route 611, turn east in Mount Pocono on Route 940, then north on Route 191. Every roll of the tires takes you farther away from civilization. Stop in Cresco to visit the **Theo B. Price Lumber Company,** a singular hardware-and-quilts store with a distinctly downhome flavor. On the street level, with its uneven wood-plank flooring, amid the nails and feed, you can find solutions for problems you didn't know you had—until you see the solutions. Upstairs are hand-sewn and handcrafted goods for the home, the friends, and the soul. Shopkeeper Maryann Miller manages the emporium, started in 1908 by her grandfather Theo, who invented tools and devices for mines. His original cash register, capable of ringing sales as high as $20, sits in the back of the place. Hours are 8:00 A.M. to 5:00 P.M., except Sunday. Call (570) 595–2501, or visit www.theobprice.com.

Eight miles up Route 191, in beautiful downtown LaAnna—wait, you missed downtown—you can visit **Holley Ross Pottery.** Daily from 9:30 A.M. to 5:30 P.M. (Sunday from 1:00 to 5:30 P.M.), you can watch pottery being made and buy Fiestaware and a variety of glass and ceramic items. The pottery showroom is closed December through April. Call (570) 676–3248, or go to www.holley ross.com for details.

Paintball is everywhere in the Poconos. It's not entirely clear what personality type likes paintball, but if you like mayhem, if you love war, paintball is for you. This competitive outdoor "sport" involves balls of water-soluble, biodegradable, nontoxic paint, which you shoot at your friends or enemies. Ride a military troop transport to a mountaintop with a beautiful view—in order to shoot paint. Your $20- to $30-per-person all-day pass entitles you to fifty paintballs, all-you-can-use carbon dioxide as a propellant, and protective headgear and face mask. You can rent a camouflage suit, which might be a good idea since the games are called "attack and defend," "hostile takeover," and "total elimination." Call ahead to reserve a field at **Skirmish** (Route 903, Jim Thorpe; 570–325–3654). There's also **Splatter Paintball Games** at Jack Frost Mountain (Route 940, Blakeslee; 800–468–2442).

For the back-to-nature gang—and even for people who prefer their nature in *National Geographic* specials—**Hickory Run State Park,** especially the **Boulder Field,** is not to be believed and never to be forgotten. This area, now a National Natural Landmark (say that fast three times) has remained essentially unchanged for 20,000 years, give or take. Boulders up to 26 feet long cover an area 400 feet by 1,800 feet, and you're welcome to climb, scramble, or sit on them—if you can. Imagine a dish of 1-inch pebbles, and imagine an ant trying to navigate the terrain. The ground beneath the boulders is totally flat and free of vegetation. Staggering.

Of course, like any self-respecting state park, Hickory Run has trails, campgrounds, and picnic facilities. You may apply for hunting and fishing licenses and try your luck in the park's 15,500 acres. You can swim in summer and snowmobile, cross-country ski, and sled in winter. But what should lure you miles out of your way—and what will indubitably entice you back—is the Boulder Field. Hickory Run is immediately southeast of the intersection of Interstate 476 and I–80, so it's hard to miss if you're in the area. You can write to the park office at State Route 534, White Haven 18661, call (570) 443–0400, or send an e-mail to hickoryrunsp@state.pa.us.

Perhaps you'd like to find the bluebird of happiness while you're in the Poconos? No problem. Take the 53-mile auto tour, with twelve stops and six suggested side trips, that follows John James Audubon's 1829 journey into the forests of the Lehigh River Valley. Audubon is the famed nineteenth-century naturalist who observed, painted, and wrote about birds and other wildlife. He lived in Pennsylvania and traveled extensively throughout the state and the rest of the country. The aim of Audubon's America Program is to help conserve,

Delaware Water Gap

restore, enhance, interpret, and protect natural and cultural resources. From Hickory Run State Park, turn east on Route 534 to Albrightsville; south on Route 903 to Jim Thorpe; west on Route 209, then north on Route 93 to Hudsondale; north on Hudsondale Drive, through Rockport; then back to Hickory Run on Route 534. Or, for kicks, travel counterclockwise. Download a map from www.audubonslehigh.org.

Delaware Water Gap

Here you are close to the ***Delaware Water Gap National Recreation Area,*** which runs along a 40-mile stretch of the Delaware River in New Jersey and Pennsylvania. Publicity calls it "the eighth wonder of the world." The town of Delaware Water Gap marks the southernmost point of the 70,000-acre recreation area, which became federal property in 1965. At the ***Dingmans Falls Visitor Center*** (off Route 209 north of Johnny Bee Road), you'll find park information and a bookstore. A full complement of programs includes a waterfall hike. For more information contact the Dingmans Falls office at (570) 828–2253. Since hours vary seasonally, you might want to visit www.nps.gov/dewa.

Even in the nineteenth century this gap attracted the well-to-do for resort holidays away from the heat. Horse-drawn carriages and rafts transported early visitors until about 1856, when the Delaware and Cobb's Gap Railroad Company opened a track to Scranton. Native Americans called the area Pohoqauline, Pahaqalong, and Pahaqualia (you choose the pronunciation), all of which mean "river passing between two mountains." Its beauty lies partly in the contrasting colors of layers of quartzite, red sandstone, and dark shale that have been revealed as the river carved its path over geologic eons.

With light hiking, you can appreciate the gap close up. Park in the Resort Point parking lot off Route 611, on the Pennsylvania side. Across the road stone steps take you to a trail paralleling a stream that goes up steeply for a short distance, then turns left onto a marked trail. The trail continues gently upward for about a mile; when you get to a waterfall, you can no longer hear the highway traffic. A little farther straight ahead, a large rock outcropping takes your breath away. It's picture-postcard pretty. In this area you can also drive into some well-marked overlooks from which you have a spectacular view without hiking. At one such place a souped-up red Chevrolet once roared in; a couple of teenagers slurping diet colas looked out, said, "There isn't anything here," and roared away. Pushing these types of people over the edge is against park regulations. For complete information on the Delaware Water Gap National Recreation Area, write to the office, River Road, Bushkill 18324, or call (570) 828–2451.

One way to see some of this without driving is to ride the **Delaware Water Gap Trolley.** Guides discuss the history, points of interest, settlers and Indians, and the entire natural splendor of the gap. The trolley operates from late March through November; the depot is on Route 611 at the center of Delaware Water Gap. The cost for adults is $8.00. Call (570) 476–9766.

The **Pocono Indian Museum** on Route 209 shows the history of the Delaware Indians in six rooms of collected artifacts. Some pottery is more than 1,000 years old, and weapons and tools have had only their handles reconstructed. As you look at the exhibits, you can listen to a half-hour recording explaining the displays. The Delaware Indians wore simple deerskin garments, cut their hair short, and wore no feathers, except perhaps for

Eagle Etiquette

"The eagles are getting so friendly," marvels Maria Vernon at the Delaware Water Gap Visitor Center. While they don't actually wave, the birds have gradually become less afraid of humans. But please, don't scare them. To view the dozen or so pairs of bald eagles along the upper Delaware shoreline, the Eagle Institute recommends using the observation blinds at viewing areas to remain hidden from view. Avoid loud noises, and use binoculars instead of moving close to the birds. And plan to do your bird-watching in midwinter—come spring, eagle parents don't want company while they're tending to their newborns (a sentiment most new mothers would share).

Maria recommends the Shohola Recreation Area, off Route 6, as a good viewing spot; Lackawaxen is good, too, she says. Basically, any spot with open, unfrozen water will afford an opportunity for viewing the raptors.

BEST ANNUAL EVENTS IN NORTHEASTERN PENNSYLVANIA

In Lackawaxen local son *Zane Grey's birthday* is cause for a special celebration at his former home and museum the last weekend in January. Call (570) 685–4871 for details.

Sometime in January or February, depending on the weather, you can watch or participate in the *Sleigh Rally* on Route 87 in Forksville. Call (570) 946–4160, or go to www.sullivanpa.com.

Mush! Each February the *Endless Mountains Sled Dog Race* pits the best teams against a 50-mile course outside Forksville. There's a carnival, too. Call the visitor bureau at (800) 769–8999.

The last weekend in April, the *Endless Mountains Maple Festival* takes place in Alparon Park, Route 14, Troy. Call (570) 673–8871 for details.

In May (usually the last two weekends) is the *Farm Animal Frolic,* a time for wee people to touch wee animals. No tours, just hens and chicks, sheep and lambs, pigs and piglets—you get the picture.

$4.00 per person. Quiet Valley Living Historical Farm; call (570) 992–6161, or go to www.quietvalley.org.

Music from the maestro: Each May for more than ninety years, Bethlehem's *Bach Festival* has showcased its famous all-volunteer choir, which has performed at the BBC Proms, the annual London Music Festival. Get the score from www.bach.org, or call (610) 886–4382 or (888) 743–3100.

Strike up the band. The Dorflinger Glass Museum holds eight outdoor (indoors if it rains) summer *concerts,* Saturday evenings at 6:00, from late June through mid-August. Most tickets cost $15 per adult, and most adults think the money is well spent. For reservations call (570) 253–1185, or go to www.dorflinger.org.

Canoe canoe? And camp? Join the *Delaware River Sojourn* the third week of June. This downstream float attracts paddlers for a day or a week. Call (609) 883–9500, or get details at www.state.nj.us./drbc/sojourn.htm.

ceremonies. Nor did they live in tepees. The museum holds a reconstructed house of the kind the Delawares made by lashing together saplings and covering them with strips of elm or oak bark. Another room exhibits artifacts from various western Indian tribes, even a 150-year-old scalp. If that seems a little gory, you can cover your eyes as you pass. The museum and gift shop are open daily 9:00 A.M. to 7:00 P.M. in June, July, and August. The rest of the year they are open 10:00 A.M. to 6:00 P.M. Admission is $5.00 for adults. For more information write to the museum at P.O. Box 261, Bushkill 18324; visit the museum at www.poconoindianmuseum.com; or call (570) 588–9338.

Even more glorious than the creations of any human hand, *Bushkill Falls,* called the Niagara of Pennsylvania, is easy to reach, 2 miles northwest of Route

One Sunday in June you can watch the *Pocono 500* at the Pocono Raceway, one of NASCAR's most competitive tracks. Call the Luzerne County tourism office at (888) 905–2872 or Pocono Raceway at (800) 722–3929.

On a Sunday in July you can watch the *Pennsylvania 500* at Pocono Raceway. Call the Luzerne County tourism office at (888) 905–2872 or Pocono Raceway at (800) 722–3929.

From July 17 to 26 every year, you can attend a *novena* at the Basilica of the Shrine of St. Ann in Scranton. Call (570) 347–5691.

Try the annual *Blueberry Festival* the first week in August in Montrose. Call (570) 278–1881.

In August Pittston holds a *Tomato Festival.* For information call (570) 693–0704, or visit www.pittstontomatofestival.com. Food fight!

In late August Towanda holds its *Riverfest.* Call (570) 265–2696.

For a lot of hot air, take in the *Shawnee Balloon Festival* in mid-October. Call (800) 742–9633 for details.

In autumn a *Harvest Festival* coincides with the weekend of Columbus Day. Since 1975 the festival has demonstrated how to make apple butter and keep bees, among other rural tricks. $6.00 per adult. Quiet Valley Living Historical Farm (570–992–6161; www.quietvalley.org).

A European-style *Christkindlmarkt* with daily outdoor music, food, trees, crafts, and St. Nick marks the holiday season in downtown Bethlehem. Get details at www.christkindlmarkt.org or give them a jingle at (610) 861–0678.

209. Easy walking over rustic bridges and a nature trail of about one and a half miles takes you through virgin forests and past a gorge with a view of eight waterfalls, the largest of which is Bushkill, dropping 100 feet. Even with a simple camera it's possible to take spectacular pictures. You may picnic, boat, and fish in the park. Some food is available. The park is open daily 9:00 A.M. to dusk April through November. Admission is $9.00 for adults. Call (570) 588–6682.

At Dingmans Ferry, farther north on Route 209 but still in the Delaware Water Gap National Recreation Area, **Dingmans Falls,** the highest waterfall in Pennsylvania, pours down over 100 feet of rock with awesome power. On the same easy trail, in woods of hemlock and ferns, **Silver Thread Falls,** not quite as high but equally beautiful, is another stop worth a few photographs. In the park's nature center, you can study an audiovisual program, pick up a map, and talk to a naturalist about the falls and good trails—including easy ones—to walk.

From Dingmans Ferry it's only about 10 miles to Milford, a good place to spend the night—or several nights if you can spare the time. An excellent choice is the *Cliff Park Inn,* completely surrounded by a golf course that has been in operation since 1913—talk about a mature course! This inn, an 1820 farmhouse, has two dining rooms serving food one guest called "a gourmet's dream." She was hooked by the quail stuffed with raisins and apples, flamed in brandy, and covered with a truffle sauce. Since the menu changes periodically, you may find not quail but some other exotic offering, such as a game pie or beef Wellington. In winter, when even the fanatics don't golf in Pennsylvania, the golf course is used for cross-country skiing. So are the nearby hiking trails. The inn has 570 acres of woods and a view that overlooks three states. You can rent golf or cross-country equipment at the inn, owned for five generations by the Buchanan family. Call ahead (570–296–6491 or 800–225–6535) to reserve one of the eighteen rooms, each with private baths. Surf the Web at www.cliffparkinn.com; or write to the inn at 155 Cliff Park Road, Milford 18337.

Can you picture one of Dingman Ferry's most famous natives, Chief Thundercloud? If you've got an old nickel, it's easy. He's thought to be the model for the famous beaked profile on the obverse of the Indian-head coin (and for the last five-dollar gold piece minted in the United States). Though he was a Boy Scout in his youth, Thundercloud went on to quite a show-biz career, traveling with Buffalo Bill's Wild West show and P. T. Barnum. He also served as a model for sculptor Frederick Remington and artist John Singer. He's buried back in his hometown cemetery on Route 6/309 in Delaware Township.

You can learn more about Thundercloud at The Columns, the home of the *Pike County Historical Society* in Milford. That's where you'll find a treasured piece of Americana reverently displayed. The Lincoln Flag is so called because it's the one that adorned the balustrade at Ford's Theatre on April 14, 1865. When the president was shot by John Wilkes Booth, the stage manager placed it under Lincoln's head. Its bloodstains, still clearly visible, have been confirmed as Lincoln's.

Located at 608 Broad Street, the Society welcomes visitors from 1:00 to 4:00 P.M. Wednesday, Saturday, and Sunday from April 1 to June 30 and September 1 to November 30, and Wednesday through Sunday in between. Admission is $5.00 for adults and $3.00 for students; children are admitted free. For information call (570) 296–8126, or visit www.pikehistory.org.

In Milford stop at the *Upper Mill,* a nineteenth-century mill where water rushing over a three-story-high waterwheel used to power a grindstone. The mill building, on the National Register of Historic Places, is open year-round with an easy-to-follow self-guided tour, and the waterwheel operates from May to Thanksgiving. The only power generated in the mill these days is retail power, but that, fortunately, is thriving. From the cafe and bar, you can watch the waterwheel. While you're there you'll also want to visit the bakery, gift shop, bookstore, and dress boutique. The mill (570–296–5141) is on Sawkill Creek at Water and Mill Streets.

From Milford, driving west on Interstate 84 for about half an hour brings you to the **Sterling Inn,** in South Sterling. It has sixty-six rooms, a third with fireplaces or Franklin stoves. The inn sits on more than a hundred acres, with hiking and cross-country skiing trails, a tennis court, and a swimming and skating pond. Call the cuisine traditional American country gourmet, and expect beef, chicken, and seafood. Since this is the health-food age, the inn presents vegetarian options, too. Saturday night entertainment is live jazz or contemporary music. For rates and reservations visit www.thesterlinginn.com; write Sterling Inn, Route 191, South Sterling 18460; or call (570) 676–3311 or (800) 523–8200.

For a different kind of stay, go northwest from Milford on Route 6 to the **Settler's Inn,** a twenty-room country lodge furnished in antiques and white wicker. The inn is run by Grant and Jeanne Genzlinger with help from family and friends. The menu, which features local produce and local trout and pheasant, changes every four months—"except for the smoked-trout appetizer, which we can't take off the menu," says Jeanne. The inn is near Lake Wallenpaupack, where you can go fishing and boating. For more information about Settler's Inn, write 4 Main Avenue, Hawley 18428; call (570) 226–2993; or visit www.thesettlersinn.com.

trivia

Lake Wallenpaupack, an artificial lake north of Route 84, east of Route 191, covers old farmlands. Divers can still see stone walls, marking the perimeters of some farmers' pastures.

Upper Delaware Wilds

The Lackawaxen area remains unspoiled. Although the land along the Delaware River and the Lackawaxen River is privately owned, the stretch of the Delaware from Port Jervis to Hancock (both towns in New York) is protected under the Wild and Scenic Rivers Act. You'll find most of the historic and natural attractions along or near Route 590. The village of Lackawaxen (an Indian word for "swift waters") is named for the river that flows into the Delaware. If you're a fishing enthusiast, you'll like the Lackawaxen Fishing and Boat Access, operated by the Pennsylvania Fish and Boat Commission, which provides good fishing where the Delaware River runs deep and slow.

Across from the fishing access is the ***Zane Grey Museum,*** representing a classic American success story. Zane Grey was a dentist. He attended the University of Pennsylvania, where he received his degree in 1896. "He played on the Penn varsity baseball team and was quite well known," says Dot Moon, curator at the museum. "Baseball was very different than it is today. College baseball was a very big thing." After college Grey played baseball for the Orange Athletic Club in the Eastern League, which was considered a "gentlemen's league." Moon says that means they played for money but did not play on Sunday as "professional" baseball players did. In the off-season Grey practiced dentistry.

Grey's first article, a fishing story, was published in 1902. He gave up baseball after the 1902 season at the urging of his future wife, who encouraged him to devote himself to writing. In 1903 he wrote his first novel, *Betty Zane,* the story of his great-great-aunt who helped save Fort Henry during the Revolutionary War. He moved to Lackawaxen in 1905 to devote himself to writing and later said the Lackawaxen area was where he first became familiar with "really wild country." Between 1902 and 1909 Grey wrote articles for popular magazines on fishing and adventure, and in 1908 he wrote about his adventures in the Grand Canyon. While he was on this trip, he began writing his first novel about the West, *Heritage of the Desert.*

After leaving Lackawaxen, Grey traveled extensively to exotic places, such as Tahiti and New Zealand, to research his books. They were so convincing that Hollywood took to them, and by 1918 he left for California to work with the people producing movies based on his books. His Lackawaxen home remains a museum containing mementos of his life. Grey and his wife are buried in the cemetery of St. Mark's Lutheran Church (built in 1848), along with an unknown soldier killed during the Battle of Minisink in 1779, during the Revolutionary War. For more details call the National Park Service at (570) 685–4871.

From the fishing access you can also see John Roebling's ***Delaware Aqueduct,*** the oldest suspension bridge in use today. Roebling (who designed the Brooklyn Bridge but died before it was built, and who also created the "Three Sisters" bridges in Pittsburgh) designed and built four aqueducts for the Delaware and Hudson (D&H) Canal; only this one remains. Completed in 1849, the aqueduct connected the canal between Lackawaxen, in Pennsylvania, and New York. The aqueduct fell into disrepair and was later restored by the National Park Service. Now it is sturdy enough to be used, a century and a half later, as an automobile thoroughfare. (Locals—and local signs—call it the ***Roebling Bridge.***)

A nice place to stay, and where owner JoAnn Jahn is deeply engrossed in local history, is the **Roebling Inn** on the Delaware. It's on Scenic Drive off Route 590 in Lackawaxen. Jahn says the white clapboard inn with green shutters and roof was built around 1870 and was used as an office for the D&H Canal company. The six guest rooms, decorated with country antiques, are modified for contemporary tastes with private baths, televisions, and queen-size beds; some rooms have fireplaces. From the inn you can walk to canoeing, golf, horseback riding, a bait shop, a lunch restaurant, a general store, white-water rafting, tennis, river swimming, and a couple of great places for dinner. (Previous editions of this guide sent many visitors to the Roebling Inn because, says Jahn, "The title of the book says it all. We really are off the beaten path.") For full details and reservations, write 155 Scenic Drive, Lackawaxen 18435; call (570) 685–7900; or visit www.roeblinginn.com.

You can find considerably more rustic accommodations at the **Sylvania Tree Farm** on the Delaware River in Mast Hope. It's a tree farm—a naturalist's paradise—where you can stay in a modern cottage or pitch your tent at a campsite. Mast Hope is one of those you-can't-get-there-from-here places. From Milford take Route 6 about 14 miles, go north on Route 434 for 3 miles, take Route 590 west to Lackawaxen, then turn right toward Mast Hope. (Ask for a brochure with full directions when you make reservations.) The destination worth the trouble is 1,250 acres on the river with woods, fields, brooks, and seclusion. The property is in the Upper Delaware Wild and Scenic River corridor, administered by the National Park Service. Watchful visitors sight bald eagles and blue herons in the valley and white-tailed deer, black bears, beavers, and foxes in the woods and fields. The fly-fishing crowd loves the farm's private stream. You can cross-country ski in winter, hike other times, and take canoe and rafting trips with nearby outfitters. In addition, the National Park Service gives tours of the river valley and several historic sites. Write Sylvania Tree Farm, 112 Mast Hope Avenue, Mast Hope, Lackawaxen 18435, or call (570) 685–7001. Find out more at www.sylvaniatreefarm.com.

trivia

A popular horse race that was 5 miles long used to take place between Camptown and Wyalusing. The race is believed to have inspired Stephen Foster, who was visiting his brother in Towanda, to write "Camptown Races." Doo-da, doo-da.

trivia

Joseph Smith, founder of Mormonism, lived in Susquehanna County in 1830 while translating the Golden Plates for the Book of Mormon. See the historical marker on Route 11 between Great Bend and Hallstead.

A Day Trip: Endless Mountains

Four adjoining counties—Bradford, Sullivan, Susquehanna, and Wyoming—form the Endless Mountains Heritage Region. More than 15,000 years ago, glaciers etched these stones, creating the North Branch of the Susquehanna River. Valleys that once held prehistoric agricultural settlements now hold modern farms—plus white clapboard churches, basket shops, and quaint bed-and-breakfasts.

On a day trip from the Scranton area, you can almost reach Versailles. At the **French Azilum Historic Site,** somebody got the bright idea that the vista looked like *la belle France.* So in 1793 they built a home-away-from-home for Marie Antoinette. Unfortunately, the planned colony never happened, and Marie never got there. She lost her head. Keep your head—and keep your eyes on the road—as you drive north on Route 6, above Wyalusing, on the banks of the Susquehanna. The grounds are open May through October, Thursday through Monday from 10:00 A.M. to 4:00 P.M. The fee is $5.00 per adult. The La Porte house is also open for tours on those days during the peak months of June, July, and August. In May, September, and October, the house is open weekends only. Call (570) 265-3376, or get the full history from www.french azilum.com.

For more information on the area, contact the **Endless Mountains Visitors Bureau,** 712 Route 6 East, Tunkhannock 18657; (800) 769-8999 or (570) 836-5431. You can also visit www.endlessmountains.org.

Easton

Color me beautiful and lime green. Take a tour of the **Crayola Factory,** where you can see how Crayola makes red, blue, and chartreuse crayons. Roll up your burnt sienna sleeves and enjoy the interactive projects and activities. Let your child—and the child in you—see things through rose-colored Magic Markers. Friends will be green with envy when you tell them you painted the museum pink. Get silly with Silly Putty. Have a perfectly periwinkle time. The factory and gift shop are at 18 Centre Square. Admission is $8.00 per person over age two. For more information call (610) 515-8000 or (800) CRAYOLA, or color in www.crayola .com. It's colorful—and noisy, with all the kids. Don't miss it.

> ## trivia
>
> A plaque on the riverbank in Easton claims it's the site of America's first Christmas tree.

The Crayola Factory shares Two Rivers Landing with the **National Canal Museum** (610-559-6613)—a natural for Pennsylvania, given the oceans of human-made waterways that crisscrossed the state in the nineteenth century. Two floors of exhibits examine the building and working of the canal system. Ten minutes out of town, at Hugh Moore Park, you can board the mule-drawn *Josiah White II* and float the 6 miles of the old Lehigh Canal that have been restored here. The *Josiah White II* sails May through September; adult admission is $6.00. Get details from the museum at www.canals.org.

For more information on northeastern Pennsylvania, call (800) 229–3526, or visit www.visitnepa.org. Or you can go to the visitor center on Montage Mountain Road, off exit 182 (old exit 51) of I–81. It is open daily 8:30 A.M. to 6:00 P.M.

Places to Stay in Northeastern Pennsylvania

BETHLEHEM

Sayre Mansion,
250 Wyandotte Street;
(610) 882–2100;
www.sayremansion.com

CLARKS SUMMIT

Inn at Nichols Village,
1101 Northern Boulevard;
(800) 642–2215;
www.nicholsvillage.com

FRACKVILLE

**Granny's Motel
and Restaurant,**
115 West Coal Street;
(570) 874–0408

HAZLETON

Hazleton Motor Inn,
615 East Broad Street;
(570) 459–1451

JIM THORPE

Hotel Switzerland,
5 Hazard Square;
(570) 325–4563

Inn at Jim Thorpe,
24 Broadway;
(800) 329–2599;
www.innjt.com

SCRANTON

**Radisson Lackawanna
Station Hotel,**
700 Lackawanna Avenue;
(570) 342–8300;
www.radisson.com

STROUDSBURG

Clarion Hotel,
1220 West Main Street;
(570) 420–1000

WILKES-BARRE

Woodlands Inn & Resort,
1073 Route 315;
(570) 824–9831;
www.thewoodlands
resort.com

Places to Eat in Northeastern Pennsylvania

ASHLAND

Snyder's,
2114 Center Street;
(570) 875–3320

BETHLEHEM

Apollo Grill,
85 West Broad Street;
(610) 865–9600;
www.apollogrill.com.
New American cuisine;
serves lunch and dinner
Tuesday through Saturday.

CLARKS SUMMIT

**Ryah House at Inn at
Nichols Village,**
1101 Northern Boulevard;
(570) 587–4124

EASTON

Pearly Baker's Ale House,
11 Centre Square;
(610) 253–9949

HAZLETON

Library Restaurant,
615 East Broad Street;
(570) 455–3920;
www.libraryrestaurant.com.
Closed Sunday and Monday.

JIM THORPE

Emerald Restaurant and
Molly Maguires Pub at the
Inn at Jim Thorpe,
24 Broadway;
(800) 329–2599;
www.innjt.com

JT's Steak & Ale House at
the Hotel Switzerland,
5 Hazard Square;
(570) 325–4563

MILFORD

Dimmick Steak House,
at the traffic light;
(570) 296–4021;
www.dimmickinn.com

MOUNTAINHOME

Mountainhome Diner,
Routes 191 and 390;
(570) 595–2523

SCRANTON

Cooper's Seafood House
& Ship's Pub,
Washington Avenue and
Pine Street;
(570) 346–6883

SHAWNEE-ON-DELAWARE

Saen,
Shawnee Square;
(570) 476–4911;
www.smugglerscove.net.
Thai cuisine. Closed Monday.

SHOHOLA FALLS

Le Gorille,
814 Twin Lakes Road;
(570) 296–8094.
Closed Monday and
Tuesday.

Stonehill,
Route 6;
(570) 296–2624

SNYDERSVILLE

Snydersville Diner,
Business Route 209;
(570) 992–4003

TANNERSVILLE

Smuggler's Cove,
Route 611;
(570) 629–2277;
www.smugglerscove.net

A Selection of Pennsylvania's Covered Bridges

Adairs Covered Bridge Built 1864, rebuilt 1904. One of four covered bridges that span Sherman's Creek. Bridge is 150 feet long; Burr-truss construction. Route 274, east of Andersonburg, west of Loysville; southwest Madison Township, Perry County.

Aline Covered Bridge Built 1884, this bridge spans the North Branch of Mahantango Creek. Span is 67 feet long; Burr-truss construction. Route 104, north of Meiserville, Snyder County.

Bank's Covered Bridge Bridge is 121 feet long; heavily reinforced underdeck of Burr-truss system. Crosses Neshannock Creek. Halfway between Volant and New Wilmington, Lawrence County.

Bartram's Covered Bridge Built 1860 by Ferdinand Wood. Span is 60 feet long, 18 feet wide, 13 feet high; Burr-truss construction. Bartram family was instrumental in having bridge built. West of Newtown; Willistown and Newtown Townships, Bucks County.

Bells Mills Covered Bridge Built 1950. Bridge is 104 feet long; Burr-truss construction. Connects Sewickley and South Huntingdon Townships and connects Route 136 to I–70. Last remaining covered bridge in Westmoreland County. Near Wyano and Herminie.

Bistline Covered Bridge Built 1884. One of four covered bridges across Sherman's Creek. Also called Book's Covered Bridge. Span is 70 feet long; Burr-truss construction with multiple king posts. Route 274, southwest of Blain, northeast of New Germantown; Jackson Township, Perry County.

Blaney Mays Covered Bridge Built 1882, this bridge spans Middle Wheeling Creek. Queen-post-truss design, vertical plank siding, covered gable roof. Bridge is 31 feet long, 12 feet wide. J. Blaney once owned land near here. Southeast of West Alexander on Donegal Road, Claysville, Washington County.

Bogert Covered Bridge Built in 1841, it's the oldest bridge in the country. Span is 145 feet long across Little Lehigh River. Fish Hatchery Road, south of Allentown in Little Lehigh Park, Lehigh County.

Bucher's Mill Covered Bridge Built 1892. Also called Cocalico Bridge, it crosses Cocalico Creek. Span is 64 feet long, 15 feet wide; Burr-truss construction. Cocalico Road, off Route 272, south of Denver; East Cocalico Township, Lancaster County.

Cerl Wright Covered Bridge Crosses north fork of Pigeon Creek. King-post-truss system. Has outlived records of its builder and date of construction. Great view from I–70. Sumney Road, northwest of Bentleyville overlooking east-bound I–70; Somerset Township, Washington County.

Crawford Covered Bridge Queen-post-truss construction. Bridge crosses Robinson Fork of Wheeling Creek, 6 miles west of Finley, then 0.7 mile north of town on Route 3037, Washington County.

Ebenezer Covered Bridge Spans south fork of Mingo Creek. Queen-truss construction. Mingo Creek County Park, Kammerer, Washington County.

Jack's Mountain Covered Bridge Built 1894. Crosses Tom's Creek. Bridge is 75 feet long, 14.5 feet wide; Burr-truss construction. State-owned; open to vehicles. Hamilton Township, southwest of Fairfield near Iron Springs, Adams County.

Jackson's Mill Bridge Built 1875. Span is 95 feet long, 14.5 feet wide; Burr-truss support. Drivable. Township Route 412, 3.5 miles south of Breezewood, Fulton County.

Kidd's Mill Covered Bridge Built 1868, restored 1990. Crosses the Shenango River. Span is 120 feet long; all-wooden-truss design patented by Robert Smith of Tippecanoe City, Ohio. Last historic covered bridge in Mercer County. Five miles south of Greenville on Route 18, then east.

Knapp's Covered Bridge Burr-arch timber bridge constructed about 1860 over Brown's Creek. Span is 88 feet, 10 inches long. Said to be the highest covered bridge in Pennsylvania, at 36 feet above the stream bed. Burlington Township, Bradford County.

Kramer Bridge C. W. Eves built the bridge in 1881 for $414.50. Named for Alexander Kramer, a local farmer, who also bid on its construction. Span is 50 feet long across Mud Run, a tributary of Green and Fishing Creeks, south of Rohrsburg on Rohrsburg Road, Columbia County.

McConnell's Mills Covered Bridge Built 1874 over Slippery Rock Creek, just downstream from McConnell's Mill. Span is 96 feet long; built with Howe-truss support system. McConnell's Mill State Park, Slippery Rock Township, Lawrence County.

Sachs Covered Bridge Built 1852 by David S. Stoner across Marsh Creek. Also called Sauck's Bridge. Red bridge is 100 feet long; lattice-truss design. Pedestrians only. Both Union and Confederate troops used the bridge in 1863. Waterworks Road between Cumberland and Freedom Townships; near Gettysburg, Adams County.

Pennsylvania's Caves

Crystal Cave
963 Crystal Cave Road
Kutztown 19530
(610) 683–6765
www.crystalcavepa.com

Laurel Caverns
200 Caverns Park Road
Farmington 15437
(724) 438–3003 or (800) 515–4150
www.laurelcaverns.com

Indian Caverns
5347 Indian Trail
Spruce Creek 16683
(814) 632–7578
www.indiancaverns.com

Lincoln Caverns
Route 22, RR #1, Box 280
Huntingdon 16652
(814) 643–0268
www.lincolncaverns.com

Indian Echo Caverns
368 Middletown Road
P.O. Box 188
Hummelstown 17036
(717) 566–8131
www.indianechocaverns.com

Penn's Cave
222 Penn's Cave Road
Centre Hall 16828
(814) 364–1664
www.pennscave.com

Thomas Mill Covered Bridge This rural bridge in the midst of the state's biggest metropolis is 97 feet long and 14 feet wide. Access it by foot, bicycle, or horse along Forbidden Drive (so named because cars were always forbidden) between Valley Green Inn and Bells Mill Road, or from Germantown Avenue down Thomas Mill Road. Chestnut Hill section of Philadelphia.

Wertz's Red Bridge Longest single-span covered bridge in Pennsylvania. Northwest of Reading on US Route 222; Bern/Spring Townships, Berks County.

Take a Hike

Appalachian National Scenic Trail Approach this 232-mile segment of the Appalachian Trail from Rouzerville, Franklin County. Its highest elevation is 2,000 feet. Along the beautiful route you'll find laurel and rhododendron blooming in late spring, historic sites, fall hawk migration, and fall foliage. For more information call (304) 535–6331, or visit www.appalachiantrail.org.

Black Forest Trail Start in Haneyville and hike a 9.8-mile loop trail that gains 1,220 feet in elevation. Allow about six hours, and you will be rewarded with a section of the Black Forest Trail along Pine Creek Gorge. Pass a waterfall and the historic remains of the Black Forest Railroad, built to log much of this area. For more information call Tiadaghton State Forest, (570) 327–3450.

Eddy Lick Run This trail is 7.3 miles long, and it takes more than four hours to hike. Starting at the trailhead at 2,292 feet, the loop gains another 950 feet in elevation. Walk past a logging railroad and traces of a splash dam, which permitted logging along streams that were too small to float logs, even in the spring flood. Most splash dams were made of logs and soil, so they were temporary, but this one was built largely of rock and is well preserved. For more information call Sproul State Forest, (570) 923–6011.

Maple Summit to Ohiopyle To walk this trail, the southernmost section—and one of the most scenic bits—of the Laurel Highlands Trail, start in Confluence. The 11.3-mile-long trail requires several steep climbs—all worth the effort—for a total elevation gain of 1,700 feet. Allow at least six hours. The trail is contained within State Game Lands, No. 111. For more information call (724) 455–3744.

Table Rock You can access this 4.2-mile easy trail near Dauphin and can cover it in a couple of hours. Allow time to take in the views from Table Rock. The wide swath cut for power lines allows for great vistas of the Susquehanna River.

For more trails—many more—visit www.trails.com. At last count it listed 265 Pennsylvania off-the-beaten hiking paths.

Final Resting Places of Prominent People

Adams, Earl John "Sparky" (1894–1989). Slick infielder for Cubs, Pirates, Cardinals, and Reds. Starting third baseman for Cardinals' "Gas House Gang" of early 1930s. Tremont Reformed Cemetery; Tremont, Schuylkill County.

Ashburn, Richie (1927–1997). Baseball Hall of Famer who was twice National League batting champ with the Philadelphia Phillies. Also an original New York Met and a Phillies broadcaster for more than thirty years. Gladwyne Methodist Church Cemetery, southeast corner, directly behind the church; 316 Righter's Mill Road, Gladwyne, Montgomery County.

Bailey, Pearl (1918–1988). African-American vocalist and movie and stage actress. Began as dancer, won amateur contest in Philadelphia in 1933, sang with Big Bands. Starred in *Hello, Dolly!* Hosted a TV variety show. Autobiography: *The Raw Pearl*. Rolling Green Memorial Park; 1008 West Chester Pike, West Chester, Chester County.

Barry, Commodore John (1745–1803). Born in Ireland, Barry went to sea early and settled in Philadelphia by 1760. Commanded two ships. Became senior captain in U.S. Navy. Called Father of the U.S. Navy. Saint Mary's Catholic Church; 252 South Fourth Street, Philadelphia.

Pennsylvania Wineries

The Web site www.pennsylvaniawine.com offers a taste of wine-making activities throughout the state (though the most productive vineyards tend to be in the northwestern counties, near Lake Erie, and the southeastern part of the state). Winemakers say that the climate and soil hereabouts is similar to the Bordeaux and Burgundy regions of France; ergo, it augurs well for wine-making. Since wine is a subject with as many opinions as there are tasters, you'll just have to find out for yourself.

Here are a few of the wineries that have been consistent award winners in national and international tastings the past few years:

Blue Mountain Vineyards
7627 Grape Vine Drive
New Tripoli 18066
(610) 298–3068
www.bluemountainwine.com

Nissley Vineyards
140 Vintage Drive
Bainbridge 17502
(717) 426–3514
www.nissleywine.com

Chaddsford Winery
632 Baltimore Pike
Chadds Ford 19317
(610) 388–6221
www.chaddsford.com

Pinnacle Ridge Winery
407 Old Route 22
Kutztown 19530
(610) 756–4481
www.pinridge.com

Clover Hill Vineyards
9850 Newtown Road
Breinigsville 18031
(888) 256–8374
www.cloverhillwinery.com

Presque Isle Wine Cellars
9440 West Main Road
North East 16428
(814) 725–1314
www.piwine.com

Naylor Wine Cellars
4069 Vineyard Road
Stewartstown 17363
(800) 292–3370
www.naylorwine.com

Winery at Wilcox
1867 Mefferts Run Road
Wilcox 15870
(814) 929–5598
www.wineryatwilcox.net

Barrymore, John (1882–1942). Stage and film actor, born in Philadelphia. Brother of Ethel and Lionel Barrymore, he debuted in 1903 and became a matinee idol. Triumphed as a stage Hamlet in 1922, then turned to films and radio. Married four times. Mount Vernon Cemetery; Ridge and Lehigh Avenues, Philadelphia.

Britt, Elton (1913–1972). "World's greatest yodeler" lies here—listen. Most famous song: "There's a Star-Spangled Banner Waving Somewhere." Independent Order of Odd Fellows Cemetery; Broadtop City, Huntingdon County.

Buchanan, President James (1791–1868). Fifteenth U.S. president and the only one born in Pennsylvania. Woodward Hill Cemetery; Lancaster.

Calder, Alexander S. (1870–1945). Sculptor and painter, "Sandy" Calder was most famous for creating sculptures that move; artist Marcel Duchamp named them "mobiles." Artist Jean Arp named Calder's stationary sculptures "stabiles." West Laurel Hill Cemetery, Pencoyd Section, Lot 200; 215 Belmont Avenue, Bala Cynwyd, Montgomery County.

Croce, Jim (1943–1973). Top-ten folk-rock singer and instrumentalist. " 'Cause every time I tried to tell you, the words just came out wrong, so I'll have to say I love you in a song." Haym Solomon Cemetery, Section B/B; Frazer, Chester County.

PENNSYLVANIA WEB ADDRESSES

www.1fghp.com/pa.html
fishing guide

www.fallinpa.com
a virtual tree of autumn leaves

www.gophila.com
tourism in Philadelphia

www.hauntedpa.com
ghoulish getaways and haunted happenings

www.pafairways.com
link to the links

www.pagroundhog.com
eternal replays of February 2

www.pahuntandfish.com
visit 17 million acres of forest

www.parailways.com
dozens of passenger railroads

www.pasportstalk.com
who's ahead?

www.pavisnet.com
tourism in Pennsylvania (commercial site with links to accommodations, parks, etc.)

www.pennsylvaniawine.com
wineries

www.scenicroute6.com
virtual drive across the northern tier

www.shoppinginpa.com
from one-of-a-kind to outlet malls

www.trails.com
off-the-beaten-highway paths

www.visitpa.com
tourism in Pennsylvania (official state site)

www.visitpittsburgh.com
tourism in Pittsburgh

www.winterinpa.com
cool destinations and winter playgrounds

Day, William Howard (1825–1900). Prominent abolitionist, minister of A.M.E. Zion Church, orator, editor, and educator. Born in New York City; traveled in United States, Canada, and Britain on behalf of antislavery and free blacks. Lived after 1870 in Harrisburg, where he edited the newspaper *Our National Progress.* First African American elected to the Harrisburg School Board; later served as its president. Lincoln Cemetery; Lincoln and Carlisle Streets, Steelton, Dauphin County.

Dorsey, Jimmy (1904–1957). One of the musical Dorsey Brothers, he was a saxophonist, playing with his trombonist-brother Tommy (1905–1956). Together they were key figures of the Big Band era. Began their musical careers in Shenandoah, Pennsylvania, performing together until 1935. Later they led separate orchestras for eighteen years before reuniting. Annunciation Cemetery; Schuylkill Avenue, Shenandoah Heights, Schuylkill County.

Drexel, Saint Katharine (1858–1955). Raised with status and wealth, she devoted herself to serving Native and African Americans and established many missions. She was beatified in 1988, canonized in 2000. 1663 Bristol Pike, Bensalem, Bucks County.

Ennis, Del (1925–1996). Slugging outfielder for the Phillies in 1950s, three-time All-Star, and member of 1950 "Whiz Kids." Hillside Cemetery, Lawnview Section, Lot 102; 2556 Susquehanna Road, Roslyn, Montgomery County.

Fine, Governor John S. (1893–1978). Governor of Pennsylvania from 1951 to 1955. Oak Lawn Cemetery; Wilkes-Barre, Luzerne County.

Forrest, Edwin (1806–1872). Actor born in Philadelphia; excelled in tragic roles. His rivalry with actor William Macready led to the 1849 Astor Place Riots in New York, where thirty people were killed during a fight. Episcopal Community Services; 225 South Third Street, Philadelphia.

Foster, Stephen C. (1826–1864). Popular nineteenth-century composer of folk songs and ballads. Penned "Oh! Susannah," "Camptown Races," and "Beautiful Dreamer." Lived in the Pittsburgh area most of his life. Allegheny Cemetery; 4734 Butler Street, Pittsburgh.

Franklin, Benjamin (1706–1790). An American superstar, Franklin signed the Declaration of Independence; proved that lightning is an electrical phenomenon; wrote, printed, and published widely; and invented bifocals. Also known as diplomat, philanthropist, statesman, and scientist. The eighteenth century's most illustrious Pennsylvanian built a house in Franklin Court starting in 1763 and lived there the last five years of his life. Christ Church Burial Ground; southeast corner of Fifth and Arch Streets, Philadelphia.

Frick, Henry (1849–1919). A Pittsburgh industrialist and philanthropist, Frick was instrumental in the organization of the coke and steel industries. His controversial management style while chairman of Carnegie Steel led to the bloody Homestead Strike in 1892. Homewood Cemetery; 1599 South Dallas Avenue, Pittsburgh.

Furness, Frank (1839–1912). Influential Philadelphia architect. Designed Victorian buildings between 1870 and 1900. Laurel Hill Cemetery, Lot 94, Section S; 3822 Ridge Avenue, Philadelphia.

Garroway, David (Dave) (1913–1982). Television host. Originally a disc jockey on Chicago radio, he appeared on NBC-TV. First host of *Today* show (1952–1961); hosted *Wide, Wide World* (1955–1958). West Laurel Hill Cemetery, Washington Section, Lot 49; 215 Belmont Avenue, Bala Cynwyd, Montgomery County.

Gathers, Hank (1967–1990). Hank "The Bankman" Gathers was the last college basketball player to lead the NCAA in both scoring and rebounding. Mount Lawn Cemetery; Eighty-fourth Street and Hook Road, Sharon Hill, Delaware County.

Gridley, Captain Charles Vernon (1844–1898). Commander of Dewey's flagship USS *Olympia* in the Battle of Manila Bay, 1898. Dewey's order, "You may fire when you are ready, Gridley," opened the battle in the Spanish-American War. Lakeside Cemetery; East Lake Road, Erie.

Hopper, Hedda (1890–1966). Gossip columnist, born Elda Furry in Hollidaysburg, Pennsylvania, one of nine children. Worked in theater, became a fashion commentator on a Hollywood radio station. Eventually her column appeared in 85 metropolitan papers, 3,000 small-town dailies, and 2,000 weeklies. Rose Hill Cemetery; Altoona, Blair County.

Jarvis, Anna (1864–1948). Her mother had hoped "sometime, somewhere, someone will found a Mother's Day." When her mother died, Jarvis, living in Philadelphia, did it. The first Mother's Day was May 12, 1907. President Woodrow Wilson made it official in every state, and the day is celebrated now in more than forty countries. West Laurel Hill Cemetery, River Section, Lot 499; 215 Belmont Avenue, Bala Cynwyd, Montgomery County.

Kahn, Louis I. (1901–1974). This twentieth-century architect designed the Salk Institute for Biological Studies in La Jolla, California, and the Yale Center for British Art and Studies in New Haven, Connecticut. He taught at Yale and Penn. Montefiore Cemetery; 600 Church Road, Jenkintown, Montgomery County.

Mansfield, Jayne (1933–1967). Actress born Vera Jayne Palmer in Bryn Mawr, Pennsylvania. Known for sultry movie and stage roles, including *Too Hot to Handle* and *Will Success Spoil Rock Hunter?* Fairview Cemetery; Plainfield near Pen Argyl, York County.

McKean, Thomas (1734–1817). Signed the Declaration of Independence. Laurel Hill Cemetery, Section G, Lot 210; 3822 Ridge Avenue, Philadelphia.

Mead, Margaret (1901–1978). Anthropologist who redefined and expanded the field of anthropology, the science of human culture. Born in Philadelphia, she was ambitious and always controversial. Did field work in Polynesia, Melanesia, and Nebraska, among other sites. President Jimmy Carter awarded her the Presidential Medal of Freedom. Buckingham Friends Cemetery; Lahaska, Bucks County.

Moore, Marianne (1887–1972). Modernist poet. Studied at Bryn Mawr College and Carlisle Commercial College; worked at U.S. Indian School. Famous for her eccentricity, devotion to baseball, and keenly intelligent poetry. Evergreen Cemetery, Lot 91, Area G, Grave 5; 799 Baltimore Street, Gettysburg, Adams County.

Peale, Charles Willson (1741–1827). Portrait painter who was a Democratic member of the Pennsylvania Assembly. He established the Portrait Gallery of the Heroes of the Revolution (1782) and founded the Peale Museum of natural history and technology (1786). His most famous painting is *The Staircase Group* (1795), portraying his sons, Raphaelle and Titian. Married three times, he had seventeen children, many of whom were artists. St. Peter's Churchyard; occupies a city block bounded by Third, Pine, Fourth, and Lombard Streets, Philadelphia.

Pitcher, Molly (1754–1832). Mary Ludwig Hays McCauley was dubbed Molly Pitcher while carrying pitchers of water to her husband and other thirsty soldiers during battle; heroine at Battle of Monmouth. Old Graveyard; South Hanover Street between Walnut and South Streets, Carlisle, Cumberland County.

Rizzo, Frank (1920–1991). Commissioner of police department of Philadelphia, where he lived all his life. Called himself "toughest cop in America." Twice elected mayor of Philadelphia (1972 and 1975). Holy Sepulchre Cemetery, Section S, Range 1, Lot 136; Cheltenham Avenue and Easton Road, Cheltenham Township, Montgomery County.

Rush, Benjamin (1742–1813). Signed the Declaration of Independence. Christ Church Burial Ground; Fifth and Arch Streets, Philadelphia. Other Signers buried at Christ Church Burial Ground include Jacob Broom (1752–1810), Pierce Butler (1744–1822), Joseph Hewes (1730–1779), Francis Hopkinson (1737–1791), Robert Morris (1734–1806), and George Ross (1730–1779).

Russell, Lillian (1861–1922). Actress and singer born in Clinton, Iowa. This popular, flamboyant blonde beauty was known for her unreliability. Starred in twenty-four musicals between 1881 and 1899. Allegheny Cemetery; 4734 Butler Street, Pittsburgh.

Sully, Thomas (1783–1872). Learned art from relatives, began painting portraits in 1801. Studied with Gilbert Stuart and Benjamin West. Returned to Philadelphia; painted technically polished and elegant portraits. Laurel Hill Cemetery, Section A, Lot 41; 3822 Ridge Avenue, Philadelphia.

Indexes

Entries for Pennsylvania museums also appear in the special index on page 173.

GENERAL INDEX

PENNSYLVANIA MUSEUMS

About the Author

Christine O'Toole is a writer and editor who has written extensively about Pennsylvania for the *New York Times, International Herald-Tribune, Continental Airlines Magazine, Washington Post, USA Today, Pittsburgh Post-Gazette,* and other publications. A native of Newtown Square, Delaware County, she has lived and worked in Philadelphia, Harrisburg, Washington, D.C., and Pittsburgh. She contributed to *Travelers Tales: Prague and the Czech Republic* (Travelers Tales, 2006). She is a contributing writer to *Pittsburgh Magazine* as well as *Mt. Lebanon Magazine* in the town where she now lives and works.